BOOKS BY PAULA WOLFERT

The Cooking of South-West France

Couscous and Other Good Food from Morocco

Mediterranean Cooking

Paula Wolfert

MEDITERRANEAN
COOKING

MEDITERRANEAN COOKING

by Paula Wolfert

THE ECCO PRESS

NEW YORK

Acknowledgments

Some of the Italian and Greek recipes have previously been published in slightly different form in the CBS International Home Dining series, written and edited by the author.

The recipe for *Marmelade de pêches* is from *French Provincial Cooking* by Elizabeth David. Copyright © 1960 by Elizabeth David. It is reprinted by permission of Harold Ober Associates, Incorporated.

The recipe for *Bourride des pêcheurs* is from *The Secrets of the Great French Restaurants* by Louisette Bertholle. Copyright © 1974 by Macmillan Publishing Co., Inc. It is reprinted by permission of Macmillan Publishing Co., Inc.

Copyright © 1977 by Paula Wolfert
All rights reserved
Issued in 1985 by The Ecco Press
18 West 30th Street, New York, N.Y. 10001
Published simultaneously in Canada by
Stoddart, a subsidiary of General Publishing Co., Ltd., Don Mills
Published by arrangement with Quadrangle, New York Times Book Co.
Printed in the United States of America
Library of Congress Cataloging in Publication Data
Wolfert, Paula.
Mediterranean cooking.
Reprint. Originally published: New York:
Quadrangle/New York Times Book Co., 1977
Bibliography: p. 341
Includes index.
1. Cookery, Mediterranean. I. Title.
TX725.M35W64   1985   641.59′182′2   84-13685
ISBN 0-88001-075-4

For Bato and Leila

Contents

Introduction   *ix*

Garlic and Oil   3

Olives   45

Eggplant, Tomatoes, Peppers, and
    Other Mediterranean Vegetables   75

Chick-Peas, Lentils, and Beans   119

Pasta, Couscous, and Other Mediterranean
    Farinaceous Foods   139

Herbs, Spices, and Aromatics   169

Yogurt   209

Cheese   225

Nuts   251

Honey   275

*Lemons, Oranges, Figs, Dates, and
Other Mediterranean Fruits*   285

Suppliers and Sources for Ingredients and Materials   333

Weights and Measures   340

Bibliography   341

Index to Recipes by Course and Country   343

Index   355

Introduction

THERE's something special about the Mediterranean that draws people like me to live around it. I used to think it was the clarity of the light—luminous, strong, direct—that makes everything look sharp and intense. But as time passed, and I shuttled back and forth between Tangier and New York (the two poles of my existence these last eighteen years), I began to look upon it as a refuge from our North Atlantic culture, a repository of a lifestyle both sensual and humane.

Humanism was born here, and to a diminishing extent still pervades the lands that border on this sea. Architecture here is on a human scale. One lives for satisfaction and finds it in simple things. The North Atlantic scramble for money, status, and fame becomes irrelevant in an olive grove. After living here a while one finds oneself gentled. What better place, it seems to me, to drop out of the rat race and seek solace in clean air, good humor, love, culture, and delicious food.

This is my Mediterranean myth, and I find it difficult to maintain today. The world is becoming more and more the same. Rude manners and high-rise developments are already entrenching themselves around Mediterranean shores. The robust sensual style is rapidly giving way to the grasping affluence-seeking madness of Paris, Tokyo, and New York. The air and sea are polluted, the beaches are being tarred, and the landscape is being ravaged in the names of "economic development" and that awful thing, "the camping village." The hotels are beginning to look the same, and from place to place the menus are becoming interchangeable. The marvelous little inns where the great regional specialties were served are becoming artifacts of the past.

Still I cannot renounce my attachment for these shores or give up this love affair that has consumed so many years. There are places (and Tangier is one) where Mediterranean life can still be lived. Sometimes, though, Moroccan friends disturb me with tales of the great hotels to be erected from Point Malabata to Cap Spartel. They seem not to have heard of all the awful things that come with "development": beaches strewn with plastic, wild forests cut down and spoiled, uniqueness and nationality that self-destructs. When I try to warn them they look at me as though I'm mad. Who can blame them? They are still Mediterranean at heart—regret and fear have yet to taint their lives.

This book is based on the myth of a way of life that is hard to find today. It still exists on certain Greek islands, in unspoiled Spanish, French, and Italian towns, in a Turkish fishing village, or a corner of Sicily which by luck has been bypassed by a modern road. As these words are written Beirut is tearing itself apart, Alexandria is a shadow of whatever it was, and Genoa is a nightmare of cloverleaf interchanges and automobile fumes. Air-conditioned buses full of tourists are crowding the roads of the Mediterranean. Clever people from Paris, Beirut, and Rome are searching out little villages which they can adorn with instant "rustic" bars and clusters of overpriced boutiques. Look at Torremolinos! Is that the future? If so then I suffer from "future shock."

When I set out to write this book I didn't intend a swan song, but as I worked on it I began to think that that's what it might become. The regional specialties of Mediterranean lands are rapidly blurring into the undistinguished and undifferentiated mush that I call, pejoratively, "international gourmet food." From Istanbul to Tangier, Tunis to Cannes, one sits down to watery onion soup, flavorless limp chicken, and sawdust textured chocolate mousse. I have never found a restaurant couscous that could compare to one made in the home, and rarely a restaurant paella that was not a shadow of what paella ought to be. Thank God one can still eat a great cassoulet in Toulouse and a superb *bourride* in Provence, but in Athens even a good *avgolemono* soup is becoming difficult to find. All of this, I'm afraid, is another symptom of the disease of which a world bathed in Coca-Cola may be the terminal stage.

But enough of gloom. There is still the food, alive and well in various places, based on marvelous ingredients in fresh and plentiful supply. Ingredients—I'm convinced they are the key, and thus the organization of this book. One can discuss Mediterranean food in terms of courses (appetizers, entrées, desserts, etc.), or in terms of national schools. But it seems somehow more appropriate, and also more Mediterranean, to organize the dishes in terms of certain flavors and tastes: the fresh aromas of wild herbs, the tang of lemons and orange, the soft textures of olives and dates, the striking and often unexpected combinations of garlic and oil, honey and nuts. Eggplants, tomatoes, and peppers, chick-peas, lentils, and beans, yogurt and cheese, pasta, couscous and figs—these are the things that Mediterranean food is all about. These ingredients comprise the bounty of the Mediterranean, the stuff of which its cuisines are built. They are available in its sun drenched markets; they are the raw materials that in its regions are combined in so many different ways.

The Mediterranean Sea has always been a medium of cultural interaction, and its culinary glories a great result. In a long history of occupations and conquests, food ideas have crossed national boundaries and stuck when they were good. A good half of the region, from Yugoslavia in the east to Algiers in the west, shows the strong culinary influence of the Turks. Moorish cooking impacts upon the food of southern Spain; Catalonia interacts with Languedoc and Provence; and there is Italy, not unified until the time of Cavour, a land of regions, each with its own style of cooking, showing traces of Turkey (in Venice), North Africa (in Sicily), Spain (in Sardinia), France (in Naples), and nearly everything else. For this reason, perhaps, there are a great number of Italian recipes in this book.

In any event I ought to confess that I have not sought to write a balanced book. Greek cooking is very nice, but can't compare in stature to Moorish or Provençal. I've made no attempt to give equal due to the different national schools, or to present a balance between hors d'oeuvres, main courses, and desserts. My criteria have been completely different, and it might be well to list them at the start.

This is a personal book, a book of food that interests me. I present no rationale to conceal this fact—I just can't bear to write about dishes I don't like. In the main, I was interested in four things: Great and famous dishes for which I could find superb recipes (my *pistou marseillaise*, for example—I've never seen a recipe for *pistou* written this way, nor eaten one nearly as good); odd and unusual dishes, culinary curiosities (usually described, though presented here sometimes in recipe form such as *acqua cotta di Maremma* and *Kouski bil hout*); dishes that illustrated contrasting or similar uses of the same materials (an endless fascination in the Mediterranean region, allowing one to move about at will and probe cross-cultural connections); and, delicious dishes that had not been published before. This last task was the most difficult, since there've been so many books about Mediterranean food. But I found a few wonderful things, family recipes secreted away in old handwritten ledgers, and it's a pleasure to present them here for the first time: *olio verde, torta di cavolo, tourte Tante Vivienne*, and several more, as well as a good number of little known North African specialties.

In the category of famous dishes, in addition to my *pistou*, I particularly recommend spinach and cheese dumplings with gorgonzola sauce, the Provençal fish soups, and the Yugoslav way of stuffing cabbage. In some cases, such as sauce *puttanesca*, I've tried to seek out an unusual recipe, which I felt tasted better than the typical restaurant presentation. I would make the same claim for my pesto, a little different from the classic Genoese recipe, coming as it does from the nearby town of Nervi. And the same could be said, too, for my garlic soup from southwestern France and my Greek baked fish with tomatoes and onions.

Some of the recipes here are easy to prepare and others take a great deal of time. I personally like complicated dishes when I can cook them quietly and without a lot of rush. I've always been seduced by recipes that are off the beaten track—odd ways of doing things that result in the expected taste plus a twist. There seemed little point in giving just another classic recipe for couscous, thus my *seksu Tanjaoui* with its unusual touch of herbal *smen*.

A word here about one country which I've nearly ignored. Israel is a young nation, with a population drawn from many lands. Its citizens cook as well as anyone, usually their native foods. But at the risk of being taken to task, I think Israel itself has yet to develop a first-rate cuisine. No reason why it should—it took hundreds of years in other lands. The Israelis are beginning now to work with their native ingredients, such things as oranges and avocados. I have no doubt that with their typical ingenuity they will come up with something very good.

Though I spent only two years traveling, tasting, and testing for this book, many of the recipes here are old favorites collected over the past eighteen years from Mediterranean friends. I've been particularly fortunate, I think, in having spent over seven years on and off in Tangier. This is still a wonderful cosmopolitan town full of French, Italians, Tunisians, Lebanese, Spaniards, and Greeks. As a result I've been able to call people and check important points, and many of my fellow "Tangerines" have given me excellent recipes, too.

Before I thank the many people who've helped I want to tip my hat to my favorite food writer, whom I know only through her work. It is Elizabeth David, author of many excellent cookbooks whose classic *A Book of Mediterranean Food* (*Mediterranean Food* in some editions) seems to me the single work of merit of the many Mediterranean cookbooks that have been produced. Her uncanny ability to see to the heart of a recipe, and her distinguished prose have been an inspiration to this work and a delight.

And now for thanks. A special lot of it to Countess Simonetta Ponzone-Lanza of Tangier, and Mario Ruspoli of Paris. Also Tony May, of the Rainbow Room in New York, Francesca Baldeschi-Balleani, and Maria Theresa Silvestri gave much help and advice on Italian cuisine. For Greek recipes I want to thank George Karamalis, Nina Vranopoulous, and Olga Thomas. For Spanish recipes Elena Spencer and Loli Martinez y Fernandez. For Turkish Hakki Anli and Aydemir and Jetta Balkan. Radoje Prica and Emilia Jovanovic taught me much about Yugoslav cooking, and on Tunisian I was advised by Ahmed Laribi and Safia Hamadi.

Claude Thomas, Annie Magnard, and Jacqueline Pacquant helped with French recipes, as did an old and modest friend who asked me to call her "Tante Vivienne." On Lebanese, Syrian, Egyptian, and Palestinian cooking I owe thanks to Ammeh Fakhry, Maha Abdul Majeed, and a certain "Madame A." of Beirut. Finally in Tangier many friends helped with research and recipes: Baronne Marie Emilie de Troostemburgh, Sarah Scoville, Kathy Jelen, Kate Bouveau, and Orford St. John. Special thanks too to Madeleine van Breughel of Marrakech, Bill Bayer of Tangier and New York, and my loyal helper in the kitchen, Fatima benLahsen Riffi.

MEDITERRANEAN COOKING

Garlic and Oil

I T isn't everyday, even in Tangier, that a friend calls up and says: "Come over and taste a wild boar's head." Without a moment's hesitation I rushed to her house.

Her husband had shot the boar near the Moroccan mountain town of Chauen. The carcass hung for a few days, then was set in a marinade. When I arrived I found my friend in the act of opening the oven door to tuck a large sprig of fresh rosemary beneath the wild pig's jaw. The head had been roasting the entire morning and already the skin was crusty and brown. As I peered in to look at it, the marvellous aroma of garlic hit me full in the face.

She'd prepared the head by rubbing it with salt, pepper, some chopped parsley, seven cloves of garlic, and plenty of olive oil. She'd also started on a sauce, simmering three heads of garlic (about forty cloves), then peeling them and pressing them through a sieve. I helped her add cream to the garlic pulp, and season this sauce with salt and pepper.

The boar's head was delicious, and I think it was due to the garlic sauce as well as the garlic and oil rubbed into the flesh. These two—garlic and oil—are among the great combinations in cookery, essential and inevitable in Mediterranean cuisine.

Herodotus wrote that the workers who built the great

Pyramids were fed raw garlic for health and strength. The Egyptians certainly thrived on garlic, learned to grind it with oil into a sauce, and this discovery led to a great chain of crosscultural culinary inventions, a cycle of sauces—*ali-oli, aillade, aïoli, aglio e oglio**, *skordalia, tarator* and eventually garlic-free mayonnaise (see page 41 for a full analysis)—that when plotted on a map form a crescent across the north shore of the Mediterranean Sea.

There are all sorts of myths about garlic, and for all I know they're true. One is that it gives energy, and another that it kills germs. Certainly it is strong in its raw state, though when cooked it becomes subtle and sublime. In France young early-picked garlic is called *la fleur de l'ail*; it is delicate in flavor, and has earned the title: "truffle of the poor." There's a theory that one's breath won't smell from eating garlic-flavored foods if one swallows a whole clove before the meal. I haven't found this true for myself, but I have friends for whom it's a way-of-life.

If you have trouble chopping garlic because the little pieces keep flying away from your knife, chop it along with a little salt. This will keep it close to the knife, absorb some of the oil and soften the flavor a bit—particularly important in America since our garlic is stronger than the Provençal kind.

If garlic is an essential flavoring, olive oil is a cooking medium without which Mediterranean food could not exist. Fish, meat, poultry, game, vegetables, salads, sauces, and in Provence and the Balkans even pastries are made with olive oil. The Mediterranean cook can do without butter if she must. She can even work without fat or lard. But without oil she is lost.

The flavor of olive oil is difficult to define: let's just say that it is fruity and warm, with a particular bouquet that the so-called "neutral" ground nut oils cannot duplicate. You can substitute vegetable oils if you like, but in my opinion your food will not taste the same.

The best quality is called "virgin," and comes from the first pressing of the olives. Virgin oil is expensive and so is used most often in dishes where it's raw: mayonnaise, salad dress-

---

* Neapolitan dialect.

ings, cold herbal sauces. For the second and third pressings the olive oil makers add water to the pulp. These pressings result in stronger tasting oils, which are generally used for cooking. There are even fourth pressings, but the oil from them goes into soaps and shampoos. And the final last pressing of the pits produces oil not much good for anything except lubrication.

In this chapter I sometimes look at oil dishes that contain no garlic, and at garlic dishes that contain no oil, but in the main I'm interested in the robust quality that comes from the combination of the two.

GAMBAS AL AJILLO

Shrimp in garlic sauce (Spain)

This is a typical Spanish *tapas* dish, one of the many kinds of delightful hors d'oeuvres served with beer or sherry at neighborhood bars. On a recent trip to Seville we went faithfully every evening at eight to the Hosteria del Laurel, one of the best *tascas* (taverns) in Spain. Along with several glasses of *Pando*, a very dry sherry served ice-cold, we'd gobble up *gambas al ajillo*, little fillets of swordfish, cold squid in mayonnaise, little plates of veal stew, tiny pork cubes, and a half dozen other delicious goodies. The Hosteria del Laurel is charming, with its handpainted ceilings, and hanging hams. The customers are mostly university students and artists who live in the Barrio de Santa Cruz, and the whole drinks-and-*tapas* experience there is delightful. At about ten we'd trudge off to dinner, our stomachs already full.

Ingredients

    1 pound small raw shrimp
    ½ onion, chopped
    ¼ cup olive oil
    3 cloves garlic, peeled and crushed
    2 tablespoons finely chopped parsley
    ¼ cup dry white wine
      Salt and freshly ground pepper

Equipment

   Large skillet

Working time: 20 minutes

Cooking time: 7 minutes (approximately)

Serves: 3 to 4

   1. Shell and devein the shrimp.
   2. In a skillet cook the onion in oil until soft and golden.
Add the garlic and half the parsley, and cook 1 minute longer,
stirring. Add the shrimp. Cook, over brisk heat, 3 minutes or
until they turn pink, stirring constantly. Add the wine and season with salt and pepper. Cook, stirring, 2 to 3 minutes longer.
Serve hot sprinkled with remaining chopped parsley.

TARAMASALATA

Carp roe dip (Greece)

   This oil-based dip is rightfully famous and very easy to
make. A good *taramasalata* should have the texture of mayonnaise. *Tarama* or carp roe can be found in bottles in most
Greek and middle eastern food stores, and sometimes, at a good
Greek market it is sold directly from the keg.

Ingredients

   ⅓ cup *tarama*
   1 cup torn crustless white bread (about 2 slices)
        soaked in water and squeezed dry
   1 tablespoon grated onion
   ¼ cup freshly squeezed lemon juice
   ¾–1 cup olive oil
        Finely chopped parsley

Equipment

Electric blender

Working time: 5 minutes

Serves: 6 to 8

Place the *tarama*, bread, onion, and lemon juice in the blender jar. Add ⅓ cup oil and blend until smooth. With blender on, gradually add the remaining oil in a slow steady stream. Scrape the resulting cream into a shallow serving dish. Surround with toast, crackers, celery ribs, cucumber strips, or pitted black olives stuck with toothpicks. Serve cold with a garnish of finely chopped parsley.

Note: Another sort of fish roe called *poutargue* is produced in southern France. It is firm and served sliced on bread with a little olive oil, lemon juice, and a good grinding of black pepper. In Italy, it is served with figs or prosciutto.

ANCHOÏADE CORSE

Anchovy oil canapes (Corsica)

This is a modern version of an ancient traditional dish. In the classic version anchovies which had been put up in brine were soaked, cleaned, filleted, and placed in an earthenware jar. They were covered with oil and a few drops of lemon juice or vinegar, then spiced with pepper. The jug was placed near a woodburning stove until, after many hours, a rich thick creamy sauce was obtained. It was then spread on bread. Now there are many modern variations including the famous one from Provence called *anchoïade de Croze* which includes chopped figs, red peppers, and walnuts.

Ingredients

    5 slices firm stale white bread, trimmed, toasted,
         and cut into 4 squares
    1 2-ounce tin flat anchovy fillets, rinsed and drained
    ½ teaspoon finely chopped garlic
    1 tablespoon finely chopped scallion
    1 tablespoon finely chopped fresh parsley
    1 teaspoon lemon juice
       Freshly ground black pepper
       Pinches of cayenne
    3 tablespoons olive oil

Equipment

    Baking sheet · Mixing bowl

Working time: 5 minutes

Baking time: 8 to 10 minutes

Serves: 4, makes 20 canapés

    1. Arrange the toasted squares side by side on a baking sheet.

    2. Mash the anchovy fillets to a puree; add garlic, scallion, parsley, lemon juice, pepper, and cayenne; mixing well. Beat in the olive oil teaspoon by teaspoon. The anchovy mixture should be thick and creamy.

    3. Spread a small spoonful on each bread square. Let stand 30 minutes. The bread will soak up the oil.

    4. Preheat the oven to 425 degrees.

    5. Set the toast in the hot oven to bake 10 minutes. Serve hot with drinks.

Note: This sauce can be stirred into Provençal fish soups instead of *sauce rouille* (see pages 18 and 19).

GAZPACHO AJO BLANCO

Gazpacho with garlic, almonds, and green grapes
from Malaga (Spain)

Gazpacho needn't be red with tomatoes, though most often it is. Originally the word is Arabic and means "soaked bread." The dish came to Spain with the Moors who made it of garlic, bread, olive oil, lemon juice, water, and salt. Just at the time the Moors finally left Spain, Columbus returned from America with tomatoes and peppers—two vegetables that soon found their way into the soup. But still today, in Andalusia, there are many versions of gazpacho that contain no tomatoes at all.

Gazpacho ajo blanco is one of these, and perfect for those who love garlic. The ground almonds and the green grapes temper the force of the garlic, and make this a delicious and particularly refreshing cold summer soup.

You can make a good sauce out of this recipe for small fried fish like red mullets or for freshly boiled green beans. Follow the recipe exactly, but leave out the ice water at the end.

Ingredients

⅔ cup (4 ounces) shelled whole almonds, blanched
1 teaspoon (2 cloves) chopped garlic
1 teaspoon salt
½ cup crustless Spanish- or Italian-style bread, soaked in water and squeezed to extract excess moisture
⅓ cup olive oil
1½ tablespoons red or white wine vinegar
1 cup seedless green grapes, peeled and halved

Equipment

Electric blender · Large bowl

Working time: 5 minutes

Serves: 4

Place the almonds, garlic, salt, and ½ cup water in a blender jar. Whirl until smooth. Add the bread and a little more water if necessary and whirl again. Slowly add the oil in a thin steady stream with the blender on. Pour into a bowl; whisk in the wine vinegar, gradually stir in 3 cups ice cold water and readjust the seasoning to taste. Pour into soup bowls and garnish with green grapes.

CRÈME À L'AIL

Garlic soup from southwestern France

This easy-to-make garlic soup is more subtle than *gazpacho ajo blanco*. Here the garlic is cooked, with the result that you'll enjoy the perfume of it, without suffering from too forceful a taste. It's elegant enough for a dinner party, and will convert people who are normally reticent about garlic.

Actually this is the Languedoc version of the classic *soupe à l'ail* of Provence. There they simply simmer garlic cloves and herbs in stock, then serve the mixture over toasted bread with grated cheese and sometimes a poached egg. (There's an almost identical soup in Spain, *sopa de ajo*.) But what makes this Languedoc version so special is the liaison of oil and egg yolks instead of egg yolks and cream. It thickens the soup nicely and gives it a "southwestern touch."

When I was in Languedoc I learned a good way to make bread croutons. You brush slices of stale bread with egg white and then set them in the oven to toast. At first it looks as though the bread will fall apart, but the slices soon firm up and sparkle with crispness.

Ingredients

> 4 slices stale French or Italian bread, brushed with egg white
> 4–6 large cloves garlic, unpeeled
> 2 egg yolks
> 3 tablespoons olive oil
> 4–5 cups beef or chicken stock
>   Salt and freshly ground black pepper
>   Chopped parsley

Equipment

> Garlic press (optional) · Large and small saucepans
> Whisk and small bowl

Working time: 10 minutes

Cooking time: 20 minutes

Serves: 4

1. Toast the bread slices in the oven until golden brown.
2. Drop the garlic cloves into boiling water and allow to cook at the boil 15 minutes.
3. Drain, rinse under cold running water, then peel. Mash to a puree or push through a garlic press into a mixing bowl. Beat with egg yolk and oil until thickened.
4. Bring the stock to a boil. Off heat stir in the garlic mixture. Cook, stirring, 5 minutes until thickened. Do not allow the soup to boil. Correct the seasoning. Serve with bread slices and sprinkle with chopped parsley.

ACQUA COTTA DI MAREMMA

Tuscan vegetable soup with olive oil and sage (Italy)

This dish, favored by workmen in the countryside around Maremma in Tuscany, is for lovers of olive oil—*and only for them!* Frankly it contains too much oil for me, but I include it because it's odd and fun.

It's from the *Petit Breviaire de la Cuisine* by my good friend Mario Ruspoli who counsels that the bread chunks must fill half the soup tureen. But even this enormous amount doesn't absorb all the oil.

Ingredients

    2 bunches of fresh sage leaves, or ¼ cup dried
    1 cup virgin olive oil
    3 cloves garlic, unpeeled
    1 cup shelled green peas
    1 cup shelled fava or lima beans
    1 cup diced carrots
    ½ cup diced celery
    4 raw artichoke hearts, cleaned and halved
    2½ quarts water
    Salt and freshly ground black pepper
    1 dried red pepper, crumbled
    8 large chunks of coarse country-style bread,
       toasted in the oven then rubbed with garlic
    4–6 fresh eggs
    Grated parmesan or pecorino cheese

Equipment

5½-quart casserole or deep wide earthenware dish set over an asbestos pad · Large soup tureen

Working time: 30 minutes

Cooking time: 20 minutes

Serves: 4 to 6

1. Scatter the sage leaves on the bottom of the casserole or dish. Pour over the olive oil. Add the garlic. Cook over very low heat 5 minutes. Add all the vegetables and cook, stirring, over

brisk heat 2 to 3 minutes. Add the water, salt, pepper, and red pepper. Slowly bring to the boil and cook at the simmer until the vegetables are tender.

2. Fill a soup tureen halfway with the prepared country-style bread. Poach the eggs in the simmering soup for 5 minutes. Carefully transfer the soup and the eggs to the tureen. Sprinkle with grated cheese. Serve lukewarm or, better still, cold the next day.

BOURRIDE DES PÊCHEURS

Provençal fishermen's soup (France)

(Recipe from the restaurant Lei Mouscardins in St. Tropez, as published in *The Secrets of the Great French Restaurants*, selected and edited by Louisette Bertholle, translated by Paula Wolfert. New York, Macmillan, 1974.)

Bourride des pêcheurs is an old and venerable fish soup from Provence, nearly as famous as Provençal bouillabaisse. The distinguishing feature of *bourride* is the addition of *aïoli*, a garlic mayonnaise. Actually for a *bourride* one makes the *aïoli* a little differently than for poached salt cod or hot or cold vegetables. One uses more egg yolks, and the *aïoli* becomes a soup thickener rather than a sauce. To make ordinary *aïoli* (the *aïoli* for the *bourride* is included in the recipe) count a garlic clove per person plus one "for the pot." Peel the garlic. In a heavy mortar crush it, then beat with one or two egg yolks until pasty and thick. Add olive oil drop by drop until you obtain a thick creamy emulsion resembling a very thick mayonnaise. Season with salt and pepper and a squeeze of lemon juice at the end. You should use only the very best quality virgin olive oil for an *aïoli* sauce. The egg yolks and oil must both be at room temperature.

Ingredients

3 pounds assorted lean white firm-fleshed fish. Choose at least
3 kinds of fish from the following list: rockfish,
mullet, halibut, flounder, redfish, pollock, gray sole,
haddock, whiting, bass, porgy or scup, baby cod
or tomcod, hake, scrod, red snapper or ocean perch.
A few soft-shell crabs and other shellfish (optional)

The vegetables
1 onion, sliced
2 leeks, white part only, sliced
4 cloves garlic, peeled
2 potatoes, peeled and sliced
Bouquet garni: parsley sprigs, bay leaf, thyme, 1 slice dried
orange peel; all wrapped in a cheesecloth bag
Salt and freshly ground black pepper

The aïoli
8 cloves garlic, peeled and crushed
6 egg yolks, at room temperature
1 cup olive oil, at room temperature
Salt and freshly ground black pepper
Lemon juice or vinegar
1 tablespoon mixed *fines herbes* (parsley, chervil, chives,
and tarragon)

The garnish
12 rounds French bread, fried in butter or oil until
golden brown

Equipment

Large earthenware saucepan or enameled or stainless steel
saucepan · Heavy large mortar or mixing bowl with
pestle · Whisk · Large mixing bowl · Food mill or
strong wire sieve (*tamis*) · Soup tureen

Working time: 35 minutes

Cooking time: 20 minutes

Serves: 4

1. To prepare the fish and the vegetables: Have the fish cleaned and scaled and cut into large chunks or slices. Clean the crabs and remove the tail flaps. Spread the vegetables in a large earthenware saucepan. Arrange the pieces of fish (crabs and shell-fish, too) on top. Just cover with boiling water, season with salt and pepper, and bring to a rapid boil. Throw in the herb bouquet and cook for 15 minutes over brisk heat.

2. Make the *aïoli*: pound the garlic cloves to a very smooth paste in a mortar or small mixing bowl with a strong pestle. Add egg yolks and pound together until thick and well blended. Stir in a little salt. Then add the oil, drop by drop, beating continuously with a wire whisk until the mixture begins to look and feel heavy. Now add the oil in a slow steady stream, beating all the time. When half the oil is in, add a few drops of lemon juice or vinegar and continue beating steadily while adding the remaining oil at a faster speed. Season and fold in the herbs. Transfer to a large mixing bowl.

3. To serve: As soon as the fish is cooked, transfer to a hot platter and keep warm. Set vegetables aside separately. Set a food mill or strong wire sieve over the large mixing bowl filled with *aïoli* and press the fish broth through, beating briskly with a whisk to combine the two preparations. Pour this mixture into the earthenware saucepan and stir in the reserved vegetables. Reheat gently, stirring continuously with a wooden spatula until the soup is thickened. Place the fried bread in the tureen and pour the soup over. Fish and soup are eaten together in large warmed soup plates. Suggested wine: a well-chilled very dry white wine.

SAUCE ROUILLE

Hot pepper and garlic sauce for Provençal fish soups and stews
(France)

Before getting into other Provençal fish soups and bouilla-baisse, I think it's best to begin with a common denominator, *rouille*, a fiery oil-based accompanying sauce. The word *rouille* means "rusty," which describes its reddish (red pimento) coloring. *Rouille* is an excellent sauce for saffron-flavored fish soups and stews and is served occasionally, too, with *bourride*. (I tasted it once that way at La Voile d'Or in Saint Raphael.) A good *rouille* should be thick, with the consistency of a light mayonnaise. Serve it in a side dish with a very small spoon—otherwise your guests may take too much, and set their mouths on fire.

Rouille can also be served with a Camargue eel dish, *catigau d'anguilles*, and an old and interesting fish stew called *L'ail cremat*. *L'ail cremat* is made with sea eel and assorted fish cooked together in a white wine and garlic-flavored fish broth. In Roussillon, where it's still popular, the hot pepper sauce is made with lard instead of oil.

Ingredients

>　2　large cloves garlic, peeled
>　1　roasted red pepper, cut up
>　1　dried red pepper, soaked in warm water until soft
>　1　2-inch slice French bread soaked in water or fish stock
>　　　　and squeezed to rid it of excess moisture
>　2　tablespoons olive oil
>　　　Salt and freshly ground black pepper
>　½　cup hot fish stock

Equipment

>　Mortar and pestle or electric blender

Working time: 5 minutes

Serves: 6

In a mortar crush the garlic with the peppers and the bread until pasty. Gradually work in the olive oil and blend until thick and smooth. Season with salt and pepper. Stir in the hot fish stock. Serve in a small sauceboat or bowl. This sauce comes out very well when made in an electric blender. In this case use 2 tablespoons water or stock to moisten and blend the garlic, red peppers, and bread mixture before adding the oil.

Here are two Provençal saffron-flavored fish soups, both similar to bouillabaisse and practical, since, for reasons I shall explain, it is impossible to make a true *bouillabaisse* in America.

Soupe de poissons "L'Aïgo-Sau" is made with one kind of fish; *Soupe de poissons "Kathy Jelen"* is made with at least four.

B O U I L L A B A I S S E

Please make either a *soupe de poissons "L'Aïgo-Sau"* or a *soupe de poissons "Kathy Jelen,"* and know that you are serving up a superb fish soup from Provence. If anyone should ask why you haven't given them bouillabaisse please recite one or all of the following reasons—my own not-too-serious reasons why it's impossible to make a bouillabaisse in North America:

1. For a true bouillabaisse you need a base broth made from at least a hundred tiny Mediterranean rock fish. (Clam juice *simply won't do.*)

2. For a true bouillabaisse you need a rascasse, and you cannot find rascasse in American waters. (A *rascasse* is a hideous red thing that you really shouldn't touch unless you have a Provençal fishmonger first remove its poisonous fins.)

3. For a true bouillabaisse you need vives and galinettes. (Substitutes such as wolf-fish, black drum and Gulf groupers *simply won't do.*)

4. It is indispensable for a true bouillabaisse that it be made with some water taken from the fishing grounds off Hyères, and that it be cooked in air no further than 100 kilometers from Marseilles. (The fact that both the waters and the air are now polluted does not invalidate this principle in the least.)

5. Finally, because no matter what you do there will be some silly snob who will say: "This is a rather nice fish soup, my dear—but, of course, not a true bouillabaisse."

SOUPE DE POISSONS "L'AÏGO-SAU"
Simple Provençal fish soup (France)

Ingredients

⅓ cup olive oil
1 cup chopped onions
1 leek or 2 scallions, chopped
½ teaspoon finely chopped garlic
1 cup fresh red ripe tomatoes, peeled, seeded, and chopped
Bouquet garni: sprigs of parsley, 1 crumbled bay leaf, fresh or dried thyme leaves, a few fennel leaves, or seeds, and a piece of dried orange peel; tied together
¼ teaspoon pulverized saffron
Pinch of cayenne
Salt and freshly ground black pepper
2½ pounds fresh, white-fleshed, saltwater fish, cleaned, cut into 1¼-inch chunks or slices, plus heads and trimmings
4 potatoes, peeled and cut into ½-inch rounds
½ stale French bread, cut into thin rounds, browned in olive oil, and rubbed with ½ clove of garlic
Sauce rouille (see page 16)

Equipment

5½-quart heavy enameled casserole · Large sieve set over a bowl

Working time: 30 minutes

Cooking time: 40 to 50 minutes

Serves: 4 to 5

1. In the casserole heat the oil and in it cook the onions and the leek until soft but not browned. Add the garlic, tomatoes, herbs, spices, and salt. Simmer, uncovered, 5 minutes, stirring frequently. Pour over 1½ quarts boiling water. Quickly bring to the boil. Add the fish heads and trimmings and cook 20 minutes.

2. Strain the cooking liquid. Pour back into the casserole and bring back to a rapid boil. Add the potatoes and the fish and cook at the boil 15 minutes or until the fish and the potatoes are just tender. Adjust the seasoning of the soup.

3. Serve in wide soup plates with the accompanying *rouille* and the fried bread rounds.

SOUPE DE POISSONS "KATHY JELEN"

Kathy Jelen's fish soup (France)

Ingredients

> 4½ pounds fresh saltwater fish (at least 4 kinds);
>   keep heads, tails, and trimmings
> 1 onion stuck with 2 cloves
> 1 onion, quartered
> 2 leeks, chopped
> 2 small carrots, scraped and chopped
> 2 bay leaves, crumbled
> 1 sprig fresh thyme
> 3 sprigs parsley
> 3½ tablespoons tomato paste
> 2 cloves garlic, peeled and halved
> ⅓ cup dried mushrooms, soaked in water until soft
>   Pinch of pulverized saffron
>   Salt and freshly ground pepper
> 1 pound (3–4) live crabs; blue, stone, or rock;
>   each about 3 inches across
> 1½ tablespoons cornstarch
>   Bowl of *sauce rouille* (see page 16)
>   Bowl of bread cubes that have been fried in oil until
>   golden with a little chopped garlic

Equipment

Large soup kettle · Food mill · Basin

Working time: 40 minutes

Cooking time: 1 hour 10 minutes

Serves: 6 to 8

1. Place the fish heads and trimmings, onions, leeks, carrots, herbs, tomato paste, garlic, mushrooms, saffron and 2½ quarts water in the soup kettle. Add salt and pepper. Simmer, covered, 45 minutes.

2. Meanwhile clean the crabs: drop the crabs into a basin of hot water. Allow to stand 10 minutes then drain. Pull off the tail flaps and discard the intestinal vein. Remove and discard the gills. Force the shell halves apart; remove and discard the head and stomach. Add the crabs to the simmering fish broth or cook separately in boiling salted water. Simmer, uncovered, 5 minutes longer. Remove the crabs and pick out as much meat as possible. Set aside.

3. Strain the fish broth through a food mill, pressing the vegetables and fish heads to extract all their juices. Return the fish broth to the soup kettle. Bring to the boil. Slip in the firm fish. Cook over brisk heat 10 minutes. Add the tender-fleshed fish and continue to cook 10 minutes longer. Lift out the fish, remove the bones. If the soup seems too thin thicken with cornstarch diluted in a little cold water. Bring back to the boil, stirring until thickened. Return the fish and the crabmeat to the simmering soup and allow to heat through. Serve in wide soup plates. Pass a bowl of *sauce rouille* and a bowl of toasted bread cubes.

CALAMARES EN SU TINTA #1

Squid in its own ink with garlic and almonds (Spain)

This inky black sauced dish of squid is rich and full of garlic (7 cloves). It makes an excellent *tapa*, or can be served as a main course over rice. (See page 98 for another version with tomato sauce.)

Ingredients

> 2 pounds squid
> ½ cup whole almonds
> 2 tablespoons chopped parsley
> 7 cloves garlic, peeled
> 2 1-inch slices Italian-style bread soaked in water
>   and squeezed dry
> ⅓ cup olive oil
> 2 cups dry white wine
> 1 cup water
> Salt and freshly ground black pepper

Equipment

> Mortar and pestle · Skillet · Sieve set over a small bowl

Working time: 40 minutes

Cooking time: 1 hour

Serves: 4 as a main course, 6 as a *tapa*

1. Clean the squid. Remove the sac from the head and set aside the tentacles. Peel off the outer mottled skin, discard the entrails and the thin bone. Put the ink sacs in the sieve. Wash the squid, inside and out, and the tentacles under cold running water; cut into bite-size pieces.

2. Chop the almonds then pound them in the mortar with

the parsley, garlic, and bread. Fry this paste in oil 2 to 3 minutes, stirring. Add the squid, the wine, and water. Season with salt and pepper. Simmer, covered, 45 minutes.

3. Crush the ink sacs and collect the ink in the bowl. Stir into the sauce, bring to the boil, season with salt and pepper, and cook at the simmer 10 minutes longer. Serve hot with boiled rice.

CACCIUCCO DE POLPI

Fricassee of squid, cuttlefish, or octopus
in the style of Populonia (Italy)

If you like squid but find *calamares en su tinta* a little too garlicky, you might want to try this recipe. It was given to me by Mario Ruspoli—filmmaker, whaling expert, renaissance man, and gastronome extraordinaire.

Among the relics of ancient Greece are a number of wine jugs decorated with little pictures of squid. This implies to me a recognition, even then, of a delightful connection. In this *cacciucco* the squid is simmered in wine, and the result is pure bliss.

Ingredients

    2 pounds squid, cuttlefish, or octopus
    ⅓ cup olive oil
    1 cup chopped onions
    1½ teaspoons finely chopped garlic
    ¼ cup finely chopped fresh parsley
      Salt and freshly ground black pepper
    1 cup dry red wine
    1 cup fresh tomato puree
      Toasted thin slices of Italian-style bread
        rubbed with garlic

Equipment

Shallow flameproof baking dish preferably earthenware with cover or aluminum foil

Working time: 30 minutes

Cooking time: 1 hour 35 minutes

Serves: 4

1. Preheat the oven to 325 degrees.
2. Wash the squid under cold running water. Peel off the outer mottled skin, remove the tentacles and reserve, discard the entrails, thin bone, and ink sac. Wash the body and tentacles carefully; cut into bite-size pieces. To clean octopus, cut away the eyes, entrails, and hard protruding parts. Pound with a cleaver to soften the flesh then cut into thin slices.
3. Heat the oil in the baking dish; stew the onions, garlic, and 3 tablespoons parsley in the oil until soft and golden. Add the squid or octopus and cook, stirring over high heat 2 to 3 minutes. Sprinkle with salt and pepper. Add the wine and the tomato puree. Cover and set in the oven to bake 1 hour or more, stirring often. When the squid is tender transfer to a warm serving dish, sprinkle with the remaining parsley, surround with toasted bread slices, and serve at once.

SCABETCH

Pickled fried fish (Algeria)

You find pickled fish all over the Mediterranean. This recipe is based on a dish I ate in Oran last year, undoubtedly *pied noir* in origin, since one finds similar things in southern France and Spain.

In Sète I ate anchovies "cooked" in a vinegar marinade like South American seviche. This kind of raw pickling is delicious, but unfortunately one can't find raw anchovies in the United States. However, in case you find yourself living around the Mediterranean sometime, here is how you do it.

If you want to eat the anchovies right away, wash and clean them, place them in a clean wide-mouthed jar and cover them with red or white wine vinegar. When the anchovies have turned white pour off the vinegar, and cover again with olive oil, salt, chopped garlic, parsley, and a bay leaf.

If you want to preserve the anchovies, clean them, place a layer in the jar, add a little salt, vinegar, and oil in equal quantities, then finely chopped garlic and a bay leaf. Cover and refrigerate 3 to 4 days before serving.

Ingredients

1½ pounds small fresh fish such as smelts or sardines
    Flour seasoned with salt and freshly ground black pepper
1 cup olive or vegetable oil
1 small carrot, sliced
1 small onion, sliced
4 large cloves garlic, peeled but left whole
⅔ cup white wine vinegar
¼ cup dry white wine
    Bouquet garni: imported bay leaf, thyme, parsley, and celery leaves, tied together
1 dried red pepper, or ¼ teaspoon cayenne
1 teaspoon salt
3–4 black peppercorns
    Chopped fresh parsley

Equipment

Enameled or stainless steel skillet · Deep glass or porcelain serving dish

Working time: 10 minutes

Cooking time: 35 minutes

Serves: 4

1. Wash and dry the fish, roll in seasoned flour, and fry in hot oil until golden on both sides. Remove, drain carefully, and place in the serving dish. Pour off half the frying oil.
2. Reheat the oil in the skillet and in it gently cook, stirring, the carrot, onion, and garlic cloves until softened but not

browned. Pour in the vinegar and the wine. Add the herbs, red pepper, salt, and peppercorns. Cook at the simmer 25 minutes.

3. Pour the contents of the skillet, still hot, over the fish. Allow to cool then refrigerate at least 36 hours before serving. Sprinkle with parsley just before serving.

Note: a teaspoon of tomato paste is sometimes added to the pan with the herbs.

BRANDADE DE MORUE EN CROUSTADE
Salt cod mousse in puff pastry shells with poached eggs (France)

I had a bite of this sublime dish off a friend's plate when I dined one time at the triple-starred L'Oustau de Baumanière in Les Baux-de-Provence. Later, when I tested it in Tangier, I served an Alka-seltzer cocktail first, and a good thing, too: the *brandade* contains almost a cup of olive oil, the hollandaise-*mousseline* is rich with whipped cream and egg yolks, the *vol au vents* are butter rich, and then there are the poached eggs!

Leftover *brandade* can be used as an omelet filling, or spread on toast, sprinkled with some grated gruyère, and grilled under the broiler until golden brown. With a little mashed potato beaten in it can be made into delicious *beignets:* drop globs of the mixture into oil heated to 375 degrees, deep fry until golden, and serve with lemon wedges.

I don't have my own recipe for *pâte feuilletée.* For years I made it as I'd been taught by Dione Lucas, then switched to the better directions of Julia Child. If you want to make your own *vol au vents* rather than use frozen packaged patty shells I refer you to Beck and Child, *Mastering The Art of French Cooking,* Volume Two.

Ingredients

    1 pound salt cod
      Bouquet garni
    1 onion, quartered
    3 cloves garlic, peeled

Continued

    3–4 black peppercorns
         About ⅓ cup milk or light cream
         About ⅔ cup virgin olive oil
         Vinegar
      6 eggs
      6 puff pastry patty shells, ready to bake
      2 egg yolks
      3 tablespoons lemon juice
         Salt and freshly ground white pepper
     ¼ pound unsalted butter
     ¼ cup heavy cream, stiffly whipped

Equipment

    Large basin · 1 large heavy saucepan · 2 small
    saucepans · Wooden pestle or heavy wooden spoon ·
    Electric blender · Baking sheet

Working and cooking time: 45 to 50 minutes

Serves: 6

    1. In a large basin soak the salt cod in cold water for 24 to 36
hours, changing the water at least 3 or 4 times. Rinse the cod; cut
into 3 or 4 pieces, place in the large heavy saucepan and cover
with fresh cold water. Add bouquet garni, quartered onion, 1
garlic clove, halved, and black peppercorns. Bring almost to the
boil and cook at a bare simmer 10 minutes.
    2. Drain; carefully remove the skin and bones of the fish, and
and flake finely. Crush the cod flakes with 2 garlic cloves in the
heavy saucepan over low heat.
    3. Put the milk in one of the small saucepans and the oil in
the other and set both over very low heat until they are warm but
not hot. Using a wooden pestle or heavy spoon pound the cod
with 2 tablespoons of the warmed oil until it becomes pasty.
Rinse the blender jar with very hot water, drain, and dry thoroughly. Place half the cod, a little more warm oil, and some of the
warm milk in the jar. Blend until smooth and creamy. Gradually
and alternately add the remaining cod, warm oil, and warm milk,

still blending. If the mixture seems too thick, thin with warm milk or oil. When creamy and somewhat resembling the texture of mashed potatoes, correct the seasoning. There will not be any need for salt.

4. In a saucepan bring vinegared water to the boil, lower to the simmer, and poach the eggs. Remove the eggs to drain on a towel.

5. Bake the patty shells

6. Make a hollandaise sauce: in a blender jar put 2 egg yolks, 2 tablespoons lemon juice, ¼ teaspoon salt, and a pinch of ground white pepper. Cover and hold. In a small saucepan melt the butter and when almost foaming blend the ingredients in the blender at high speed for 2 seconds. Uncover the jar, slowly add the foaming butter in a thin steady stream at high speed. The sauce should be thick and creamy. Add more salt, pepper, and lemon juice to taste. For this dish the sauce should be quite lemony. Keep warm.

7. Place 1 tablespoon of the prepared cod mixture into the bottom of each baked patty shell; set a drained poached egg on top and cover with more cod mixture. Top with the pastry cover. Fold the whipped cream into the sauce and spoon into a warmed sauceboat. Serve the filled pastry shells at once and pass the sauce in a sauceboat.

POULET AUX 40 GOUSSES D'AIL

Chicken with 40 cloves of garlic (France)

This is a real garlic-lover's dish; it'll fill your whole house with its perfume.

It's famous in Provence, but my version has a southwestern touch—an accompaniment of fried fennel bulbs. For 40 garlic cloves you'll need about 3 heads of garlic.

My advice is to seal the pot very well so that the garlic doesn't burn. When you serve the dish give a few cloves to each person. They can unpeel them with a knife and fork and spread them on toasted French bread.

Ingredients

    1 3½-pound ready-to-cook chicken
       Salt and freshly ground black pepper
    2 bouquets garni of Provençal herbs:
         bay leaf, parsley, thyme, celery leaves, savory,
         and a little rosemary
  ¼ cup olive oil
 40 cloves of garlic, unpeeled
    2 tablespoons anisette, pastis or anisina
       Flour and water paste
    2 pounds small fennel bulbs, quartered lengthwise
       Juice of 1 lemon
       Flour
    1 egg
       Breadcrumbs
       Oil for frying
       Slices of French bread, ½-inch thick, toasted golden
         brown in the oven

Equipment

3-quart oval casserole with tight-fitting cover, preferably earthenware · Skillet and slotted spoon · Kitchen twine · Saucepan

Working time: 20 minutes

Cooking time: 1 hour 15 minutes

Serves: 4 to 5

    1. Preheat the oven to 350 degrees.
    2. Rub the chicken with salt and pepper. Stuff with one of the herb bouquets then truss the chicken. Place in the casserole. Combine oil, garlic cloves in their skins, anisette, salt and pepper, and remaining herb bouquet and dump over the bird. Cover and seal the casserole with a ribbon of flour and water paste. Set in the oven to bake 1 hour 15 minutes.

3. Meanwhile cook the fennel in boiling salted water 20 minutes or until barely tender. Refresh under cold running water; drain. Sprinkle with lemon juice, salt and pepper, roll in flour, egg, and breadcrumbs. Fry in hot oil until golden brown on both sides. Drain on paper towels and keep hot until ready to serve.

4. Remove the casserole cover at table and serve directly from it. Pass a basket filled with toasted bread rounds and the fennel.

FARAREEJ MASHWI

Broiled chicken with oil, lemon, and garlic sauce (Egypt)

Ingredients

    1 small chicken, quartered
      Salt and freshly ground black pepper
    4 large cloves garlic, peeled and crushed
    ¼ cup freshly squeezed lemon juice
    3 tablespoons fruity olive oil
    1 tablespoon chopped parsley

Equipment

Broiling pan with rack

Working time: 5 minutes

Broiling time: 25 minutes (approximately)

Serves: 2

1. Season the chicken with salt and pepper. In a shallow dish filled with a mixture of garlic, lemon juice, oil, and parsley, roll the chicken quarters to coat them. Allow to marinate at least 1 hour.

2. Preheat the broiler. Drain the chicken, reserving the marinade. Set the broiling rack about 7 inches from the heat. Place the quarters, skin side down on the broiling rack, and broil

10 minutes, basting often with the cooking juices and a little of the marinade. Turn the quarters over and broil the chicken 10 minutes longer. Turn and brush twice more until both sides are golden brown and crusty. Pour over the remaining oil mixture. Serve at once.

POLLO TONNATO

Poached chicken with tuna fish sauce (Italy)

This is a Sicilian variation on the North Italian *vitello tonnato*. The sauce is exactly the same, a tuna-enriched mayonnaise.

Ingredients

- 2 teaspoons coarse salt
- 2 celery ribs, chopped
- 2 small onions, sliced
- 2 carrots, cut in 4
- 1 tomato
- 5 black peppercorns
- 4 parsley sprigs
- 1 3½–4-pound chicken, cleaned
- 2 egg yolks, at room temperature
- 1 cup olive oil, at room temperature
  Salt and freshly ground black pepper
- ¼ cup lemon juice
- 1 4-ounce can tunafish packed in olive oil, drained
- 3 flat anchovies, rinsed
- 2 tablespoons capers

For decoration: lemon quarters, sliced gherkins, and rinsed small capers

Equipment

Large soup kettle with cover · Electric blender · Mixing bowl · Whisk · Strainer

Working time: 35 minutes

Cooking time: 1 hour

Serves: 8 as a first course, 5 to 6 as a main course

1. To be prepared one or two days in advance. Place the salt, celery, onions, carrots, tomato, peppercorns, and parsley in the kettle with plenty of water. Bring *almost* to the boil; slip in the chicken, partially cover the kettle, and cook at the simmer for 1 hour or until the chicken is tender, skimming the surface often.

2. Remove the chicken, allow to cool completely, cut into serving pieces. Reduce the cooking liquid to 1 quart. Strain and reserve ½ cup for the sauce. Use the remaining broth for some other use.

3. Beat the egg yolks with the salt in a mixing bowl until thick and sticky. Add the olive oil drop by drop while beating constantly until you have a sauce the consistency of thick mayonnaise. Stir in 1 tablespoon lemon juice. Set aside.

4. Put tuna, anchovies, 1 tablespoon capers, and remaining lemon juice in the blender jar; whirl until smooth. If too thick, thin with a little chicken cooking liquid. Fold into the prepared mayonnaise. Stir in the remaining capers. Taste for salt and pepper.

5. Arrange half the chicken pieces on a flat serving dish. Spread over half the sauce, cover with the remaining chicken, and then the rest of the sauce. Refrigerate. When ready to serve decorate with lemon wedges, gherkins, and capers. Serve cool.

GIGOT D'AGNEAU FARCI

Stuffed boned leg of lamb from Languedoc (France)

This is a superb farmhouse dish from Languedoc. The lamb is boned and then stuffed with a mixture of ground pork, mushrooms, herbs, and breadcrumbs made from home-made whole wheat bread. It's roasted on a bed of diced bacon surrounded with potatoes and whole garlic cloves. In Languedoc roasting lamb is lavishly basted with bacon (or pork or goose) fat and rarely with wine or stock.

When serving, present the garlic as a vegetable, or spread on thin slices of glazed toasted French bread (see introduction to *crème à l'ail*, page 10 for instructions).

Ingredients

> 1　4-pound boned leg or shoulder of lamb
> Salt and freshly ground black pepper

> *Stuffing*
> 1　medium onion, finely chopped
> 1　tablespoon oil or fat
> ½　cup finely chopped mushrooms
> 1　cup crumbled stale bread, crusts removed, moistened
> 　　with ⅓ cup meat stock or water
> 2　tablespoons finely chopped parsley
> 1　teaspoon mixed dried herbs: thyme, bay leaf, savory,
> 　　rosemary
> ½　pound ground pork (3 parts lean and 1 part fat)
> ½　teaspoon finely chopped garlic

> ¼　cup melted bacon, pork, or goose fat
> ½　cup diced bacon
> 2½–3　pounds potatoes, peeled and quartered
> 2　heads garlic, broken into unpeeled cloves
> 1　imported bay leaf, crumbled
> 2　good pinches of crumbled fresh thyme, or dried thyme
> 1　tablespoon finely chopped parsley
> ½　cup dry white wine

Equipment

> Small saucepan　·　Skillet　·　Skewers or kitchen string
> Large roasting pan

Working time: 35 to 40 minutes

Roasting time: 2 hours

Serves: 8

1. Rub the lamb all over with salt and pepper.
2. Slowly soften the onion in oil. Add the mushrooms and continue cooking 5 to 8 minutes, stirring often, until most of the liquid in the pan has evaporated. Off heat combine with bread-crumbs, herbs, ground pork, chopped garlic, salt, and plenty of ground black pepper, mixing well. Cool.
3. Preheat the oven to 450 degrees.
4. Stuff the lamb and close up the opening with skewers or string. Rub the pan with melted bacon, pork, or goose fat. Scatter the diced bacon on the bottom and place the stuffed lamb on top. Surround with the potatoes and garlic cloves and sprinkle with more pepper. Gently warm the remaining fat with bay leaf, thyme, and parsley. Allow to steep a few minutes then pour over the lamb and potatoes. Roast, uncovered, 30 minutes.
5. Lower the oven heat to 375 degrees. Continue to roast the lamb about 1½ hours, basting often with the pan juices, for medium lamb.
6. Transfer the lamb to a carving board. Place the potatoes and the garlic cloves on a heated platter. Pour off most of the fat in the pan then deglaze with white wine. Boil down by half. Taste for seasoning. Carve the lamb and arrange in overlapping slices. Pour over the pan juices and serve at once.

GASCONNADE

Leg of lamb with garlic sauce (Languedoc, France)

When I was in Languedoc and asking for dishes with garlic I was overwhelmed with recipes for lamb. The combination is natural and sublime, as this and the preceding recipe seem to prove.

Note that the sauce for this *gasconnade* requires 20 to 25 garlic cloves.

Ingredients

    1 5-pound leg of lamb
      Salt and freshly ground black pepper
    1 onion, quartered
    1 carrot, scraped and chopped
    1 celery rib, chopped
    1 bay leaf, few parsley sprigs, a little thyme
    2 large cloves garlic, peeled and finely chopped
    6 anchovy fillets (half a 2-ounce tin), rinsed and mashed
    3 tablespoons olive oil
    1 tablespoon mixed fresh chopped herbs: parsley, thyme,
        rosemary, and savory
    2 heads garlic (20–25 cloves)
   ½ teaspoon meat extract such as Bovril or Liebig

Equipment

    Boning knife · Greased roasting pan · 2 saucepans ·
    Garlic press

Working time: 20 minutes

Roasting time: 1½ hours (approximately)

Serves: 8

    1. Preheat the oven to 425 degrees.
    2. Partially bone the lamb by working a thin-bladed knife around the hip end of the leg. Loosen the flesh around the bone until you reach the joint, then twist to remove. You do not remove the shank bone. Rub the cavity with pepper and very little salt.
    3. Make 2 cups lamb stock with the lamb bone, trimmings, onion, carrot, celery, and bay leaf, parsley, and thyme. Simmer 1 hour.
    4. Combine chopped garlic, anchovies, 1½ tablespoons oil, and the fresh chopped herbs and rub into the cavity of the lamb. Rub the surface with the remaining oil and set in a roasting pan. Roast 15 minutes. Reduce the oven heat to 350 degrees and con-

tinue to roast, basting with the pan juices, until cooked to desired doneness—10 to 12 minutes per pound for medium-rare lamb.

5. Meanwhile drop the garlic cloves in boiling water and cook at the boil 5 minutes. Drain, rinse under cold running water, and peel. Mash to a puree or push through a garlic press. You should have about ¼ cup pureed garlic.

6. Strain the lamb stock and reduce to 2 cups if necessary. Add the garlic puree and simmer 10 minutes.

7. When the lamb is cooked, remove and allow to settle a few minutes before carving. Meanwhile pour off the pan fat and discard. Add the garlic flavored stock and cook, stirring, over high heat until reduced by half. Stir in the meat extract and correct the seasoning. Serve the lamb sliced and pass the sauce in a sauceboat.

CHULETAS DE CORDERO A LA BRASA CON ALI-OLI

Lamb chops with oil, garlic, and egg sauce (Spain)

Ali-oli is a thick rich garlic mayonnaise, closely related to *aïoli*.

Ingredients

3 cloves garlic, peeled and crushed
About 1 cup olive oil, at room temperature
1 egg yolk, at room temperature
Juice of ½ lemon
Salt and freshly ground black pepper
8 thick lamb chops
2 tablespoons oil or butter for frying

Equipment

Mortar and pestle   ·   Whisk and mixing bowl   ·   Skillet

Working time: 10 minutes

Cooking time: 6 minutes (approximately)

Serves: 4

1. In a mortar pound the garlic with a few drops of olive oil to make a paste. Add the yolk and beat until thick and smooth. Transfer to a slightly warmed mixing bowl. Add the oil drop by drop in a thin stream, beating constantly. Mix in the lemon juice and season with salt and pepper. Scrape into a small serving dish.

2. Brown the chops in hot oil; lower the heat and cook until desired degree of doneness. Serve at once with the sauce.

ORTIKIA SKARA

Grilled quail (Greece)

In this recipe the quail are marinated in oil before grilling. Quail, like squab and other small birds, absorb oil very well, but the birds should always be fresh—never aged or hung.

Ingredients

　　4 quail, freshly killed, cleaned, and eviscerated
　　　Olive oil
　　1 tablespoon dried oregano or marjoram
　　2 bay leaves, crumbled
　　　Salt and freshly ground black pepper
　　2 lemons

Equipment

　　Glass or porcelain bowl · Cleaver · Charcoal
　　broiler (optional)

Working time: 10 minutes

Broiling time: 15 minutes

Serves: 4

1. Split the quail down the back and with a cleaver flatten each one on a hard work space. Place in a large bowl, sprinkle with olive oil, oregano, bay leaves, and salt and pepper. Cover the bowl and let stand in a cool place for a few hours, turning the quail once or twice.

2. Place the quail on the grid over hot coals or under a heated broiler. Broil, basting with oil, until cooked and golden brown on both sides. Serve with lemon wedges.

SPINACI AGLIO OLIO

Spinach with garlic and oil (Italy)

Ingredients

    2 pounds fresh spinach
4–5 tablespoons olive oil
2–3 cloves garlic, peeled but whole
      Freshly grated nutmeg
      Salt and freshly ground black pepper
    4 tablespoons parmesan cheese

Equipment

    Enameled or stainless steel saucepan with cover
    Colander · Enameled or stainless steel skillet

Working time: 25 minutes

Cooking time: 10 minutes

Serves: 4

1. Wash and trim the spinach. Place in the saucepan without water and cook, covered, over medium heat 5 minutes or until bright green and wilted. Dump into a colander; drain then press to remove excess water.

2. Heat the oil in the skillet. Add the garlic and fry until browned; remove and discard the garlic. Add the spinach to the skillet and toss over medium high heat until the spinach glistens and is well coated with oil. Season with salt, pepper, and grated nutmeg. Place in a serving dish and sprinkle with cheese.

OLIO VERDE

Genoese herbal oil for spaghetti (Italy)

Ingredients

¼ cup each: chopped fresh parsley, basil, and tarragon,
      or 2 tablespoons dried tarragon
2 tablespoons each: chopped rosemary, dried sage leaves
1 teaspoon each: dried marjoram or
      oregano, and fennel seeds
2 crumbled bay leaves
2 dried red peppers, crushed
1 cup fruity olive oil
    Salt
1½ pounds spaghetti
1 cup parmesan cheese

Equipment

Small mixing bowl · Food mill · Large pot ·
Small saucepan

Working time: 15 minutes

Cooking time: 5 to 10 minutes

Serves: 8

1. Combine the herbs and the peppers in the mixing bowl. Pour over olive oil to cover. Stir, pressing down on the herbs. Let stand 12 hours or more.
2. Press the herbal oil through the finest blade of a food mill.

The oil should be a deep green color and very aromatic. Discard the herbs. Salt to taste.

3. Cook the spaghetti al dente in boiling salted water. Heat the oil in a saucepan without boiling. Drain the spaghetti, toss with the oil, and serve at once with plenty of grated parmesan cheese.

SKORDALIA

Garlic sauce (Greece)

There are two ways to make *skordalia*: with mashed potatoes or with bread and nuts. Because of these additions it's thicker than the French *aïoli*.

The Greeks serve it with fried eggplant or zucchini, batter fried salt cod, or over sliced fried fish, boiled beets in a salad, or cold hard-boiled eggs.

Skordalia should be absolutely smooth. You can make it in a blender like mayonnaise, or follow the more traditional method below.

It's an ancient dish, and in its more primitive peasant version the egg yolks are left out.

Ingredients

      3 large cloves garlic, peeled and crushed
   ¾ cup (3½ ounces) walnut meats
      2 2-inch-thick slices stale Italian-style bread, soaked in water
            for a few minutes and squeezed dry
      2 egg yolks, at room temperature
   ¾–1 cup olive oil
      3 tablespoons lemon juice
         Salt

Equipment

   Mortar and pestle   ·   Mixing bowl and whisk

Working time: 5 minutes

Makes: 1⅓ cups, serves 4 to 6

In a mortar pound the garlic, nuts, and bread to a very smooth paste. Beat the egg yolks until thick in the mixing bowl. Add the garlic mixture and beat to thoroughly blend. Gradually add the oil, still beating, until the sauce is very thick. Stir in the lemon juice and salt to taste.

SALSA VERDE

Green sauce (Italy)

Italian *salsa verde* is another of the garlic-oil sauces, but with an addition of anchovies and herbs. The Italians love it on *bollito misto* (boiled meats), and it's a delicious accompaniment to paper-thin slices of raw beef.

In Liguria on Italy's west coast, there's a fish salad called *cappon magro* that requires a similar sauce. Parsley, lemon juice, garlic, anchovies, capers, hard-boiled eggs, and green olives are mashed to a paste, then a cup of oil is slowly beaten in.

In Yugoslavia, on the Dalmatian coast, there's a green oil sauce for fish. The green color comes from pickled cucumbers.

Ingredients

    ½ cup chopped parsley
    1 2-ounce tin anchovy fillets, rinsed, drained, and mashed
    1 tablespoon capers, rinsed and crushed
    2 small cloves garlic, peeled and finely chopped
    1 tablespoon red or white wine vinegar
    Freshly ground black pepper and a little salt
    ¾ cup olive oil

Equipment

Whisk · Small mixing bowl

Working time: 5 minutes

Makes: 1 cup

Combine the parsley, anchovy, capers, and garlic in a small bowl; mix well. Moisten with vinegar. Beat in the oil in a thin steady stream. Season with salt and pepper.

MAYONNAISE

By my own circuitous route I'd planned to end this chapter with mayonnaise—the inevitable culmination of the many things I've been talking about all along. Strange, perhaps, since there is no garlic in mayonnaise—but then not so strange if you look closely at the history of the dish.

It all began in ancient Egypt where an oil-garlic suspension was long a part of the national cuisine. The Romans learned about it there, played around with it, used their own superior olive oils, and produced something even better, which was picked up by the people they colonized.

When the Romans brought it to southern Spain, the Catalonians created their ancient specialty, *pa-y-al*—in which oil is added drop by drop to garlic crushed in a mortar with a little salt. The result is a thick emulsion used as a spread for bread.

The next step took place in Catalonia, too: the invention of *ali-oli* (see page 35), similar to *pa-y-al*, except that less garlic is used, and often an egg yolk is added to help richen and thicken the sauce. The slow addition and rapid beating of the oil becomes a principle followed in all the variant sauces which were devised in other regions.

A quick look at these variations provides a panorama of north Mediterranean cookery. Moving east from Catalonian *ali-oli* we come upon the *aïllade* of southwestern France. Here the egg yolks are dropped, and the thickening agent becomes ground walnuts or almonds. A little further east, in Provence, we find *aïoli* (see page 14)—closer to *ali-oli* than to *aïllade*, but with a lot more egg yolks and a richer emulsion as a result. In Liguria there is *agliata*—a garlic-oil sauce for fried salt cod and liver. In Greece the suspension is called *skordalia* (see page 39)—a garlic-oil sauce without egg yolks but thickened with ground walnuts or almonds or mashed potatoes. And finally in Turkey there is *tarator*—similar to *skordalia*, but thickened with mashed pine nuts instead.

Look at the list again—garlic and oil, always together with various thickeners such as egg yolks or ground nuts added from time to time. What then is mayonnaise? An *aïoli* without garlic? Or better defined: an oil and egg yolk emulsion. It's said to have been invented in the town of Mahon on the Spanish island of Minorca, and conventional wisdom has it that the Duc de Richelieu first brought it to France. There's some question whether the people of Mahon really left out all the garlic or merely minimized the amount, but the point of mayonnaise, the secret to its marvelous versatility, is that it is a pure and most subtly flavored emulsion that gives a texture to food instead of drowning it in strong taste.

I hope now you see the progression, and why a chapter on garlic and oil *has* to end this way. I've tried to explore the wonderful connection between the two materials around the Mediterranean, and then at the end, when the garlic is finally dropped, to suggest an opening up to a wider, less robust, less regional world of food.

You can do so many things with mayonnaise that it seems superfluous to list them. And once you've made it yourself at home, I doubt you'll ever want to go back to the store-bought kind. Mayonnaise is very easy to make, even easier than in the recipe below. If you want to do it quickly you can make it in a blender—almost every cookbook will tell you how. I personally prefer the by-hand method because it gives a somewhat heavier, richer-tasting sauce.

The secret of good mayonnaise is the quality of the oil. I personally find Plagniol from France the best. Remember that the oil should always be at room temperature, and so should the eggs, which must be very fresh. If by chance your mayonnaise should begin to curdle you can save it by starting again. Simply beat a teaspoon of oil into a new egg yolk, then slowly add the curdled mixture, beating as you go along. The two will emulsify together and the end result should be creamy and smooth.

A combination of salad and olive oil is suggested to those who object to the strong taste of olive oil.

Ingredients

    2 egg yolks, at room temperature
   ½ teaspoon Dijon mustard
    2 teaspoons vinegar
   ½ teaspoon salt
    2 pinches ground white pepper
 1¼ cups virgin olive oil, or salad oil,
        or a combination of the two
    1 tablespoon lemon juice

Equipment

Whisk · Warmed mixing bowl

Working time: 5 minutes or less

Makes: 1½ cups

Combine the egg yolks, mustard, vinegar, salt, and pepper in the mixing bowl. Stir briskly until well blended. Slowly add the oil drop by drop, beating vigorously without stopping. When the mixture is thick, add the remaining oil in a slow steady stream. Stir in the lemon juice.

Olives

ALL about the Mediterranean you find them—gnarled, wind-swept, thick, craggy, ancient trees. There is one in my garden in Tangier, a young *olivier*, perhaps no more than one hundred years old. Even among the jacarandas and fruit trees, it is the most stately, the one that looks most like it belongs.

Athena, say the Greeks, brought forth the olive tree, her gift of plenty to man. And ever since it has symbolized Mediterranean agriculture, the richness of the fruits of the earth. The olive branch has long meant peace; even now it's featured on the United Nations' flag. But to me it symbolizes even more—it is the sign of the Mediterranean, the sign that tells me I am in the place where man first learned how to live.

Of course its main bounty is oil, the great medium for cooking around the sea. But the fruit itself is eaten too, though differently in different places. Draw a line across the sole of the Italian boot, along the eastern shore of Sicily then across the water to the Tunisian–Libyan frontier. You will have cut the Mediterranean almost precisely in half, and divided opinion on the olive, too. To the east—Yugoslavia, Greece, Turkey, Syria, Lebanon, Egypt, and Libya—men eat the olive marinated or cured, but never cooked along with their food. But to the west—Italy, southern France, and Spain, and in the countries of the Maghreb—the olive is essential to cooking, appearing in every cuisine. Why?

Why is it that this fruit grown about the entire sea is eaten only as a fruit in one half of the region while it is a component of dishes in the other? I have never figured it out. A great gastronomic mystery, perhaps, still waiting to be solved.

Olives can be collected when still green and unripe, then put into solutions to soak. If the farmer waits a while longer his olives will turn purple, and if he waits longer still they will become black. But even then, black and dried by the sun, they must be put in brine or oil before their bitterness goes away. All sorts of herbs are used to flavor them: bay leaves, rosemary, orange or lemon peel, fennel, oregano; and thus the many qualities and varieties, dependent on tree, soil, and cure.

Impossible to imagine a *salade niçoise* without the famous black olives of Nice. Or a picnic in Majorca without the fat salty green Spanish ones stuffed with almonds, anchovies, or peppers from Murcia. I'll never forget a sunset on Skiathos facing the Aegean, with corn fields and olive trees surrounding the cove. I nibbled on Greek *kalamatas* and drank a chilled white St. Helena wine.

In Italy you find them in pizzas, used in stuffings for all sorts of meats, game, and poultry, in Sicilian caponata, cooked with cauliflower or broccoli, and on spaghetti, of course, in *puttanesca* sauce. In Malta they appear in a turtle stew, along with apples, chestnuts, and tomatoes, raisins, capers, and nuts. You cannot conceive of Moroccan food without thinking of chicken, lemon, and olives. In Tunis there is a *ragoût aux olives farcies*, and in Algeria the *pied noirs* have honored the olive by creating an olive tart. In Catalonia olives are used as a stuffing for freshwater fish, along with mushrooms, almonds, and parsley. In Malaga they are braised with fresh tuna; in Seville they are roasted with loin of pork.

If you eat a steak in Toulon you my find on olive wrapped in an anchovy strip on the side of your plate. In Provence they will turn up in numerous daubes of beef, turkey, rabbit, or duck. And in Languedoc they have invented something sublime, *capon à la carcassonnaise*, a capon stuffed with olives, sausage, and chicken livers, its neck stuffed separately with garlic and breadcrumbs, then the whole trussed and roasted on a spit.

What more is there to say? Olives are *the* Mediterranean food, whether eaten plain as *mezzes* (appetizers) in the Levant, or in countless culinary masterpieces in Italy, France, North Africa, and Spain. What follows is a sampling, some of the best olive dishes I know. If you merely read you may sometimes think that olives are just another item on an ingredients list. But if you cook and taste I guarantee you will know the olives are there.

ELYES

Marinated olives (Greece)

Here's the Greek way of marinating olives, simple and good to know because you can use it for either black or green olives, or even combine the two if you wish.

Marinated olives are served as an hors d'oeuvre all over the Mediterranean region. In Provence they're gently crushed, soaked and then marinated in a brine with herbs for flavoring. In Lebanon where they're put up in jars either with lemon or oil and spices, they're often served with other *mezzes*—stuffed grape leaves, *hummus*, or on a little plate, nestled among fresh sprigs of rocket or arugula.

One of the most famous ways of marinating olives, the Calabrian *olive schiacciate* has been described by Waverly Root in *The Food of Italy*: Hard green olives are crushed into a paste with a pestle, then left in their brine for several days, pressed by a weight. Afterwards they're sprinkled with garlic and pimento and preserved in vinegar.

Ingredients

　　2　cups imported black or green olives, packed in brine
　　1　lemon, halved then thinly sliced
　　1　tablespoon dried oregano or thyme
　　2　cloves garlic, peeled and slightly bruised
　　2　small Salonika peppers or 2 bruised red hot chili peppers
　　　　Imported virgin olive oil

Equipment

>   Cleaver · Mixing bowl · 2 very clean Mason jars

Working time: 10 minutes

1. Rinse the olives under cold running water. Drain. Gently crush each one with the side of a small cleaver. The skin and the pulp should tear but do not break the pit.

2. In a mixing bowl combine olives, lemon slices, and herbs. Toss. Pack tightly in mason jars. Top each jar with a clove of garlic and a hot pepper. Cover completely with olive oil, close tightly, and let stand 1 week before using.

TORTINO RIPIENO DI SCAROLE E OLIVE

Neapolitan "cake" stuffed with escarole and black olives (Italy)

If you stroll the streets of Naples late in the afternoon you might look up and see Neapolitans consuming this delicious filling cake on their balconies. And in the surrounding countryside, especially near Sarno, you'll find this same filling in the local pizzas.

Ingredients

>   1 package dry active yeast
>   ½ teaspoon sugar
>   ¼ cup lukewarm water
>   2 cups all-purpose flour, sifted
>   ⅓ cup melted and cooled lard or butter
>   Salt and freshly ground black pepper

Filling
>   5 tablespoons olive oil
>   3–4 very small heads escarole, shredded
>   1 cup juicy dark olives (preferably *gaetas*), rinsed, pitted
>   and chopped
>   ½ cup yellow raisins, previously soaked in warm water

½ cup pine nuts
1 tablespoon capers, rinsed
1 clove garlic, chopped
2–3 tablespoons chopped parsley

1 egg white

Equipment

Mixing bowl · 5-quart casserole · A 10-inch deep cake pan, oiled

Working time: 30 minutes

Baking time: 45 minutes

Serves: 4

1. Dissolve the yeast in ¼ cup sugared warm water. Set in a warm place until bubbly. Place the flour in a mixing bowl. Make a deep hollow in the center. Add the bubbling yeast, 3 tablespoons of the lard, 1 teaspoon salt, and ½ teaspoon black pepper. Work to form a smooth elastic dough, adding more flour or lukewarm water as necessary. Cover the dough loosely with a damp towel and let rise in a warm place 1 hour or until doubled in bulk.

2. Meanwhile heat 4 tablespoons of the olive oil in the casserole. Add the shredded escarole and cook, stirring, for 10 minutes. When most of the liquid in the pan has evaporated, add olives, raisins, pine nuts, capers, garlic, and parsley. Continue cooking 10 minutes, stirring often. Season well with pepper and a little salt. Remove from heat, drain completely and allow to cool to room temperature.

3. Punch down the dough in the bowl, turn out onto a lightly floured board and knead for 3 minutes. Work in the remaining lard and continue to knead until the dough is smooth. Cut into 2 equal parts. Lightly press one part into an oiled cake pan. Spread the well-drained escarole filling evenly over the dough and cover with the remaining dough pressing and pushing

it to cover the filling completely. Brush with the remaining table-spoon of oil, cover, and let rise a second time until almost doubled in bulk.

4. Preheat the oven to 375 degrees.

5. Brush with egg white beaten with 1 teaspoon water. This will make a shiny crust. Set in the preheated oven to bake for about 45 minutes. Serve lukewarm or cold.

PISSALADIÈRE

Onion, anchovy, and olive tart (France)

There are two ways of doing this "Provençal pizza"—with tomatoes, or without. I prefer the tomato variation, but if you want to make the other, just leave the tomatoes out and increase the amount of onions. Also, if you want to serve little squares of pissaladière as an hors d'oeuvre, forget the pizza pan and use a rectangular or square baking sheet, then cut the pie with a serrated knife.

Ingredients

Pastry
  1 package dry active yeast
  ½ teaspoon sugar
  2 cups all-purpose flour, sifted
  1 teaspoon salt
  1 tablespoon olive oil

Filling
  ¼ cup strong fruity olive oil
  3 large Bermuda onions, halved then thinly sliced
  2 small cloves garlic, chopped
3–4 tablespoons breadcrumbs
  2 cups fresh or canned peeled, seeded,
       and chopped tomatoes
     Salt and freshly ground black pepper
  2 teaspoons fresh thyme, basil, or rosemary or
       1 teaspoon dried

¼ cup grated parmesan or gruyère cheese
2 2-ounce cans flat anchovy fillets, drained
12 imported pitted black olives

Equipment

Mixing bowl · 12- to 14-inch skillet · Oiled pizza pan

Working time: 50 minutes

Baking time: 20 to 25 minutes

Serves: 4 to 6

1. Dissolve the yeast in ⅔ cup warm sugared water and set in a warm place until bubbly.

2. Place the flour in the mixing bowl and make a well in the middle. Add salt, bubbling yeast, oil, and enough warm water to form a soft dough. Turn the dough out onto a lightly floured board and knead hard until smooth and elastic, about 10 minutes. Cover the dough loosely with a damp towel and let rise in a warm place until doubled in bulk, about 1 hour.

3. Meanwhile heat half the olive oil in the skillet, add the onions and garlic, and cook over low heat for 20 to 25 minutes, stirring often, until the onions are very soft and golden. Season with salt and pepper. Allow to cool.

4. Preheat the oven to 400 degrees.

5. Punch the dough down then roll out evenly into a circle 1 inch larger than the pan. Transfer to the oiled pizza pan. Sprinkle the surface with breadcrumbs and cover the dough to within 1 inch of its edges with the cooked onions. Mix tomatoes with salt, pepper, herb, and cheese and spread over the onion. Arrange the anchovy fillets lattice fashion on top and place an olive in each section. Dribble remaining olive oil over all. Bake 20 to 25 minutes or until the edges of the dough are cooked and browned. Serve, hot, lukewarm, or cold.

TAPENADE

Provençal olive paste (France)

This is a typical Provençal way of treating olives, resulting in a somewhat salty and sharp spread, delicious on toast. In parts of Provence *tapenade* is used in a fresh cheese tart, brushed onto the pastry with olive oil, spread with cheese, sprinkled with herbs, and baked in the oven.

Ingredients

  1 2-ounce tin anchovy fillets, rinsed and drained
  1 cup black Mediterranean-type olives, pitted, and roughly chopped
  2 tablespoons capers, rinsed and drained
  1 tablespoon lemon juice
  ½ teaspoon Dijon mustard
     Freshly ground black pepper
  2 tablespoons cognac
  ¼–½ cup fruity olive oil

Equipment

Electric blender

Working time: 10 minutes

Makes: 1 cup (approximately)

Blend anchovy fillets, olives, capers, lemon juice, mustard, freshly ground pepper to taste and cognac until pasty. Still blending pour in just enough olive oil in a steady stream to obtain a smooth thick sauce. Scoop into a pretty pottery bowl and chill well before serving.

SPAGHETTI ALLA PUTTANESCA

Spaghetti with olive sauce (Italy)

There are numerous ways of doing this famous dish. Here are three variations, all of them superb. Conventional wisdom has it that spaghetti alla puttanesca was invented by the whores of Naples as quick and lusty fortification, and also to lure customers with a delicious aroma of olives, garlic, and anchovies simmering in rich tomato sauce. But my informants tell me otherwise. *They* say that *puttanesca* is an ideal dish for a respectable woman enjoying an illicit affair between five and seven in the afternoon. She can prepare it in advance, let it marinate while she is out on her adventure, then dash home and in five minutes serve it up to her famished spouse.

Ingredients

- ½ pound juicy black Greek olives, rinsed, pitted, and finely chopped
- ½ pound green olives, rinsed, pitted, and finely chopped
- 1 2-ounce tin anchovy fillets, rinsed and mashed
- 1 tablespoon capers, rinsed and drained
- 2–3 tablespoons chopped pickled or raw mushrooms (optional)
- 2 tablespoons chopped parsley
- 2–3 fresh basil leaves, chopped (optional)
- 2–3 cloves garlic, finely chopped
  - Freshly ground black pepper
  - Olive oil
- 2 pounds spaghetti
  - Salt

Equipment

Mixing bowl · Large pot · Saucepan

Working time: 25 minutes

Marinating time: 2 hours

Serves: 10 to 12

1. Combine olives, anchovies, capers, mushrooms, herbs, garlic, and pepper in the mixing bowl. Pour over enough olive oil to cover. Allow to stand and marinate 2 hours, turning the ingredients often and adding more oil if necessary to keep the olive mixture completely covered.

2. Cook the spaghetti in boiling salted water until tender. Meanwhile in a saucepan heat the olive and oil mixture but do not allow it to boil. Drain the spaghetti, pour over the sauce and serve at once. Serve *without* grated cheese.

VARIATION # 1

This variation may sound peculiar, but I assure you that the touch of raisins blends perfectly with everything else.

Ingredients

2½ ounces black Greek olives, rinsed, pitted, and chopped
4 ounces green olives, rinsed, pitted, and chopped
½ cup yellow raisins, soaked
¾ cup pine nuts, chopped
3 anchovy fillets, rinsed and mashed
Cayenne
Olive oil
1 pound spaghetti

Equipment

Same as above

Working time: 20 minutes

Marinating time: 2 hours

Serves: 6

Proceed as directed above. Before serving taste the sauce—it should be fiery.

variation # 2

This is the traditional *puttanesca*, the one you will find on the menu of a chic trattoria. It is certainly good, but to me nowhere as good as the other two.

Ingredients

    1 cup black olives, rinsed, pitted, and chopped
    5 anchovy fillets, rinsed and mashed
    1 tablespoon capers
    2 cloves garlic, finely chopped
    1 tablespoon finely chopped parsley
      Cayenne
      Olive oil
    2 cups prepared tomato sauce, heated
    1 pound spaghetti

Equipment

Same as above plus a skillet

Working time: 20 minutes

Serves: 6

Combine olives, anchovy fillets, capers, garlic, parsley, and cayenne. Heat a little olive oil in the skillet and in it sauté the olive mixture 2 to 3 minutes. Add the tomato sauce and readjust the seasoning. Simmer 5 minutes. Serve on spaghetti that has been freshly cooked, without grated cheese.

IMPANATA DI PESCA (SPADA) ALLA MESSINESE

Swordfish pie in the style of Messina (Italy)

I think this unusual pie is best with swordfish, but any firm-fleshed fish such as tuna or bass will do. You can substitute potatoes for the zucchini, but be sure to keep the olives, raisins, and pine nuts, for a very special Sicilian taste. Actually this dish is similar to the famous Maltese lampuki pie. (Lampuki is a fish found in Maltese waters in late summer and early fall.) In Malta they use cauliflower instead of zucchini and sometimes leave out the raisins and pine nuts. But to my mind this sort of simplification defeats much of the point. The sugar crust dates back to the Saracens.

Ingredients

Sweet pastry dough
   3 cups all-purpose flour, sifted
   ½ cup granulated sugar
     Salt
   8 tablespoons unsalted butter, or lard, or a mixture
   2 egg yolks
   ¼ cup ice water

Filling
   6 small zucchini, cut into long thin strips
     Flour seasoned with salt and pepper for dredging
   1 egg, beaten
     Olive oil
   1 pound firm-fleshed fish, cut into ¾-inch chunks
       (about 2 cups)
     Juice of 1 lemon
     Salt and freshly ground black pepper
   ½ cup finely chopped onion
   4 ripe tomatoes, peeled, seeded, and chopped

¼ cup chopped celery
1 cup rinsed and pitted green olives
2 tablespoons yellow raisins, soaked in water until plump then drained
2 tablespoons pine nuts
2 tablespoons capers
1 egg yolk beaten with 1 teaspoon water for glaze

Equipment

Large mixing bowl · Skillet · Slotted spoon
Deep 8- or 9-inch cake pan · Small funnel or
1½-inch parchment tube

Working time: 45 minutes

Baking time: 1 hour (approximately)

Serves: 6 to 8 as a first course

1. To make the pastry: mix flour, sugar, and a little salt. Rub in the butter or lard. Mix in the egg yolks and enough ice water to form a ball of dough. Knead until smooth. Chill 2 to 3 hours.

2. Dip the zucchini into seasoned flour, beaten egg, and flour again. In a skillet sauté the prepared zucchini in hot oil until golden brown on both sides. Remove to drain on paper towels.

3. Discard the burned oil. Add 3 to 4 tablespoons fresh oil to the skillet and in it lightly brown the fish chunks. Remove to a side dish and sprinkle with lemon juice, salt and pepper.

4. In the same oil gently cook the onions until soft. Stir in the tomatoes and celery and cook, uncovered, 10 minutes, stirring often. Add the olives, raisins, pine nuts, and capers. Raise heat and reduce the contents of the pan by half. Salt and pepper to taste. Pour over the fish chunks and allow to cool completely.

5. Preheat the oven to 375 degrees.

6. Roll out half the pastry into a large circle and carefully fit into the cake pan. Arrange half the fried zucchini in one layer, cover with the fish-tomato mixture, and then with the remaining zucchini. Roll the remaining pastry and cover the pie. Crimp the

edges and trim neatly. Make a hole in the center and insert a small funnel or a 1½-inch long paper parchment tube. This allows the steam to escape during the baking. Glaze the top with beaten egg and set the pie in the oven to bake 1 hour. Serve hot.

HANCHA BIL SALSA OU ZEETOON

Eel with tomatoes and olives (Tunisia)

In the autumn of 1974 I took a long trip through the Mahgreb with a friend who was writing a novel about the nineteenth-century adventuress Isabelle Eberhardt, and was retracing her footsteps. We spent several weeks in Tunis and in several Tunisian homes we were served this dish with the fish mérou. Mérou is the favorite Tunisian fish, but alas it doesn't exist in America. I was wondering what to substitute in its place when unexpectedly my problem was solved. The city of Tunis is very cosmopolitan, the most Parisian of North African towns. At a fine little French bistro near the Africa Hotel I came upon this splendid variation with eel.

Ingredients

    1¾ pounds fresh eel
        Salt and freshly ground black pepper
        Flour
    ¼ cup oil
    ½ cup chopped onion
    2 garlic cloves, chopped
    1 cup tomato sauce, fresh or canned
    ½ teaspoon *harissa* (see page 182)
    1 bay leaf
    3 sprigs parsley
    1 cup juicy black olives, pitted
        Juice of 1 lemon
        Chopped parsley for garnish

Equipment

    Large enameled skillet · Tongs

Working time: 10 minutes

Cooking time: 20 minutes

Serves: 4 to 6

    1. To remove the skin broil under high heat until the skin blisters. Cut the eel into 1-inch pieces. Season each piece with salt and pepper then roll in flour.

    2. In the skillet lightly brown the pieces of eel in hot oil on both sides then add the onion and garlic. Cook 2 to 3 minutes. Add the tomato sauce, *harissa*, herbs, and 1½ cups water. Cook, covered, 10 minutes. Add the olives and continue cooking, uncovered, until the eel is tender. Add lemon juice. Serve on a heated platter and decorate with chopped parsley.

DJEJ BIL ZEETOON

Chicken with olives, Tangier style (Morocco)

    Chicken with lemon and olives is one of the most famous of all Moroccan dishes. I didn't have room in my book *Couscous and Other Good Food from Morocco* for this Tangier variation, which is the one I serve most frequently.

Ingredients

    1 2½–3-pound chicken, quartered
    3 cloves garlic, peeled and crushed (optional)
       Salt
   ½ cup vegetable oil
 1½ cups chopped onion
   ½ teaspoon freshly ground pepper
    1 teaspoon ground ginger

Continued

½ teaspoon turmeric
2 ripe tomatoes, peeled and chopped
4 sprigs each: fresh coriander and parsley
1 preserved lemon (see page 287)
1 cup green olives (such as Greek Royal, Victoria, Agrinon, or Napfpiou), or Spanish green olives, pitted

Equipment

Large heavy casserole with tight-fitting lid

Working time: 20 minutes

Cooking time: 1 hour (approximately)

Serves: 4

1. Wash and drain the chicken. To purify the chicken, North Africans blend the garlic with 1 tablespoon salt to make a paste which is then rubbed into the cavity and flesh of the chicken. The bird is rinsed well and then dried with paper towels. This step is optional.

2. Brown the chicken quarters in hot oil. Add the onions and stir-cook 3 to 4 minutes. Add salt, pepper, ginger, and turmeric. Cook over medium heat 5 minutes, tossing and turning the chicken quarters often. Add the tomatoes. Cook over high heat until the pan juices are well reduced. Add ½ cup water and cook over moderate heat, stirring, until evaporated. Add another 1½ cups water, a little at a time, stirring constantly. When the pan juices are thick, add the herbs. Cover tightly and cook over low heat until the chicken is tender.

3. Rinse and cut up the preserved lemon. Drop olives into boiling water, simmer 2 to 3 minutes then drain. Add the lemon and olives to the casserole 5 minutes before serving. Uncover the casserole and cook over high heat to reduce the sauce slightly.

DJEJ BIL ZEETOON MESLALLA

Chicken smothered in green olives (Morocco)

Ingredients

    1 3½-pound chicken, whole
    3 cloves garlic, peeled and crushed (optional)
       Salt
    ½ teaspoon ground ginger
    ½ teaspoon ground black pepper
       Pinch of pulverized saffron, or ¼ teaspoon turmeric
    ¼ teaspoon ground cumin
    ¼ teaspoon sweet paprika
   1½ teaspoon finely chopped garlic
    ½ cup grated onion
    ¼ cup finely chopped parsley
    ¼ cup finely chopped fresh coriander
    3 tablespoons oil
    1 1-pound jar green olives packed in brine
    4 tablespoons lemon juice, or more to taste

Equipment

Large heavy casserole   ·   Small saucepan   ·   Olive pitter

Working time: 30 minutes

Cooking time: 1 hour

Serves: 4

1. Wash the chicken then drain. The remainder of this step is optional; the North Africans do it to purify the chicken. Blend the garlic with one tablespoon salt to make a paste. Rub the paste into the cavity and the flesh of the chicken. Rinse well.
2. Place the chicken in the casserole with the spices, garlic,

onions, herbs, oil, and 2 cups water. Simmer, covered, 30 minutes, turning the chicken often in the cooking liquid.

3. Meanwhile pit the olives. To rid them of their bitterness boil them 3 times, changing the water each time.

4. Add the drained pitted olives and the lemon juice to the casserole and continue cooking until the chicken is very tender. Transfer the chicken to a serving dish. Using a slotted spoon remove the olives and place around the chicken. Meanwhile reduce the cooking liquid in the casserole to a thick sauce. Adjust the salt and lemon juice to taste. Pour over the chicken. Serve at once.

POULET À LA CAMARGUAISE

Chicken prepared in the style of the Camargue (France)

This chicken and olive dish, completely different in procedure and flavor from the more familiar chicken and olive dishes of North Africa, is from one of my favorite parts of France—the flat rough wild cowboy country of the Camargue. In the Camargue one would accompany this dish with the delicious local rice and braised white onions.

Ingredients

> 1 3–3½-pound chicken, cut into serving pieces
>   Salt and freshly ground black pepper
> 3 tablespoons olive oil
> ½ cup diced bacon
> ½ cup chopped onion
> 2 teaspoons finely chopped garlic
> ½ cup dry white wine
> 1 cup fresh or canned tomato sauce
> 1 cup rich chicken stock
> 3 tablespoons finely chopped parsley
> 1 bay leaf
> ¼ teaspoon crumbled thyme leaves, or a pinch of dried
>   thyme
>   Cayenne

About 12 juicy black olives, rinsed and pitted
About 12 green olives, rinsed and pitted

Equipment

3½-quart heavy casserole with tight-fitting lid

Working time: 20 minutes

Cooking time: 45 minutes

Serves: 4 to 5

1. Season the chicken pieces with salt and pepper. Heat the oil in the casserole and in it brown the chicken pieces on both sides. Remove the pieces of chicken and keep warm and moist.

2. Add the bacon, onion, and garlic to the pan drippings and cook, stirring, for 3 to 4 minutes. Pour in the wine, raise the heat, and cook, stirring, until most of the wine evaporates.

3. Return the chicken to the casserole and add the tomato sauce, chicken stock, half the parsley, and the herbs. Season with salt, pepper, and cayenne to taste. Simmer, covered, 30 minutes or until the chicken is tender. If the cooking juices are thin raise the heat and rapidly boil down until thick.

4. Five minutes before serving stir in the olives and correct the seasoning. Sprinkle with the remaining chopped parsley.

FRITTO MISTO ALLA MARCHIGIANA

Mixed fry as prepared in the Marches (Italy)

Of course there are as many versions of *fritto misto* in northern Italy as there are of bouillabaisse in Provence, but what's interesting about this particular recipe from the Marches is that it includes olives, and stuffed olives at that. For this alone it's unique in Italian cuisine.

In Spain, of course, olives are frequently stuffed with anchovy butter, almonds, tuna, red pepper, and ham. In Seville they are even stuffed with chicken and eggs, then roasted along with a loin of pork. But in this dish the stuffing is ingenious—the very stuffing used in Tuscan *agnolotti*. Then, the olives are rolled in batter and fried.

If you don't have any leftover *agnolotti* filling and want to mix up something fairly fast, make a small mixture of cooked, ground veal, breadcrumbs, and grated parmesan cheese, bind it with a small beaten egg, and then season with salt, pepper, and grated nutmeg.

Ingredients

       1 pound calf's brains (2 pairs)
       2 tablespoons vinegar
         Salt
       1 package frozen artichoke hearts
       1 raw chicken breast, skinned, boned,
            and cut into ½-inch slices, cross-wise
       1 lemon
         Freshly ground black pepper
       4 small zucchini, cut into ½-inch slices
       2 dozen extra large green olives, pitted
      ¼ cup leftover filling from ravioli
            or *agnolotti Toscani* (see page 143)
         Flour
       2 beaten eggs
     1½ cups soft breadcrumbs
         Vegetable oil for frying
         Lemon quarters

Equipment

     Saucepan · Deep fat fryer or deep skillet · Slotted
     spoon · Paper towels · Shallow bowl

Working time: 45 minutes

Frying time: 30 minutes

Serves: 4

1. Soak the brains in cold water acidulated with 1 tablespoon vinegar. Let soak for 2 to 3 hours. Meanwhile defrost the artichoke hearts.

2. Drain the brains and trim away the outer membrane and blood spots. Rinse well. Place the brains in a saucepan; cover with a quart of water to which 1 tablespoon vinegar and 1 teaspoon salt have been added. Bring to a near boil and cook below the simmer 15 minutes. Allow the brains to cool in the cooking liquid. Drain and pat dry with paper towels. Cut the brains into bite-size pieces. Place in a shallow bowl with the sliced chicken breast and artichokes; sprinkle with the juice of 1 lemon and season with salt and pepper. Let stand 30 minutes.

3. Sprinkle the zucchini with salt and let stand 30 minutes. Meanwhile stuff the olives with the prepared filling.

4. Rinse the zucchini slices and pat dry with paper towels. Also pat dry the artichokes, the calf's brains, and the slices of chicken. Dip each ingredient including the stuffed olives, into flour seasoned with salt and pepper, beaten eggs, and finally breadcrumbs.

Dish can be prepared ahead of time to this point.

5. Heat the frying oil to 375 degrees and deep fry the prepared ingredients a few at a time until nicely browned on all sides. Drain on paper towels and serve hot. Serve with lemon quarters.

ANITRA CON OLIVE

Genoese duck with green olives (Italy)

Here's an Italian variation of the famous classic French dish, *canard aux olives*. It's especially nice, I think, because it has an Italian *battuto* of chopped carrot, celery, onions, and bacon at its base, and carries the aromatic flavor of fresh rosemary.

Ingredients

>   1 4½–5-pound duck, cut into serving pieces
>   Salt and freshly ground black pepper
>   ½ cup chopped onion
>   ½ cup chopped carrot
>   1 celery rib, chopped
>   2 ½-inch-thick bacon slices, diced
>   1 cup dry white wine
>   1 cup chicken or duck stock
>   1 bay leaf
>   3 sprigs parsley
>   ½ teaspoon crumbled rosemary
>   1 cup large green olives, rinsed and pitted

Equipment

> Skillet · 4- or 5-quart heavy casserole with lid ·
> Strainer or food mill

Working time: 20 minutes

Cooking time: 40 minutes

Serves: 4

1. Remove the excess fat from the duck cavity and prick the skin all over with a fork. In a skillet render some of the fat and in it brown the duck pieces on all sides. Transfer to the casserole. Sprinkle with salt and pepper. Cover to keep moist and warm.

2. Pour off all but 3 tablespoons fat from the skillet. Add the onion, carrot, celery, and bacon. Cook until soft and light brown. Add wine, stock, garlic, and herbs. Simmer briefly then pour over the duck. Chop 3 or 4 of the olives and add to the casserole. Cook, covered, for 25 to 30 minutes, or until the duck is tender. Remove the duck to a warm serving dish. Skim off excess fat from the sauce. Strain or pass the sauce through a food mill pressing down to extract as much juice and flavor as possible. Stir the remaining olives into the resulting sauce. Heat through then pour over the duck. Serve hot.

PALOMBACCI ALLA PERUGINA

Wood pigeons or squab with polenta as prepared in Perugia
(Italy)

Ingredients

    2 cups red Chianti wine
    2 cups rich chicken stock
   ¾ cup chopped carrots
   ¾ cups chopped celery
   ¾ cup chopped onion
    2 whole cloves garlic, peeled
    3 bay leaves
    4 sprigs parsley
    2 sage leaves, crushed
    4 juniper berries, crushed
    6 black peppercorns
   ½ tablespoon tomato paste
      Salt
    4 1-pound squab, drawn and trussed,
         plus the livers and giblets
      Flour
      Freshly ground black pepper
   ¼ cup olive oil
   ¾ cup Italian black olives (preferably Gaeta),
         rinsed and pitted
      A squeeze of lemon juice (optional)

Equipment

5-quart enameled heavy casserole with tight-fitting lid ·
Electric blender · Strainer

Working time: 30 minutes

Cooking time: 2½ to 3 hours

Serves: 4

1. In a heavy enameled casserole combine the wine, chicken stock, vegetables, garlic, herbs, spices, tomato paste, and salt to taste. Bring to the boil and simmer for 1 hour.

2. Add the livers and giblets of the squab. Continue to cook, uncovered, over gentle heat for another hour.

3. Discard the bay leaves. Whirl the contents of the casserole in a blender then push through a strainer. You should have about 2 cups smooth sauce. Thin with more chicken stock if too thick.

4. Dust the squab in flour seasoned with salt and pepper. In a large casserole heat the olive oil over medium heat until hot. Brown the squab in oil on all sides. Remove to a side dish, pour off the excess oil, and return the squab to the casserole. Add the sauce. Heat to the simmer, cover tightly, and continue to cook over gentle heat for 30 minutes.

5. Add the olives to the casserole and cook, uncovered, 10 minutes more.

6. Remove the squab from the casserole and place them on a hot serving dish. Readjust the seasoning of the sauce. If very rich, a squeeze of lemon may be necessary. Spoon the sauce over the squab and serve at once with sautéed or toasted polenta slices.

To make polenta: Slowly sprinkle 1 cup polenta into 4 cups simmering salted water, stirring. Reduce the heat and continue cooking, stirring constantly in one direction for 20 minutes. The polenta must be very thick and pull away from the sides of the saucepan. Pour the polenta onto a large flat plate. Allow to cool completely. Cut with taut string into ¼-inch-thick slices. Sauté in oil until browned on both sides or sprinkle with melted butter and grated parmesan cheese and brown under the broiler. Serve hot.

GIGOT D'AGNEAU, SAUCE AUX OLIVES

Leg of lamb with olive sauce in the style of Provence (France)

This is an absolutely splendid sauce for roast lamb, one of the best ways to serve it that I know. And remember, in Provence lamb is basted with hot fat, not with wine or stock.

In Languedoc there's a similar sauce served with boiled calf's head.

Ingredients

> ½ pound lamb breast or a few lamb bones
> 3 carrots, cut up
> 3 onions, cut up
>   Bouquet garni: bay leaf, parsley, thyme, few celery leaves, tied together
>   Salt and freshly ground pepper
> 1 5-pound leg of lamb
> 3 cloves garlic, peeled and slivered
>   Olive oil
> 1½ cups juicy black Mediterranean-type olives, rinsed, pitted, and chopped
> 1 2-ounce can anchovy fillets, rinsed and mashed
> 2 tablespoons finely chopped parsley
> 1 teaspoon finely chopped garlic
>   Juice of ½ lemon
>   About ¼ teaspoon cayenne

Equipment

Saucepan · Roasting pan · Meat thermometer · Sieve

Working time: 20 minutes

Cooking time: 1 hour

Roasting time: 1 hour 20 minutes (approximately)

Serves: 6

1. Prepare a lamb broth with the lamb breast or bones, carrots, onions, herbs, and 3 cups water. Season with salt and pepper. Cook, covered, 1 hour.

2. Preheat the oven to 400 degrees.

3. Make a few incisions near the lamb leg bone and insert the slivers of garlic. Rub the meat with salt, pepper, and olive oil. Place in a roasting pan and set in the oven to start browning for 15 minutes.

4. Reduce the heat to 325 degrees, and continue to roast the lamb, basting often with the lamb drippings and more oil, until the desired degree of doneness. Pink lamb registers 140 degrees on a meat thermometer.

5. Remove the lamb to a heated platter and keep warm. Spoon off the excess fat in the pan and discard. Degrease and strain lamb broth. Add 1 cup broth to the pan juices. Set the pan over medium heat and stir to scrape up all the brown particles that cling to the pan. Add the remaining broth, stirring. Boil down to 2 cups. Add olives, anchovies, chopped parsley, garlic, lemon juice, and cayenne. Heat, stirring, until well combined. Correct the seasoning. Keep hot.

6. Carve the lamb and serve with the sauce in a warmed sauceboat.

LA DAUBE DE BOEUF PROVENÇALE

Beef, wine, mushroom, and olive stew as prepared in Provence (France)

This daube is so good that I include it even though it's one of the few which cannot be presented closed. We all love to break open the *daubière* before our guests and flood the dining room with the aroma of Provence. In this version, however, the olives and mushrooms are added 10 minutes before the dish is served. The loss of dining room drama is more than compensated by olives and mushrooms which have retained their own flavors and thus set off the blended taste of the rest of the stew.

Ingredients

> *Wine marinade*
> ½ cup sliced carrots
> ¼ cup sliced celery
> ¼ cup chopped onion
> 3 tablespoons olive oil
> 2 tablespoons mixed herbs: parsley, thyme,
>   crumbled bay leaf, and rosemary or savory
> 2 teaspoons chopped garlic
> 2 cups dry red or white wine
>   Salt and 12 black peppercorns
>
> 3 pounds grainy chuck beef, cut into 15–18 serving pieces,
>   each larded with a small piece of pork fat back
> 2 medium onions, thinly sliced
> ½ cup very lean salt pork, cut into ¼-inch-by-1-inch lardons
>   then blanched, rinsed, and dried
> 2 pounds fresh ripe tomatoes, peeled, seeded, and chopped
>   Bouquet garni: bay leaf, parsley sprigs, thyme leaves,
>   and a piece of dried orange peel, 2 inches by 2 inches,
>   tied together
>   Flour and water paste
> ¼ pound fresh mushrooms, sliced
> 2 dozen salt-cured black olives, rinsed and pitted
> 2 tablespoons chopped parsley

Equipment

> Skillet · Glass or porcelain bowl · An earthenware
> casserole (*daubière*), or a heavy enameled casserole with
> a tight-fitting lid

Working time: 30 minutes

Cooking time: 4 to 5 hours

Serves: 6

1. *The day before:* Make the wine marinade. In a skillet over gentle heat soften the carrots, celery, and onion in olive oil. Add the herbs and the garlic and continue cooking, stirring, until the flavors are released. Moisten with the wine and add salt and pepper. Bring the liquid to the boil and allow to simmer 10 to 15 minutes. Remove from heat and allow to cool completely.

2. Place the beef cubes in the bowl; pour over the cooled marinade, cover with foil, and set in a cool place overnight turning the meat once or twice.

3. Preheat the oven to 350 degrees.

4. Place the meat and the marinade in the *daubière.* Scatter the sliced onions over the meat; add the pork lardons, tomatoes, fresh herbs, and the orange rind. Cover and seal with a thick flour and water paste. Set the daube in the oven to cook slowly for 4 to 5 hours. After 1 hour lower oven temperature to 250 degrees.

5. Ten minutes before serving break the flour and water seal and discard. Set the *daubière* on top of the stove over very gentle heat (to avoid breaking, place the earthenware casserole on an asbestos pad or trivet set over the flame). Add the mushrooms and the olives. Continue cooking until the mushrooms are tender. Remove the herb bouquet and skim the grease from the top of the cooking liquid. Readjust the seasoning. Sprinkle with chopped parsley. Serve with freshly cooked macaroni.

Note: Daubes are very good reheated or eaten cold.

CARNE FIAMBRE

Stuffed beef roll (Spain)

This is an ideal dish for a summer buffet and, indeed, one of my favorite meat dishes from Spain.

Ingredients

> 2½ pounds flank steak in 1 piece
>   Salt and freshly ground black pepper
> 1 teaspoon crushed garlic
> 3 eggs

¼ cup olive oil
½ pound ground lean pork
⅔ cup green olives, rinsed and pitted
4 thin carrots, each about 6 inches long
3 roasted sweet red peppers, cut into long thin strips
¼ cup diced *cornichons* (small French pickles—optional)
2–3 tablespoons chopped parsley
Flour
1 chopped onion
2 cloves garlic, peeled and bruised
1 cup dry white wine
2 cups beef stock
1 bay leaf
1 tomato, peeled, seeded, and chopped
1 carrot, chopped

Equipment

Cleaver · Skillet · Kitchen string · 4- or 5½-quart
heavy casserole with tight-fitting lid · Strainer

To serve cold: weights and a deep dish

Working time: 30 minutes

Cooking time: 1½ hours

Serves: 6 to 8

1. Butterfly the meat lengthwise using a sharp knife. Place the meat between sheets of waxed paper and flatten with the side of a cleaver. Rub with salt, pepper, and crushed garlic.

2. Beat the eggs with salt and pepper until the whites and yolks are well combined. Heat 1 tablespoon olive oil in the skillet and make a firm omelet. Cool then cut into ½-inch strips.

3. Spread the pork evenly over the meat, arrange the omelet slices, olives, carrots, sweet peppers, and *cornichons* on top in rows. Sprinkle with parsley and season with salt and pepper. Roll the meat into a cylinder and tie securely with string.

4. Roll the meat in flour. Heat remaining olive oil in the casserole and in it brown the meat on all sides. Add chopped onion and garlic, and cook until golden. Moisten with wine and stock. Add bay leaf, tomato, carrot, and season with salt and pepper. Simmer, covered, 1½ hours.

5. To serve hot: remove the meat and discard strings. Allow to rest 5 to 10 minutes before slicing. Strain the cooking liquid. Arrange slices overlapping on a heated long dish and moisten with some of the cooking liquid. Serve with sautéed potatoes.

To serve cold: place the meat in a deep dish, pour over enough strained cooking liquid to cover the meat completely. Weight the meat. Be careful of an overflow of hot liquid. When cool spoon off fat. Serve thinly sliced.

Eggplant, Tomatoes, Peppers, and Other Mediterranean Vegetables

IF you come to live around the Mediterranean you will soon discover that the people here eat with the seasons. You won't find every vegetable available in the markets every month of the year, as in the stores of North America. In late summer there will be piles of eggplants, zucchinis, peppers, and tomatoes and you will know it's the season for ratatouille. In fall there will be mushrooms, artichokes, okra, and fennel; in winter leeks, and the root vegetables, turnips and carrots; in spring a plentitude of asparagus, radishes, and lettuce. And it will be the same with the fruits: melons, peaches, and plums in summer; grapes, quince, and pears in the fall; oranges and grapefruit in winter; cherries, strawberries, and figs in the late spring.

The American who moves to these parts is often frustrated the first few months. You want to serve asparagus with autumn game, but in autumn you won't find hot house asparagus in the market and if you do it will be at an extravagant price. But as one settles into Mediterranean life the frustration will give way to delight. It's a joy to eat with the seasons, to face peppers and

eggplants for four or five months out of the year and discover all
the good things that can be done with them. And there's the joy
of anticipation, too—the wait for the next seasonal change. Little
piles of artichokes appear in early September, growing larger and
larger each week while the zucchini piles decline. A new season
has arrived and with it new produce. It's time for new recipes to
come into play.

One of the best things about seasonal vegetables is that they
cost least when they're at their peak. The newcomer soon learns
the great role of Mediterranean food shopping: buy what you see
in quantity and don't go to market with a preconceived idea.
Following this you will end up with fresh produce at the height of
its quality, and will save a lot of money besides.

The seasonal approach has had a good effect on Mediterranean cookery, forcing cooks to come up with numerous uses for
food which would be boring if always served the same way. The
result is that Mediterranean cooks have devised a great number of imaginative uses for their produce, and the people of the
region associate each season with a different kind of feast.

Vegetables always look good in Mediterranean markets—
sprinkled with water, lovingly arranged, bathed in brilliant Mediterranean light. If you live around the region for a while, and
then for some reason return to a home someplace else, one of your
fondest memories will be of the markets where you shopped.

I spent a summer in the early 1960s in the village of Gruz on
the Dalmatian coast, and I still have a vivid memory of the market there—a great peasant market in a big public square, shaded
by old plane trees. It was not like the lush markets of Cannes and
Nice with their pyramids of perfectly shaped vegetables and
fruits, nor the glistening supermarkets now prevalent in Beirut
which have replaced the little alley *souks*. It bore no resem-
blance either to two other favorite markets of mine: the one in
Rome near the Trastevere, and the Fez market of Tangier where
there is an old Riffian woman who has sold me garlic on and off
for the last fifteen years. No, the market of Gruz presented an
amazing sight.

It was full of long wooden tables tended by craggy faced
peasant women, all wearing babushkas and holding antique
scales in their hands. Donkeys and trucks poured in all morning

with produce, and the market did not close until dark. But what was extraordinary, aside from a certain obvious picturesqueness, was that this market offered only one seasonal item each day. I remember once when the whole place was flooded with green peppers, and every restaurant on the square served stuffed peppers and nothing else. One morning there was nothing except peaches, and then the square looked like a field of marigolds. Another time it was all red with tomatoes, and still another it was black with eggplant. On my last morning there were onions—tens of thousands—tied together into endless chains.

I've never seen anything quite like that market at Gruz—truly, it was an extraordinary place. Its rapid changes in color, its sudden shortages and surpluses had something to do, I suppose, with fields methodically picked, and possibly with the whims of a local commissar. But its unpredictable floods of produce remain a symbol to me of all the markets of the Mediterranean, choked with the bounty of each season, telling the cook what *must* be made.

EGGPLANT

Eggplants, or aubergines as the British call them, are truly wonderful. Arabs brought them to the region 1500 years ago from India, and ever since these purplish egg-shaped vegetables, some very small and narrow, others huge, have been a mainstay of Mediterranean cuisine. The Turks have more than 30 ways to prepare them, and the other Middle Eastern countries do nearly as well. They are good mashed, fried in oil, braised, or stuffed and boiled.

The Greeks like to remove the pulp, sauté it in oil with onions, then mix it with feta cheese, eggs, parsley, salt, and pepper, restuff the shells, top them with tomato slices, sprinkle them with more oil, and bake them in the oven.

The Moroccans like to add them to couscous, and they make a big thing about the little nugget under the eggplant stem which they slice up and add to stews to impart a mushroom taste.

The Italians sometimes prepare eggplant bits like mushrooms, and in Israel they use eggplant for a dish they call "mock liver." The Italians also like to pickle them, and in southern Italy they sometimes use slices of fried eggplant instead of bread as the outer leaves of a tomato and cheese sandwich.

The Lebanese are great picklers of eggplant. They have a dish called *torshi batinjan* consisting of partially boiled eggplants stuffed with crushed salted walnuts. They are put up in jars with olive oil, vinegar, a red pepper and garlic cloves, and left to pickle two weeks.

In Spain there's a mixture of potatoes, ham, mushrooms, onions, white wine, and eggplant called *berenjenas duquesa*. In Provence there's an eggplant *timbale* called *papeton d'aubergines*, lightened with egg whites and served with an herbal tomato sauce. The Egyptians top fried eggplant slices with onions, seasoned tomatoes, and sugar, and then bake them until brown, and the Jews of North Africa make an eggplant jam to serve with tea and toast.

No matter how you use them—in ratatouille, moussaka, caponata or *hunkar begendi*—you will find them versatile and always a delight.

AJVAR

Eggplant and green pepper relish (Yugoslavia)

I stayed with a buxom middle-aged school teacher named Mrs. Jovanovic the summer I lived in Gruz, and she used to make this wonderful eggplant relish all the time. A plate of it was always on the table, even for the 10:00 A.M. *second* breakfast! In the evening she'd serve *ajvar* as an accompaniment to a grilled beef dish called *ćevapčići*, always served, too, with a plate of chopped raw onions. I include her recipe for *ajvar* and recommend that you try it with *ćevapčići*.

Ingredients

 1 pound eggplant
 4 small, elongated, light-green Italian peppers
 1 long hot green pepper
 ½ teaspoon finely chopped garlic
 2 tablespoons grated onion

2½ tablespoons lemon juice or wine vinegar
6 tablespoons fruity olive oil
Salt and freshly ground black pepper

Equipment

Baking sheet · Charcoal grill (optional) ·
Mixing bowl and wooden spoon

Working time: 10 minutes

Baking and broiling time: 35 minutes (approximately)

Makes: 2 cups (approximately)

1. Pierce the eggplant with a fork in 2 or 3 places. To give the eggplant a good smokey flavor and still have time for other kitchen work start the eggplant off in a preheated 375 degree oven to bake 20 minutes, turning midway. Place the peppers (sweet and hot) on a baking sheet and set in the oven to bake 30 minutes, turning them midway too.

2. When the eggplant has baked 20 minutes set over a gas flame or over hot coals and cook until it is completely soft and the skin is black and blistery. Rub the black parched skin off under cold running water then squeeze gently to remove any bitter juices. Chop the pulp fine.

3. Remove the peppers when soft, cover with a towel, and allow to cool. Core, seed, and slip off the skins of the peppers; chop fine and mix with the eggplant. Add garlic, onion, and lemon juice. Stir in the oil a tablespoon at a time. Season with salt and pepper to taste. Chill.

ĆEVAPČIĆI

Finely ground skewered beef (Yugoslavia)

Ingredients

  1½ pounds finely ground lean beef (ground 3 times)
   1 clove garlic, crushed
      Salt and freshly ground black pepper
      Bowl of finely chopped raw onion
      Ajvar (see page 79)

Equipment

   Charcoal grill (optional) · 10 10-inch skewers

Working time: 10 minutes

Broiling time: 10 minutes

Serves: 4 to 5

1. Mix meat, garlic, salt and pepper to taste. Knead well. With wet hands, separate the meat into 40 small sausage shapes, packing them around the skewers, 4 on each one.

2. Broil quickly on both sides, 2 to 3 inches from a broiler flame or over hot coals, until done to taste. Serve, at once, and pass a bowl of chopped onion and the *ajvar*.

HUNKAR BEGENDI

"Sultan's Delight"—an eggplant cream (Turkey)

Here is the recipe for the famous "Sultan's Delight" and also three variations. The master recipe is from Turkey, the place where most Levantine and Middle East cooking derives. The Greek variation is extremely simple, with olive oil instead of a cheese-milk sauce as the base. The Syrians add yogurt, and the

Lebanese and Egyptians add sesame seed paste, rename it *baba ghanoush* and use it as a dip.

"Sultan's Delight" is delicious with grilled kebabs and roasted meats. The smokey flavor of the grilled eggplants permeates the dish.

Ingredients

> 1½ pounds eggplant
> Juice of ½ lemon
> 2 tablespoons unsalted butter
> 3 tablespoons all-purpose flour
> 1 cup hot milk
> ¼ cup grated parmesan or gruyère cheese
> Salt

Equipment

> Mixing bowl · Saucepan · Whisk

Working time: 10 minutes

Cooking time: 45 minutes (approximately)

Serves: 4

1. To give the eggplants a good smokey flavor and still have time for other kitchen work start them off in a preheated 375 degree oven to bake for 20 minutes, turning them midway. Then set over a gas flame or over hot coals and cook until they are completely soft and their skins are black and blistery. Rub the black parched skins off under cold running water then squeeze to remove any bitter juices.

2, Mash the eggplant with the juice of ½ lemon until smooth. In a saucepan melt the butter, off heat stir in the flour. Cook, stirring, until the flour turns light brown in color. Whisk in the milk and continue to cook, until smooth. Stir in the cheese and the eggplant and cook 5 to 10 minutes longer over low heat, stirring often. Season with salt and serve at once.

A GREEK VARIATION WITH OLIVE OIL

Ingredients

> 1 pound eggplant
> 2–3 tablespoons lemon juice
> 1 clove garlic, crushed
> Salt
> ⅓ cup olive oil

Equipment

Electric blender

Working time: 5 minutes

Grilling time: 35 minutes (approximately)

Makes: 1 cup

Roast the eggplant as described in step 1 for *hunkar begendi.* Place the skinned eggplant pulp in the blender jar with the lemon juice, garlic, and a little salt. Blend until smooth. Uncover jar, and still blending at high speed, pour in the oil, drop by drop. The puree will become very light. Readjust the seasoning. Serve chilled with sesame crackers.

A SYRIAN VARIATION WITH YOGURT

Recipe above mixed with ½ cup plain yogurt. A very soothing snack.

A LEBANESE VARIATION—*baba ghanoush*

Same recipe as the Greek variation plus 2 or more tablespoons sesame seed paste (tahini) added to the puree. This very popular dip is often decorated with dried or fresh pomegranate seeds, chopped parsley, or olive oil dribbled on top.

BATENJAL M'CHARMEL

Eggplant salad (Algeria)

Algiers, unfortunately, is not the city it once was. On a recent trip there we stayed at the famous Hotel St. George where we were informed that there was a law forbidding porters to carry the valises of guests, and where we discovered bare protruding wires near our bed where there'd been a service button in better days. The bar had one whiskey—an unmarked bottle that tasted like Spanish "scotch," but the food in the restaurant was still very good. We particularly liked the Algerian specialties including this salad of pureed eggplant.

In Tunisia there's a similar dish. The eggplant is mixed with spicy red *harissa sauce* (see page 182), and flavored with ground coriander, lemon juice, garlic, and oil.

Ingredients

> 2 medium eggplants (about 1 pound each)
> Salt
> Olive oil for frying
> 3–4 cloves garlic, peeled and crushed
> 1 tablespoon sharp paprika or a mixture of
> sweet paprika and 2 pinches of cayenne
> 1 teaspoon ground cumin
> 2 tablespoons vinegar or lemon juice, or more to taste

Equipment

> Vegetable parer · Colander · Skillet · Potato masher

Working time: 20 minutes

Cooking time: 20 minutes

Serves: 4 to 6

1. Remove 3 vertical strips of skin from each eggplant, leaving it striped, then cut eggplant into ½-inch-thick slices. Salt the slices and leave to drain in the colander 30 minutes. Rinse well, squeeze gently, and pat dry with paper towels.

2. Heat about ¾ inch of oil in the skillet and fry the slices a few at a time over high heat until golden brown on both sides. Drain. Mash the eggplant with the garlic and spices. Fry this puree in the oil in the skillet until all liquid evaporates and there is only oil and vegetable left. Stir the puree often to avoid scorching. Pour off the oil and season with vinegar or lemon juice to taste. Taste for salt. Serve at room temperature.

SPAGHETTI CON LE MELANZANE

Spaghetti with tomato and eggplant sauce (Italy)

This spaghetti dish is extremely popular in southern Italy. It has a warm southern feeling that comes from the blushingly obvious eggplant-tomato combination, a linkage made all over the Mediterranean region.

Ingredients

     1 medium eggplant (about 1¼ pounds)
      Salt
      Vegetable oil for frying
     2 tablespoons olive oil
     1 teaspoon finely chopped garlic
  1½ cups fresh or canned tomato sauce
     1 tablespoon chopped fresh basil, or ½ tablespoon dried
      Freshly ground black pepper
     1 pound spaghetti
    ⅓ cup grated parmesan cheese
      Bowl of grated parmesan cheese

Equipment

    Colander · Skillet and slotted spoon · Large pot ·
    Saucepan

Working time: 15 minutes

Cooking time: 20 minutes

Serves: 6

1. Peel the eggplant and cut into 1-inch cubes. Place in a colander, sprinkle with salt, and let stand 30 minutes. Rinse, drain, and pat dry with paper towels. Heat about ¾ inch of vegetable oil in the skillet and fry the eggplant over high heat until golden brown on all sides. Drain on paper towels. Season with salt and pepper and reserve.

2. In a saucepan heat the olive oil and in it gently cook the garlic without browning for 1 minute. Add the tomato sauce, basil, and salt and pepper to taste. Cook over low heat 5 minutes, stirring. Fold in the chunks of eggplant and continue cooking 2 minutes longer. Set aside.

3. Cook the spaghetti in boiling salted water until just tender. Reheat the sauce; add ⅓ cup grated cheese and correct the seasoning. Drain the spaghetti and place in a hot serving dish. Pour the sauce over it and toss together. Sprinkle with freshly ground black pepper and a little grated cheese. Pass a bowl of grated parmesan cheese separately.

RATATOUILLE

Provençal vegetable stew (France)

Here's my recipe for the great vegetable specialty of Provence, which is echoed in almost all the Mediterranean countries. Long ago people realized that eggplant, tomatoes, and peppers could make a beautiful delicious blend. In Tunisia there is a similar vegetable medley called *chachouka,* and in Spain where eggplant is not too popular there's *escallinada,* which is their version of the same thing.

In Languedoc ratatouille is used as the bed for a roasted garlic-studded monkfish, called *lotte* in French, and also "poor man's lobster." A trimmed monkfish or *lotte* is shaped something like a leg of lamb, so this ratatouille fish dish is called *gigot de mer*.

Two of the wonderful things about ratatouille are that it can be even better the second night, and that it's just as delicious cold as hot. I often spread leftover ratatouille in a gratin dish, making little indentations on the surface. When it's reheated, I break eggs into the indentations and return it to the oven until the eggs are baked.

Ingredients

        1 pound eggplant
     3–5 zucchini, each about 5 inches long
          Salt
        2 medium sweet green peppers, or 5 small
            elongated light-green Italian peppers
        1 large onion
        4 large red ripe tomatoes
     6–8 tablespoons fruity olive oil
        1 bay leaf
          Freshly ground black pepper
          Pinch of cayenne (optional)
        1 teaspoon finely chopped garlic
      ¾ teaspoon thyme leaves
        2 tablespoons chopped fresh parsley
        1 teaspoon chopped basil

Equipment

    Colander · Skillet and slotted spoon ·
    4-quart casserole with cover

Working time: 15 minutes

Cooking time: 1 hour 10 minutes

Makes: 5 cups, serves 8 to 10

1. Cut the eggplant and the zucchini into 1-inch chunks. Salt them and leave to drain in a colander 30 minutes.

2. Meanwhile seed, derib, and cut up the green peppers. Cut the onion into eighths. Peel, seed, and roughly chop the tomatoes.

3. Rinse the eggplant and the zucchini in cold water; squeeze gently, and pat dry with paper towels. Heat ¼ cup oil in the skillet and when hot lightly brown the eggplant and zucchini chunks. Transfer to the casserole.

4. Lightly brown the green peppers in the same oil. Add to the casserole. Add the onion, tomatoes, bay leaf, and the remaining oil to the casserole. Season with salt and pepper and if desired the cayenne. Simmer, covered, 30 minutes, stirring often. Stir in the garlic and the thyme. Cook 20 minuters more or until thick and well blended. Serve hot or cold. Sprinkle with fresh herbs.

AUBERGINES À LA TOULOUSAINE

Stuffed eggplants in the style of Toulouse (France)

This is one of the *bonnes recettes* of my great friend "Tante Vivienne." I thought the original way she made this dish was a little heavy, possibly because she fried the eggplant shells before stuffing them. I tried omitting that step, and found it worked better for me.

The idea of stuffing eggplants is very popular, especially around the Middle East. The most famous stuffed eggplant dish of all is the Turkish *imam bayildi*, or, literally, "the fainting priest." Those who don't think much of the dish say the priest fainted because he was overwhelmed by olive oil, and those who think highly of it say he was overwhelmed by delight.

Ingredients

   3 small eggplants, (about ¾ pound each)
     Salt
   4 thick slices of mild cured bacon, (about ¼ pound)
   1 cup finely chopped onions
   1 cup thick tomato sauce or puree

Continued

    1 teaspoon finely chopped garlic
    1 tablespoon chopped parsley
       Pinches of crumbled thyme and ground bay leaf
       Freshly ground black pepper
       Breadcrumbs
    2 tablespoons olive oil

Equipment

    Grapefruit knife · Colander · Skillet ·
    Greased ovenproof dish (about 10 inches by 10 inches)

Working time: 20 minutes

Baking time: 1 hour

Serves: 6 as a first course

    1. Remove and discard the eggplant stems. Halve the eggplants lengthwise and cut out the centers, using a grapefruit knife and spoon, leaving a ½-inch-thick shell. Sprinkle the hollowed-out shells and the center pulp with salt; let stand 30 minutes in a colander.

    2. Dice the bacon. In a skillet lightly brown the bacon then remove to drain on paper towels. Pour off ½ the bacon fat. Rinse the eggplant pulp under cold running water; drain, pat dry, then dice. Brown the pulp in the bacon fat. Add the onions and cook until soft but not brown. Add the tomato sauce, garlic, and herbs and continue cooking 5 minutes to blend flavors. Fold in the bacon then taste for salt and pepper.

    3. Preheat the oven to 375 degrees.

    4. Rinse the eggplant shells under cold running water, drain, and pat dry. Arrange hollow side up in one layer in the baking dish. Fill each shell with about ⅓ cup filling, sprinkle with breadcrumbs, dribble over a little olive oil, and set in the preheated oven to bake 1 hour. Serve hot or lukewarm.

CAPONATINA

Seafood and vegetable medley in the style of Syracuse (Italy)

This is an adaptation of the recipe that appears in Anna Gosetti della Salda's *Le ricette regionali Italiane*.

I can think of no better way to describe the unique process of this unusual dish than to quote from Waverly Root. Writing about the *caponatina* of Catania in *The Food of Italy*, he says: "It consisted simply in cooking each of its chief ingredients—eggplant, peppers, tomatoes, onions, and celery—separately. Thus each could be sautéed in the *soffritto* most appropriate to it, with the dosage of cooking fat (chiefly olive oil) which it could most advantageously absorb. Each could be seasoned by its own selection of herbs.and spices. And perhaps most important of all, each could be allowed its optimum cooking time."

Caponatina can be served hot by itself. And it can also be served cold as a buffet dish with seafood, hard-boiled eggs and a special almond, anchovy, and chocolate sauce. Following the master recipe I give the recipe for the cold presentation. The vegetables are formed into a pyramid, decorated with the shellfish and eggs, and then coated with the sauce. The addition of chocolate pinpoints the dish as coming from Syracuse.

Ingredients

> 16 cooked small artichoke hearts (fresh, frozen, or canned)
> 1 clove garlic, peeled
>   Olive oil
>   Lemon juice
>   Salt and freshly ground black pepper
> 3 medium sweet peppers, or 8 small
>   elongated light-green Italian peppers,
>   seeded, deribbed, and sliced into long strips
> 1 cup sliced celery
>   Sugar

Continued

    2 medium eggplants, peeled, cubed, and salted
    2 tablespoons chopped parsley
    ½ teaspoon finely chopped garlic
    18 small white onions, peeled and boiled 10 minutes
        in salted water
    2 tablespoons wine vinegar
    1½ cups fresh or canned tomato puree
    1 tablespoon capers
    ½ cup green olives, rinsed and pitted
    ½ cup black olives, rinsed and pitted

Equipment

    Medium-sized skillet with cover　·　Large skillet or
    paella pan　·　Slotted spoon

Working time: 1 hour

Cooking time: 1 hour

Serves: 6

　　1. In the smaller skillet sauté the artichoke hearts with 1 clove garlic in hot olive oil for 1 minute on each side. Use a slotted spoon to transfer to the larger skillet. Season the artichokes with salt and pepper and sprinkle with lemon juice to taste. Remove the garlic clove and discard.

　　2. In the same oil, adding more if necessary, sauté the peppers and the celery slices 5 minutes, stirring often. Sprinkle with salt, pepper, and a pinch of sugar. When lightly browned, cover the skillet and cook over low heat 5 minutes. Transfer the peppers and the celery to the larger skillet next to the artichokes.

　　3. Rinse, drain, and dry the eggplant cubes. Add more oil to the skillet and in it fry the eggplant in hot oil 5 minutes, or until barely tender and light brown. Season with salt and pepper and toss with 2 tablespoons chopped parsley and ½ teaspoon chopped garlic. Transfer to the larger skillet and place next to the peppers.

　　4. Lightly brown the onions in the remaining oil in the skil-

let. Sprinkle with a little sugar, salt, and pepper. Glaze them over high heat, shaking the skillet to avoid scorching. Add the vinegar and reduce to a glaze. Transfer to the large skillet, placing between the artichokes and the peppers.

5. Add the tomato puree to the small skillet and simmer for a few minutes. Stir in the capers and the olives. Correct the seasoning adding a drop of vinegar for a sharper flavor. Pour the tomato mixture over the reserved vegetables. Cook over low heat 5 minutes. Serve sizzling hot or allow to cool completely and serve with the following seafood and sauce.

SEA FOOD

Ingredients

> 1 pound cooked shrimp, shelled
> 2 cooked lobsters, cut up into serving pieces
> 8 hard-boiled eggs, peeled and quartered

The sauce

> ¾ cup (3½ ounces) whole almonds, blanched
> 1–2 tablespoons oil
> ⅓ cup finely ground toasted breadcrumbs
> 1 2-ounce tin anchvoy fillets, washed and drained
> ¼ cup orange juice
> 1–1½ tablespoons sugar
> ¼ cup wine vinegar
> 1 ounce grated bitter chocolate
>   (about ⅓ loosely packed cup)

Equipment

Electric blender · Small skillet · Sieve and spatula ·
Enameled saucepan

Working time: 10 minutes

Makes: 1 cup sauce (approximately)

1. In the skillet brown the almonds in oil. Drain on paper towels. In an electric blender grind to a puree the almonds with the breadcrumbs, anchovy fillets, and orange juice. Scrape into a small enameled saucepan and heat gently, stirring. Add the sugar, vinegar, and ½ cup water. Cook, stirring, until well combined. Add the grated chocolate. Cook, stirring, 1 minute without boiling. Push through a sieve and allow to cool completely.

2. Assembling the *caponatina:* pile up the cooled vegetables on a serving dish—pyramid style. Use a spatula to coat the vegetables evenly with the sauce. Decorate with the shellfish and the hard-boiled eggs. Serve slightly chilled.

TOMATO

It's almost impossible to conceive of Mediterranean food without considering the tomato, but it didn't arrive in the area until the sixteenth century when the Spanish brought it back from Mexico and South America. It was first called the "love apple" and almost immediately it took the Mediterranean by storm. With good reason, too, for like the eggplant it can be mashed, braised, baked, fried, stuffed, and boiled, and, in addition, it can be eaten raw.

I only give nine tomato recipes here, but I'd write a book of tomato recipes if I could. There's a soufflé omelet flavored with tomato juice in Turkey, and a Corsican *pestu* that's absolutely divine. Flaked salt cod and tomato puree are sieved and simmered together in equal amounts, and when the combination is good and thick some mashed anchovies are added, with pine nuts, garlic, parsley, and olive oil. Elizabeth David writes of another Corsican tomato dish, the famous *pebronata* served with braised beef. It's a seasoned tomato sauce with juniper berries, red wine, and fried peppers, and it shouldn't be confused with the equally famous Sicilian *peperonata*, served lukewarm or cold with meat. In Greece, they stuff small seedless tomatoes with hazelnuts, and in the Levant they use tomatoes to flavor pilaf. In fact there are so many uses for tomatoes that it boggles the mind, and one wonders what on earth people did before the "love apple" arrived.

COULIS DE TOMATE À LA PROVENÇALE

Fresh, thick tomato sauce in the style of Provence (France)

This is my personal recipe for tomato sauce—the one I used for testing all the recipes in this book. I hope you use it, but if you don't I'll understand. There are two problems with fresh tomatoes —they cost a lot, and too often in America they lack taste. You may want to substitute canned tomato sauce.

Another approach might be to combine a little imported tomato paste with fresh tomatoes, which I think is a much better idea than using tomato paste in large quantities.

I've been a little wary of the overwhelming and slightly bitter taste of canned tomato paste since my first professional cooking experience in 1957 when I served as apprentice for a year to the late Dione Lucas, then reigning queen of New York cooking teachers. Ms. Lucas was a most proficient cook, and perhaps the best kitchen technician I've ever observed. But I was a little shocked by one thing: her "instant *sauce espagnole*" which, unfortunately, made all her main course dishes taste nearly the same. She made it out of tomato paste, meat extract, and potato flour. I've been cautious about using too much tomato paste ever since.

Ingredients

> 1 cup chopped onions
> 3 tablespoons olive oil
> 3–4 cups tomatoes, peeled, seeded, juices strained,
>   and pulp chopped
> 3 small cloves garlic, crushed
> 1 bay leaf
> 1 sprig fresh thyme, or ¼ teaspoon dried thyme
> 2 cloves
> ½ teaspoon sugar
>   Salt and freshly ground black pepper

Equipment

> Large heavy skillet · Food mill

Working time: 10 to 15 minutes

Cooking time: 25 to 30 minutes

Makes: 3 cups

In a heavy skillet cook the onions in oil until soft but not browned. Add the garlic, the tomatoes, the strained tomato juices, herbs, cloves, sugar, salt and pepper. Cook, stirring often, about 20 minutes until thickened. Push the sauce through a food mill. Readjust the seasoning.

Note: This sauce freezes well.

INSALATA CAPRESE

Tomato, mozzarella, and basil salad (Italy)

Ingredients

> 3 tablespoons olive oil
> 1 tablespoon fresh basil leaves, finely chopped
> 3 red ripe tomatoes, peeled and sliced
> 1 whole fresh mozzarella cheese, thinly sliced
> Salt and freshly ground pepper
> Wine vinegar

Working time: 5 minutes

Serves: 4

Marinate the basil leaves in the olive oil for 2 to 3 hours. Arrange alternating slices of tomato and cheese on a long serving dish. Season with salt and pepper to taste. Spoon over the oil and chopped basil. Just a drop of vinegar is used.

Here are two recipes for stuffing tomatoes, out of literally a hundred Mediterranean variations. *Pomodori ripieni alla calabrese* is served hot, and the Turkish *zeytinyagli domates dolmasi* is served cold.

POMODORI RIPIENI ALLA CALABRESE

Hot stuffed tomatoes in the style of Calabria (Italy)

Ingredients

    8 firm red tomatoes
        Salt
    ¼ loaf stale French or Italian bread
    2 cloves garlic, peeled and crushed
        Olive oil
    1 2-ounce tin anchovy fillets in oil
    ¼ cup pine nuts
    ¼ cup yellow raisins, plumped in water then drained
    2 tablespoons chopped fresh parsley
        Freshly ground black pepper

Equipment

Skillet · An oiled shallow baking dish

Working time: 10 minutes

Cooking time: 20 to 25 minutes

Serves: 4

1. Preheat the oven to 375 degrees.
2. Cut a slice off the top of each tomato, scoop out the pulp and seeds and discard or reserve for some other use. Salt the shells and set them upside down to drain.
3. Thinly slice the bread, rub with garlic, and cut into ¼-inch cubes. Brown lightly in olive oil and set aside to drain on paper towels.

4. Rinse and mash the anchovies. Mix with the bread cubes, nuts, raisins, and chopped parsley. Season the mixture with pepper and very little salt. Stuff the tomatoes; cover with the tops, arrange in the baking dish and set in the oven to bake 20 to 25 minutes. Serve hot.

ZEYTINYAGLI DOMATES DOLMASI

Cold stuffed tomatoes (Turkey)

Ingredients

> 6 firm large tomatoes
> Salt
> ½ cup olive oil
> ½ cup chopped onion
> ½ cup long-grain rice
> ¼ cup pine nuts
> 3 tablespoons black currants or raisins
> 2 tablespoons chopped fresh parsley
> 1 teaspoon dried dill weed
> 1 teaspoon crushed mint leaves

Equipment

> Skillet · 4-quart casserole with cover
> or ovenproof baking dish with cover

Working time: 10 minutes

Cooking time: 50 minutes

Serves: 6

1. Cut off and reserve the top of each tomato, then scoop out most of the pulp and reserve. Salt the tomato cups, invert and let drain. Chop the tomato pulp.

2. Heat ¼ cup oil in a skillet and in it soften the onion without browning. Add the rice and stir. Add the nuts, currants or raisins, chopped tomato pulp, and ¼ cup water. Season with salt and pepper. Simmer, uncovered, 5 minutes. Mix in the herbs.

3. Preheat the oven to 375 degrees. Fill each tomato cup halfway and cover with the reserved top. Arrange the tomatoes in the casserole. Add ¾ cup water and the remaining oil. Cover and set in the preheated oven to bake 40 minutes or cook on top of the stove, covered, over medium heat, basting often with the liquid in the pan. Serve lukewarm or cold.

GAZPACHO

Cold vegetable soup (Spain)

This is a standard gazpacho but keep in mind there are at least 20 other ways of making this cold soup. I include one other, *gazpacho ajo blanco* (see page 9). When I worked at the Chillingsworth Restaurant in East Brewster, on Cape Cod, we used to do a variation that was garnished with a dollop of mayonnaise mixed with large quantities of curry powder and chopped parsley. It's a good way to serve gazpacho, too.

Ingredients

    3 cups tomato juice
    1 cup roughly chopped onion
    ⅓ cup chopped green pepper
    ½ cup chopped peeled cucumber
    2 large red ripe tomatoes, roughly chopped
    1 clove garlic, peeled and crushed
    2 tablespoons olive oil
    2 tablespoons wine vinegar
      Salt and freshly ground pepper to taste
    1 cup water or degreased meat stock

      Garnishes: small bowls filled with chopped green pepper,
        chopped onions, chopped tomatoes,
        and cubed fresh bread

Equipment

> Electric blender   ·   Deep glass, earthen,
> or wooden serving bowl

Working time: 10 minutes

Serves: 4 to 5

Put 1 cup tomato juice in the blender jar. Add the onions, peppers, tomatoes, cucumber, and garlic. Whirl until smooth at high speed. Pour into a large bowl and whisk in the oil and vinegar. Thin with remaining tomato juice and water. Season to taste with salt and pepper. Chill at least 2 hours before serving. Serve with an assortment of garnishes.

CALAMARES EN SU TINTA # 2

Squid in its own ink with tomato sauce (Spain)

Ingredients

> 2 pounds large squid
> 1 cup chopped onion
> 3 tablespoons olive oil
> 1 tablespoon flour
> ½ cup dry white wine
> ½ teaspoon finely chopped garlic
> 2 tablespoons finely chopped fresh parsley
> 2 tablespoons tomato paste
> Salt and freshly ground black pepper

Equipment

> Enameled, earthenware, or stainless steel skillet with cover   ·
> Sieve set over a bowl

Working time: 25 minutes

Cooking time: 45 minutes

Serves: 4 to 6

1. To clean the squid, remove and discard the head but set aside the tentacles. Discard the entrails and transparent bone but keep the ink sacs. Peel off the outer mottled skin. Wash the squid, inside and out, and wash the tentacles; cut into bite-size pieces.

2. Cook the onions in hot oil until soft and golden. Add the squid and the tentacles and cook, stirring, 5 minutes. Sprinkle with flour and moisten with white wine. Add the garlic, parsley, and tomato paste. Simmer, covered, over gentle heat 30 minutes.

3. Set a sieve over a bowl, crush the ink sacs in the sieve and collect the ink. Stir into the sauce. Bring to the boil, season with salt and pepper, and allow to simmer 15 minutes. Serve with rice.

PSARI PLAKI

Baked fish with tomatoes and onions (Greece)

Ingredients

    4 fish steaks or fillets: halibut, bass, codfish, red snapper, or rockfish
    Lemon juice
    Salt and freshly ground black pepper
⅓ cup olive oil
    3 cups chopped onions
    2 cups fresh or canned tomato sauce
⅓ cup finely chopped parsley
    1 teaspoon crumbled oregano
⅛ teaspoon ground allspice or cinnamon
⅓ cup sweet red wine such as Greek Mavrodaphne, Italian Recioto, or port wine
⅓ cup finely grated breadcrumbs

Equipment

Heavy skillet with cover · 10-by-10-inch baking dish, oiled

Working time: 10 minutes

Cooking time: 45 minutes

Serves: 4

1. Wash the fish slices. Rub with lemon juice and rinse. Rub with salt and pepper and let stand 10 minutes. Rinse again and drain.

2. Preheat the oven to 350 degrees.

3. Heat the oil in the skillet and sauté the onions over medium heat for 5 minutes or until soft but not browned. Add the tomato sauce, parsley, oregano, allspice, and wine. Season with salt and pepper. Cook, covered, 10 minutes.

4. Arrange the fish slices in the baking dish. Pour the sauce over the fish. Sprinkle the surface with breadcrumbs and dribble over a little oil. Set on the middle shelf of the oven and bake 30 minutes, or until the fish is cooked and a nice crust has formed over the sauce. Serve hot, warm, or tepid.

DJEJ MATISHA MESLA

Chicken tagine with sweet tomato jam (Morocco)

A lot of Andalusian cooking is heavily influenced by Moroccan cuisine, but here's a case where the Spanish have influenced the Moors. This dish comes from the north Moroccan city of Tetuan, a great center of Moorish-Andalusian culture, which even today is strongly Spanish in character. The Spaniards, of course, were the first to bring the tomato from the New World, after the collapse of Grenada in 1492, and in Spain they make a sweet tomato jam as a filling for cakes. It seems clear that the Tetuanese were intrigued by the idea, and used it to invent this delicious chicken dish.

Ingredients

 1 2½–3-pound chicken, quartered
 4 cloves garlic, peeled
  Salt
 ¼ teaspoon ground turmeric
  Pinch of ground ginger
  Freshly ground black pepper
 2 tablespoons vegetable oil
 ¼ cup grated onion
 3 pounds fresh red ripe tomatoes, peeled, seeded,
   and chopped
 1 tablespoon tomato paste
 1 teaspoon ground cinnamon
 2 tablespoons dark heavy honey
 2 tablespoons toasted sesame seeds

Equipment

 Mixing bowl · 4-quart heavy casserole

Working time: 30 minutes

Cooking time: 1½ hours

Serves: 4

 1. The day before: wash the chicken then drain. If you choose to purify the chicken as it is done in Morocco, blend 3 crushed garlic cloves with 1 tablespoon salt to make a paste. Rub into the flesh and underside of the chicken. Rinse well then pat dry with paper towels.
 2. Put the turmeric, ginger, pepper, and remaining garlic clove, crushed, in the bottom of a mixing bowl; mix well. Moisten with oil then rub this mixture into the flesh of the chicken. Cover and refrigerate overnight.
 3. Place the spiced chicken, oil drippings, grated onion and 1 cup water in the casserole. Bring to a boil, reduce the heat, and simmer, uncovered, 10 minutes.

4. Add the tomatoes, tomato paste, cinnamon, and a little salt. Cook over high heat, turning the chicken often in the sauce until tender. Remove the chicken and keep warm.

5. Rapidly cook down the tomatoes until all the water is completely evaporated, stirring occasionally to avoid scorching and stirring continuously the last 15 minutes. When all the water evaporates the tomatoes will begin to fry in the released oil and will start to thicken very fast. Stir in the cinnamon and the honey. Reheat the chicken in this sauce, rolling the quarters around to coat evenly. Sprinkle with sesame seeds and serve hot or warm.

KEFTAIDAKIA ME SALTSA

Small meatballs in tomato sauce (Greece)

Ingredients

  1 small onion, finely chopped
  4 tablespoons vegetable oil
1½ cups fresh or canned tomato sauce
  1 tablespoon red wine vinegar
  1 teaspoon paprika
 ½ teaspoon freshly ground black pepper
 ½ teaspoon ground cinnamon
   Pinch of ground cloves
   Salt
  1 pound ground beef
  2 tablespoons grated onion
  1 clove garlic, peeled and crushed
 ½ cup breadcrumbs
  1 teaspoon crushed mint
 ¼ teaspoon dried oregano
  2 pinches ground allspice
  1 egg, lightly beaten
   Flour
  2 tablespoons butter

Equipment

1½-quart saucepan with a cover   ·   Mixing bowl   ·
Skillet

Working time: 15 minutes

Cooking time: 30 minutes

Serves: 6, as part of a Greek *mezze*

1. In the saucepan soften the onion in 2 tablespoons oil
without browning. Add the tomato sauce, vinegar, paprika, black
pepper, cinnamon, cloves, and salt to taste. Cook, covered, over
medium heat 20 minutes, stirring often.

2. Meanwhile mix the ground beef with the grated onion,
garlic, and breadcrumbs. Add the herbs, allspice, and salt and
pepper to taste. Work in the egg and blend thoroughly. With
floured hands shape into 30 1-inch balls. Fry in 2 tablespoons oil
and 2 tablespoons butter until nicely browned on all sides and
completely cooked. Drain on paper towels.

3. Drop the meatballs into the prepared sauce and allow to
simmer 2 to 3 minutes. Serve hot or at room temperature.

PEPPERS

Peppers, like tomatoes, were introduced to the Mediterranean in
the sixteenth century by the Spanish who brought them back
from the Americas. Since then they've become so popular that it's
impossible to conceive of Mediterranean food without them.

Generally speaking the larger the pepper the milder it will
be. Many people persist in believing that redness in a pepper is a
sure sign that the pepper is hot, probably because they associate
redness with hot coals and fire. In fact a red pepper is simply a
green pepper turned ripe, and more often than not a red pepper is
sweet.

Like eggplants and tomatoes, peppers just cry out to be
stuffed. In Turkey and Yugoslavia they're often stuffed with a
mixture of cheeses, then set upright in a pan and baked. All

through the Balkans and the Middle East you find peppers stuffed with meat, rice, and herbs. In Yugoslavia there's an interesting dish of pickled green peppers stuffed with red cabbage.

I've included here a classic Turkish recipe for stuffed green peppers, a Sicilian-style chicken dish with sweet red peppers (in southern Italy the pepper is as popular as the tomato), and a simple Spanish dish of rice with peppers which to my mind is very satisfying.

BIBER DOLMASI

Cold stuffed green peppers (Turkey)

Ingredients

⅓ cup olive oil
2 cups chopped onions
1 cup rice
¼ cup pine nuts
1 scant tablespoon tomato paste
1 teaspoon salt
½ teaspoon freshly ground black pepper
1 teaspoon sugar
1 scant teaspoon ground allspice
1½ tablespoons chopped fresh mint
2 tablespoons lemon juice
8 sweet green peppers
2 lemons, quartered

Equipment

Heavy skillet with cover · 5-quart casserole
with tight-fitting cover

Working time: 20 minutes

Cooking time: 1¼ hours

Serves: 8

1. Heat the oil in the skillet. Add the onions and cook, stirring, for 5 minutes. Add the rice and cook, stirring, 3 minutes longer until the grains are well coated with oil. Add the pine nuts and stir for 1 minute. Pour in 2¼ cups hot water. Add the tomato paste, salt, pepper, sugar, and allspice. Bring to the boil. Cover the skillet, reduce the heat, and cook at the simmer 20 minutes.

2. Using a fork toss the rice. Add mint and lemon juice and toss again, mixing well. Allow to cool.

3. Remove the pepper tops, pull out seeds and hard white ribs. Rinse under running cold water and drain. Stuff the peppers. Arrange them, top side up, in the casserole. Add 1½ cups water without disturbing them. Bring to the boil; cover the casserole, reduce the heat, and cook at the simmer 45 minutes or until the peppers are tender. Allow to cool in the casserole. Chill overnight and serve as a first course or part of a buffet with lemon quarters.

PUNJENE PAPRIKE

Stuffed green peppers (Yugoslavia)

Ingredients

- 8 large sweet green peppers
- ½ cup chopped onion
- 3 tablespoons vegetable oil
- 1¼ pounds ground pork or beef or a mixture
- ⅓ cup rice
  Salt and freshly ground black pepper
- 2 tablespoons finely chopped parsley
- 1 egg
- 2 cups peeled, seeded, and chopped tomatoes
- 1 cup rich beef or chicken stock
- 1 teaspoon sweet paprika
- ¾ cup sour cream

Equipment

> Saucepan and strainer · Large skillet ·
> 5½-quart heavy casserole with tight-fitting cover

Working time: 25 minutes

Cooking time: 45 to 50 minutes

Serves: 4 to 5

    1. Cut off the stem ends of the green peppers. Remove the seeds and the thick white ribs but keep the pepper whole.

    2. Cook the onion in oil until it is soft but not browned. Add the meat and cook, stirring, until browned and separated. Meanwhile cook the rice in boiling salted water 5 minutes; drain and add to the meat and onion. Sprinkle with parsley and season well with salt and pepper. Mix in the egg, blending well.

    3. Stuff the peppers and place them side by side on a bed of chopped tomatoes. Add the stock and the paprika. Cover tightly and cook over gentle heat 45 minutes. Transfer the peppers to a serving dish. Whisk the sour cream into the cooking liquid, reheat without boiling. Pour over the peppers and serve hot.

POLLO ALLA CACCIATORA CON PEPERONI

Sicilian-style hunter's chicken with sweet peppers (Italy)

Ingredients

> 1 pound large sweet red and / or green peppers
> ½ cup chopped bacon
> 2 cloves garlic, chopped
> ¼ cup chopped onion
> 1 celery rib, chopped
> ¼ cup olive oil

    1 3-pound chicken, quartered
    ½ cup dry white wine
    4 tomatoes, peeled, seeded, and roughly chopped
      Salt and freshly ground black pepper
    2 tablespoons chopped parsley

Equipment

    Baking sheet · Large skillet with cover

Working time: 20 minutes

Cooking time: 40 minutes (approximately)

Serves: 4

1. Preheat the oven to 450 degrees.
2. Wash the peppers, drain, dry, and arrange on an ungreased baking sheet. Bake for 10 minutes, then turn and continue to bake 10 minutes more, or until the skins are black and blistered. Allow to cool under a kitchen towel.
3. Meanwhile lightly brown the bacon, garlic, onion, and celery in olive oil. Add the chicken and slowly brown on both sides. This takes about 10 minutes. Pour the wine over and reduce to a glaze over high heat, turning the chicken pieces often to crisp them. Add the tomatoes and season with salt and pepper. Cook, covered, 20 minutes.
4. Core, seed, and slip off the skins of the peppers. Cut into long strips. Just before serving fold the peppers into the sauce and allow to heat through. Readjust the seasoning, sprinkle with chopped parsley, and serve hot.

ARROZ EN CALDERO

Rice with green or red peppers in the style of Murcia (Spain)

Ingredients

    3 tablespoons olive oil
    2 cloves garlic, peeled but left whole
    1 pound boneless lean pork, cut into 1-inch cubes
    1 tablespoon chopped parsley
  ¼ teaspoon pulverized saffron
      Salt and freshly ground black pepper
  ½ cup chopped onion
    1 cup peeled, seeded, and chopped ripe tomatoes
    1 pound sweet red or green peppers, deribbed,
         seeded, and cut into long strips (makes 3 cups)
    2 cups raw rice, preferably imported Spanish rice
    1 quart boiling water or beef stock

Equipment

Large casserole with tight-fitting cover

Working time: 30 minutes

Cooking time: 1½ hours

Serves: 6

1. Heat the oil in the casserole and in it brown the garlic cloves and the pork on all sides. Remove the garlic cloves when soft and brown. Mash them to a puree and return to the casserole. Add the parsley and the saffron, stirring. Sprinkle with salt and pepper. Add the onion, tomatoes, peppers, and 1½ cups water. Bring to the boil. Cook, covered, over low heat 20 minutes. Remove the cover and cook over high heat, about 5 minutes, stirring, until the mixture is thick.

2. Add the rice and cook for a few minutes. Add boiling water or stock, 1½ teaspoons salt, and pepper to taste. Bring to the boil, stirring. Cover tightly and cook over low heat 30 minutes. Uncover the casserole and let stand 5 minutes before serving.

OTHER MEDITERRANEAN VEGETABLES

Zucchini, fennel, cabbage, artichokes, carrots, spinach, Swiss chard, fresh favas, and cardoons—the list of Mediterranean vegetables goes on and on. Because these appear in Mediterranean markets in quantity in their respective seasons, the Mediterranean cook has a great repertory of recipes allowing her to cook each vegetable in innumerable ways. Here are seven recipes from various parts of the region, all typically Mediterranean in their ingenuity, a mere sampling of what can be done.

ARTICHAUTS AUX ANCHOIS
Artichokes with anchovies (France)

Ingredients

  2 tablespoons olive oil
  ½ onion, finely chopped
  1 teaspoon finely chopped garlic
  2 tablespoons finely chopped parsley
  1 2-ounce tin anchovies, rinsed and mashed
  ⅓ cup dry white wine
  6 large cooked artichoke bottoms, quartered,
       or 1 package (10 ounces) frozen artichoke hearts,
       defrosted
     Salt and freshly ground black pepper
  ½ lemon

Equipment

Stainless steel or enameled skillet with cover

Working time: 10 minutes

Cooking time: 10 minutes

Serves: 4, as a first course

Heat the oil in the skillet and in it sauté the onion until soft and golden. Add the garlic, 1 tablespoon parsley, and the anchovies. Cook, stirring, for 1 minute. Pour in the wine. Add the artichoke hearts and season with freshly ground black pepper and a little salt. Bring to the boil. Simmer the artichokes for 5 minutes, stirring often. If using frozen artichokes cover and simmer until artichokes are tender. Add lemon juice to taste. Sprinkle with remaining parsley and serve at once.

SPINACI CON PARMIGIANA
Spinach with parmesan cheese (Italy)

I learned this lovely presentation for spinach from Paolo Zappi-Manzoni.

Ingredients

> 1½ pounds fresh spinach
> ¾ cup light cream
> ¾ cup grated parmesan cheese
>   Salt
>   Pinch of grated nutmeg
>   Freshly ground black pepper
> 2 egg whites

Equipment

> 3-quart enameled saucepan · Electric blender ·
> Mixing bowl and beater

Working time: 10 to 20 minutes

Cooking time: 10 minutes

Serves: 4

1. Trim off any spinach stems. Wash the spinach thoroughly and gently squeeze to remove most of the water. Place in the saucepan and cook until tender. Drain spinach well.

2. Place the spinach in an electric blender and add the cream. Whirl for 20 seconds. Return to the saucepan and mix in the grated cheese then season with salt, nutmeg, and black pepper. Stiffly beat the egg whites and fold into the spinach. Cook over low heat 2 to 3 minutes. Place in a warmed serving dish and serve at once.

BISBAS MICHCHI
Stuffed fennel bulbs (Tunisia)

Ingredients

> 4 fennel bulbs
> 1 pound ground beef or lamb
> ¼ cup finely chopped parsley
> 1 teaspoon *tabil* (see page 202)
> 2 teaspoons freshly ground black pepper
> Salt
> ¼ cup vegetable oil
> 2 eggs, lightly beaten
> 1 tablespoon grated parmesan cheese
> 1 cup homemade or canned spicy tomato sauce

Equipment

4-quart saucepan · Mixing bowl · Skillet ·
A buttered shallow ovenproof serving dish such as a
tagine slaoui (a shallow, round, earthenware dish)

Working time: 20 minutes

Cooking time: 20 minutes

Serves: 4

1. Wash the fennel and cut off their hard bases. Cook in boiling salted water 15 minutes or until they are just tender. Drain, then cut in half lengthwise.

2. Combine the meat, parsley, spices, and salt in a mixing bowl and blend thoroughly. Fry the mixture in oil until nicely browned. Cool; then mix in the beaten eggs and cheese.

3. Preheat the oven to 400 degrees.

4. Place 4 fennel halves cut side up in the baking dish; pile on the filling, top with the remaining fennel halves, spoon over the tomato sauce, and set in the oven to bake 15 to 20 minutes. Serve hot.

FRITTATA DI FIORI DI ZUCCA

Omelet with stuffed zucchini blossoms (Italy)

I am again indebted to my friend Mario Ruspoli for this fabulous Tuscan dish. A *frittata* is a kind of stuffed flat omelet served at room temperature in Italy as a first course. *Frittatas* are also ideal for picnics, and Mario suggests that this particular one is very good cold, too. Here zucchini blossoms (or the blossoms of any squash) are stuffed with mozzarella cheese and either anchovies or prosciutto, then they're rolled in batter and fried, and added to the omelet. You can also serve the stuffed blossoms without the omelet as a first course, but in that case they should be served hot and with a wedge of lemon.

Ingredients

　　　1 cup sifted all-purpose flour
　　　5 ounces water
　　　2 tablespoons olive oil
　　　¼ teaspoon salt
　　　½ cup finely diced mozzarella cheese
　　　1 2-ounce tin anchovy fillets, rinsed and mashed

12 fresh zucchini blossoms (see note)
1 egg white, beaten
3 tablespoons vegetable oil
3 tablespoons butter
Juice of ½ lemon
6 eggs
Salt and freshly ground black pepper
2 tablespoons milk
Pinch of grated nutmeg
1 tablespoon grated parmesan cheese
1 tablespoon chopped parsley

Equipment

2 mixing bowls · 8-inch ovenproof skillet ·
Whisk · Spatula

Working time: 20 minutes

Cooking time: 15 minutes

Serves: 4

1. Place the flour in a mixing bowl. Stir in the water, the olive oil, and salt, and stir until smooth. Allow to rest 2 hours.
2. Preheat the oven to 400 degrees.
3. Blend the mozzarella cheese and the anchovies. Separate into 12 equal parts. Set aside.
4. Carefully wash the blossoms; avoid tearing them. Drain and pat dry. Stuff the blossoms with the cheese-anchovy mixture.
5. Fold the egg white into the prepared batter. Heat the oil and the butter in the skillet. Dip each stuffed blossom in the batter and slip into the hot fat. Fry until golden brown on both sides. Drain on paper towels, then sprinkle with lemon juice.

Note: Zucchini blossoms are available in Italian markets during the summer. The blossoms may also be stuffed with prosciutto and mozzarella.

6. In a mixing bowl beat the eggs with salt, pepper, milk, nutmeg, parmesan cheese, and parsley until frothy. Pour into the skillet and cook over moderate heat for 30 seconds to set the eggs on the bottom. Arrange the fried stuffed blossoms in 1 layer on top. Then transfer the skillet to the hot oven and bake for 8 minutes or until the eggs are just firm.

7. Remove from the oven; use a spatula to loosen the bottom and turn out onto a round serving dish. Serve hot, warm, or cold, cut into wedges.

HOUT MAKLI

Fried fish with zucchini and tomato sauce (Tunisia)

This is an attractive and spicy fish dish, very popular in Tunis. Here the zucchini is fried and then added on top of the tomato sauce, so that the dish looks red with little green pin wheels scattered around. The Tunisians also make a version substituting small cubes of salted eggplant for the zucchini.

Ingredients

    4 fish fillets such as flounder, sole, etc.
      Salt and freshly ground black pepper
    2 lemons
    3 zucchini, each about 5 inches long
    ¼ cup olive oil
    ½ cup chopped onion
    2 cups fresh or canned tomato sauce
    ½ teaspoon *harissa* (see page 182)
    ½ teaspoon finely chopped garlic
    1 egg, beaten
      Flour for dredging
      Oil for frying

Equipment

    Skillet · Deep skillet

Working time: 15 minutes

Cooking time: 15 minutes

Serves: 4

1. Wash and dry the fish fillets, season with salt and pepper, and sprinkle with the juice of 1 lemon; set aside.
2. Peel the zucchini and slice into ¼-inch-thick rounds. Heat the oil in the skillet and fry the rounds until brown on both sides; drain. In the same oil cook the onions until soft. Add the tomato sauce, *harissa*, garlic, salt and pepper. Cook, uncovered, over medium-high heat, stirring, for 5 minutes. Return the zucchini to the tomato sauce and continue to cook at the simmer, uncovered, 5 minutes.
3. Meanwhile heat enough oil to a depth of 1 inch in the deep skillet. Dip the fish fillets in flour, beaten egg, and flour and fry in oil heated to 375 degrees. Drain.
4. Add the juice of the remaining lemon to the tomato sauce, readjust the seasoning, and serve hot with the fish.

MARKA OMMALAH

Pickled vegetables with spiced ground beef (Tunisia)

Ingredients

    1 pound ground beef
    ¾ teaspoon salt
    ½ teaspoon freshly ground black pepper
    2 teaspoons *tabil* (see page 202)
    1 teaspoon pulverized dried mint
    1 cup pickled vegetables (see note)
    1 tablespoon capers
    ½ cup juicy black olives, rinsed and pitted
    ½ cup green olives, rinsed and pitted
    ¼ cup chopped fresh tomato
    2 tablespoons peanut oil
    1 teaspoon sweet paprika

Equipment

> Mixing bowl · Large enameled or stainless steel skillet with cover

Working time: 20 minutes

Cooking time: 45 minutes

Serves: 3 to 4

Place the beef in the mixing bowl. Add salt, pepper, *tabil*, dried mint, and a few tablespoons water; blend thoroughly. With wet hands form 16 meatballs. Place in the skillet. Add the remaining ingredients plus 1 cup water. Cook, covered, over medium low heat for 45 minutes. Serve hot.

Note: Pickled vegetables, imported from Greece, are sold in 1-pound jars in Middle Eastern markets.

SARMA

Stuffed cabbage (Yugoslavia)

I learned this recipe 15 years ago in Dubrovnik. The French stuff cabbage, of course, as do the Armenians and nearly everyone else, but *sarma* remains my favorite stuffed cabbage dish.

Ingredients

> 1   2½–3 pound cabbage
> 2–3   tablespoons chopped onion
> 1   tablespoon lard or oil
> 1   pound ground beef, or ½ pound ground pork
>   and ½ pound ground beef, or 1 pound ground pork
> ¼   cup rice, boiled 10 minutes, rinsed, and drained
> 2   tablespoons chopped parsley
> ½   teaspoon sharp paprika

Salt and freshly ground black pepper
9 slices smoked bacon, halved lengthwise
1 carrot, chopped
1 onion, chopped
2 tablespoons butter
2 cups fresh or canned tomato sauce
6 thin slices of lemon
Chopped parsley
Lemon juice

Equipment

Mixing bowl · Large kettle · Colander ·
4-quart casserole with tight-fitting cover

Working time: 30 minutes

Cooking time: 1¼ hours

Serves: 4 to 6

1. Carefully remove the outer leaves from the cabbage then cut out the core. Loosen the leaves; drop into boiling salted water and parboil for 3 to 4 minutes. Drain in a colander, allow to cool, and choose 18 large leaves.

2. Lightly brown the onions in oil or lard. Combine with the meat, cooked rice, parsley, paprika, salt and pepper. Mix until well combined. Separate into 18 portions of equal size.

3. Spread out the leaves and season with salt and pepper. Put 1 portion of meat filling on each cabbage leaf near the base; starting at the base, fold the bottom of the leaf over the filling. Fold the sides toward the center then roll up tightly. Wrap a thin slice of bacon around each roll.

4. In a heavy casserole gently fry the carrot and onion in butter. Arrange the rolls in layers on top. Add the tomato sauce and lemon slices. Cover tightly and cook over low heat for 1 hour. Sprinkle with fresh parsley and a little lemon juice just before serving.

Chick-Peas, Lentils, and Beans

CHICK-PEAS, lentils, and beans, all dried vegetables, have been cultivated around the Mediterranean since farming first began. Along with onions they are the oldest Mediterranean vegetables, but with one advantage that onions do not have— under proper conditions they can be stored almost indefinitely. High in protein, strong in nutrient value, simple to grow, store, and prepare, they are an almost perfect food.

The peoples of the Mediterranean do much with them, especially the chick-pea. According to Waverly Root the first canning of pork and beans took place in Pompeii when chick-peas and bacon were put up in sealed clay pots and exported to all corners of the Roman world. Chick-peas are a necessity for North African food, appearing in numerous couscous dishes and *tagines*. In Tunisia today there is a boiled chick-pea dish called *leblebi*, for which the diner is advised to bring a handkerchief to the table. The chick-peas are served in a large bowl over crumbled bread and half-cooked eggs, with lots of powdered cumin and a great deal of hot *harissa* sauce. The dish is so hot with spices that "the nose runs ferociously," according to a Tunisian friend, and thus the handkerchief comes into play.

The Phoenicians brought the chick-pea to Spain where it turns up in a number of fine lusty dishes. Chick-peas were grown in ancient Egypt and the Middle East in biblical times. One of the most typical of all Middle Eastern dishes is *hummus bi taheeni*, an hors d'oeuvre of mashed chick-peas and sesame paste served with olives, radishes, lemon wedges, and bread. There is a Turkish chick-pea dip called *zather*, consisting of mashed chick-peas, watermelon seed, cumin, and marjoram; and in Israel, chick-peas are seasoned with salt, pepper, cumin, and coriander in *naheet b'ob*. Chick-peas can be used in place of favas in Egyptian *tamiya*, becoming the Israeli dish *falafel*: chick-pea fritters stuffed into Arab-style bread (*pita*).

The Italians like chick-peas, too. I've included an old Tuscan recipe for *pasta e ceci*, a thick soup of chick-peas, macaroni, and chopped pork ribs in chicken broth—a hearty winter dish. But as much as the Italians like the chick-pea their real love is the bean. The Tuscans are known as the bean-eaters of the Mediterranean. They have a bean dish called *fagioli al fiasco*—beans cooked in a sealed bottle so that none of the flavor escapes. I've included a recipe for the famous *fagioli con tonno* (tuna with white beans) and the fancy restaurant version with Beluga caviar. But I've left out what must be some kind of ultimate: *lenticchie e fagioli*, literally lentils with beans!

The bean is given good treatment along the entire Spanish coast in *cocido con judías blancas*, a casserole of flavored white beans and lamb. But the lowly bean is certainly raised to the summit of gastronomic art in *cassoulet Toulousain*, the glory of Languedocian cookery.

The fava bean is ever-present on the streets of Cairo where *tamiya* is the most popular street food. If there is a fava bean equivalent of cassoulet, it is probably the Sardinian casserole *la favata*, made of favas, pork chops, homemade sausage, fennel, hot pepper, white cabbage, garlic, tomatoes, and pork fat.

Finally there are lentils, used in cooking since Roman times. In Italy *anitra con lenticchie*, is a fine presentation of braised duck with lentils, and *kushari* is an Egyptian dish of lentils and rice topped with fried onions and a spicy tomato sauce. I've included a good-tasting simple Lebanese dish called *adas be sabanigh*, a heavy soup of lentils, spinach, and lemon.

Years ago, when I first lived in Morocco, I had a Spanish maid named Loli who had a reverential attitude toward the lentil. She was from the town of Murcia and her family had fought on the Republican side of the Spanish civil war. "Lentils," she'd told me, "are blessed by God. They were all we had to eat during the war, so we owe our lives to them, and also they taste so good." She'd tell me how she'd flavor a kilo of lentils with two tomatoes and half a pork chop, and that would be enough to feed eight adults for an entire day. Unlike most people who live on one food during a war or a difficult time, and then resolve never to eat it again, Loli had fond memories of her lentil casserole, and used to make it for herself all the time.

FAGIOLI CON TONNO

White beans with tuna (Italy)

Ingredients

> 1 8-ounce can cannellini beans, drained
> ¼ cup chopped scallions
> ¼ cup olive oil
> 1–2 tablespoons freshly squeezed lemon juice
> Salt and freshly ground black pepper
> 1 7-ounce can first-quality tuna packed in olive oil
> 1 tablespoon finely chopped fresh parsley
> Pinch of crumbled oregano

Equipment

Colander · Shallow serving dish

Working time: 5 minutes

Serves: 4 to 6 as a first course

Mix the beans, green onions, oil, and lemon juice. Season to taste with salt and pepper. Pile into a serving dish. Break the tuna into small pieces and arrange on top of the beans. Sprinkle with herbs and serve at room temperature.

FAGIOLI CON CAVIALE
White beans with caviar (Italy)

This is the luxurious way of presenting white beans, served up in certain fancy Roman restaurants with Beluga caviar. It's delicious, but has always struck me as a rather expensive and decadent way to salt one's beans! Actually this dish was invented in Florence in the 1930s for a fading upper class. Then the beans were cooked with a head of garlic. The garlic was discarded before the caviar was mixed in.

Ingredients

>　2 cups dried white beans
>　1 onion, stuck with 1 clove
>　1 garlic clove
>　½ teaspoon freshly ground black pepper
>　1 bay leaf
>　⅓ cup French dressing
>　1 2-ounce jar caviar or Danish lumpfish or whitefish roe
>　　Lemon quarters

Equipment

Large saucepan　·　Colander　·　Glass serving dish

Working time: 5 minutes

Cooking time: 1½ hours

Serves: 4

1. Pick over the beans and discard any stones. Soak in water to cover overnight. Drain, cover with fresh cold water. Add the

onion, garlic, black pepper, and bay leaf. Bring to the boil, lower the heat and cook at the simmer, covered, until the beans are tender, about 1½ hours. Discard the onion, bay leaf, and garlic clove.

2. Drain the beans in a colander: place in the serving dish, add the French dressing, toss well and let cool. Add the caviar; tossing well. Readjust the seasoning. Garnish with lemon quarters and serve at once.

TAMIYA

Bean patties (Egypt)

You find *tamiya* served off little stands on every street in Cairo, even the most obscure back streets in the most wretched slums. It's the street food of the city, served up with slices of tomatoes and shredded lettuce inside Arab bread.

Ingredients

1½ cups (½ pound) shelled dried fava beans
    or substitute chick-peas
1 teaspoon finely chopped garlic
½ teaspoon ground cumin seed
2 tablespoons chopped fresh coriander
2 or 3 scallions, finely chopped
½ teaspoon double-acting baking powder
    Salt and freshly ground pepper
½ teaspoon crushed red pepper, or ¼ teaspoon cayenne
    Flour for dredging
    Oil for deep frying

Equipment

4-quart saucepan with cover · Food mill or meat grinder · Deep-fat fryer or deep skillet · Slotted spoon

Working time: 15 minutes

Cooking time: 1 hour

Frying time: 2 minutes for each set of 4

Makes: 32, serves 4

1. Soak the beans overnight in plenty of water to cover.
2. Drain and rub the beans between the palms to loosen the skin. Discard the skins. Rinse, cover with 2 quarts cold water, and cook, covered, over low heat 1 hour or until tender, stirring often. Remove and discard any skins that float to the surface. Drain thoroughly.
3. Push the beans through a food mill or meat grinder. Combine with the garlic, cumin, coriander, scallions, baking powder, salt, pepper, and cayenne, mixing until well blended. Chill at least 30 minutes in the refrigerator.
4. Shape into small balls with moistened hands, then dust with flour and arrange on a plate in 1 layer. Allow to dry for about 10 minutes before frying. Heat the fat to a depth of 1 inch in the fryer or skillet. Fry in very hot fat until golden brown on both sides. Serve hot with drinks.

HUMMUS BI TAHEENI

Chick-peas with sesame paste (Middle East)

This is undoubtedly the most famous dish of the Middle East—a delicious dip, spread, hors d'oeuvre, or what have you.

In areas of the country where hard water is prevalent, dried chick-peas should be soaked in water with ¼ teaspoon baking soda. The following day the chick-peas should be well rinsed before cooking.

Ingredients

    1 cup dried chick-peas or 1 can cooked chick-peas, drained
    ¼ teaspoon baking soda (optional)
    ¾ cup tahini (sesame seed paste)
    ¾ cup freshly squeezed lemon juice, or more to taste
    1 teaspoon chopped garlic
    1 teaspoon salt
      Pinch of sharp paprika
      About 1 tablespoon olive oil

Equipment

    2-quart saucepan with cover · Electric blender

Working time: 10 minutes

Cooking time: 1½ hours (if using dried chick-peas)

Makes: 3 cups (approximately), serves 8

1. If using dried chick-peas, pick them over and then soak overnight in water to cover. Drain; rinse well. Cook in simmering water, covered, about 1½ hours or until tender. Drain.

2. Stir up the tahini paste with the oil until well blended. Put the lemon juice and the garlic in the blender jar. Whirl while adding the chick-peas, a handful at a time. Gradually add the tahini paste and some spoonsful of water. When the mixture is smooth and creamy, adjust the seasoning with more salt, garlic, or lemon juice to taste.

3. Scrape into a serving dish. Decorate with a pinch of paprika in the center and dribble over olive oil. Use as a dip with *pita* or crackers.

PASTA E CECI

Pasta and chick-peas (Italy)

This is another recipe from my friend Mario Ruspoli for a robust peasant Tuscan dish. It's particularly good for lunch on a cold winter day.

Ingredients

> 1 cup dried chick-peas, picked over
> ¼ teaspoon baking soda (optional)
> ⅓ cup olive oil
> 2 cloves garlic, peeled and chopped
> 1 cup chopped onion
> 12 ounces pork spare-ribs, cut into 1-inch squares
> 2 cups chicken stock
> 1 sprig fresh basil (optional)
> 1 sprig fresh rosemary or ½ teaspoon dried
>   Salt and freshly ground black pepper
> 1½ cups elbow macaroni
>   Grated parmesan cheese

Equipment

Saucepan with cover   ·   Food mill or electric blender   ·
Large casserole with cover

Working time: 15 minutes

Cooking time: 2 hours

Serves: 6

1. Soak the chick-peas overnight in water to cover.
2. Drain the chick-peas and rinse well. Place in the saucepan, cover with fresh water, bring to the boil, and cook at the simmer, covered, for 1½ hours or until they are tender.

3. In the casserole in hot oil lightly brown the garlic, onion, and pork ribs. Add 2 cups stock, herbs, and seasoning. Cover and cook 1 hour over gentle heat.

4. Push half the cooked chick-peas through a food mill or puree in an electric blender. Add the puree, the whole chick-peas, and the cooking liquid to the casserole. Bring to the boil and cook at the simmer 15 minutes, stirring often.

5. Add 1 quart water. Taste the soup for seasoning and re-adjust. Bring to the boil; throw in the macaroni and cook rapidly until just tender—about 15 minutes. Serve hot and pass a bowl of grated cheese.

ADAS BE SABANIGH

Lentils with spinach and lemon (Lebanon)

Ingredients

- ½ pound lentils
- 1 cup sliced onions
- ¼ cup olive oil
- 3 cloves garlic, peeled and finely chopped
- ¼ cup chopped fresh coriander
- 10 ounces frozen spinach leaves, completely thawed and roughly chopped
- 2 medium potatoes, peeled and sliced
-   Salt and freshly ground black pepper
- ¼ cup freshly squeezed lemon juice, or more to taste

Equipment

Saucepan with cover · Large stainless steel or enameled casserole

Working time: 15 minutes

Cooking time: 1 hour 20 minutes

Serves: 6

1. Wash and pick over the lentils. Place in a saucepan and cover with water. Bring to the boil. Cook, covered, about 20 minutes.

2. Meanwhile, in a large casserole brown the onions in oil. Stir in the garlic and coriander. Add the spinach and sauté 5 to 6 minutes, stirring frequently. Add the potatoes, lentils, and enough lentil cooking liquid to cover. Season with salt and pepper. Bring to the boil, lower the heat, and cook at the simmer 1 hour or until thick and soupy. Stir in the lemon juice. Serve hot, lukewarm, or cold.

COCIDO CON JUDIAS BLANCAS

Lamb, pork, and white bean stew (Spain)

This is the Spanish version of the formidable French cassoulet.

Ingredients

> 1½ cups dried white beans
> ¼ pound salt pork
>   Parsley sprigs and 1 bay leaf
> 1 onion studded with 1 clove
> 2 pounds lamb shoulder or breast, cut into serving pieces
>   Salt and freshly ground black pepper
>   Flour
> 2 tablespoons olive oil
> 4 thick slices of bacon, diced
> 2 medium onions, halved and thinly sliced
> 2 cups beef stock
> 2 tablespoons tomato paste
> 2 cloves garlic, finely chopped
> 5–6 ounces chorizo
>   Chopped parsley

Equipment

Large saucepan · 4-quart heavy casserole with cover

Working time: 20 minutes

Cooking time: 2 hours

Serves: 6

1. Separately, soak the beans and the salt pork overnight in plenty of water. Rinse well then place in a large saucepan. Add parsley, bay leaf, onion, and enough water to cover the top of the beans by 1½ inches. Cook at the simmer 1 hour, skimming often.

2. Sprinkle the lamb with salt and pepper and dust with flour. In the large casserole, brown the lamb on all sides in olive oil. Remove to a side dish. Lightly brown the bacon and the onion in the same fat. This will take about 10 minutes. Discard all but 2 tablespoons fat. Return the meat to the casserole and moisten with the stock. Add the tomato paste, garlic, and the sausage. Simmer, covered, 1 hour.

3. Drain the beans reserving 1 cup of the cooking liquid. Cut the salt pork into cubes and add to the casserole. Add beans and reserved cooking liquid to the casserole and continue cooking 30 minutes or until the beans and the meat are very tender. Readjust the seasoning and serve hot sprinkled with chopped parsley.

DJEJ BIL HAMUS

Chicken with chick-peas (Morocco)

Ingredients

½ pound dried chick-peas or 1 can cooked chick-peas, drained

¼ teaspoon baking soda (optional—see *hummus bi taheeni*, page 124)

Continued

1 3½-pound chicken
4 cloves garlic, peeled
  Salt
½ teaspoon ground ginger
½ teaspoon ground black pepper
  Pinch pulverized saffron
½ teaspoon turmeric
2 tablespoon finely chopped parsley
1 cinnamon stick
¼ cup finely chopped onion
3 tablespoons butter
1 small onion, thinly sliced
2 tablespoons black raisins (optional)

Equipment

Mixing bowls · Saucepan · 3½-quart casserole
with cover

Working time: 30 minutes

Cooking time: 1½ hours

Serves: 4

1. The day before, pick over the chick-peas then soak over-night in water to cover.

2. To purify the chicken as it is done in Morocco, rub the flesh with a paste made with 3 cloves crushed garlic and 1 tablespoon salt. Rinse the chicken well then pat dry with paper towels. In a mixing bowl combine ginger, pepper, remaining garlic clove, crushed, and 2 tablespoons water. Rub this mixture all over the chicken. Cover and refrigerate overnight.

3. The next day, drain the chick-peas, rinse well, place in the saucepan, cover with fresh water, bring to the boil and cook at the simmer, covered, for about 1 hour or until they are tender. Drain and submerge in a bowl of cold water. Rub the chick-peas to remove their skins. The skins will rise to the surface, discard

them. (If using canned chick-peas, drain and skin them, then set aside.)

4. Place chicken, any juices in the bowl, saffron, turmeric, parsley, cinnamon stick, chopped onion, and butter in the casserole. Add 2½ cups water and bring to a boil. Cover and cook at the simmer 1 hour, turning the chicken frequently in the sauce. Remove the chicken and keep warm and moist.

5. Add the finely sliced onion, cooked chick-peas, and raisins, if using them, to the sauce and cook until the onions are soft and the sauce has reduced to a thick gravy. Return the chicken to the sauce to reheat. Taste the sauce for salt, and add a pinch of pulverized saffron for a good yellow color.

6. To serve, place the chicken in a deep serving dish, spoon over the chick-pea sauce, and serve at once.

ANITRA CON LENTICCHIE

Braised duck with lentils (Italy)

Ingredients

1¼ cups lentils, picked over (see note)
1 5-pound duck, quartered
1 cup chopped onions
3 ounces prosciutto, chopped or substitute smoked ham
1 cup dry red wine
2 cloves garlic, chopped
2 parsley sprigs
1 bay leaf
   Salt and freshly ground black pepper
1 chopped carrot
1 chopped celery rib
¼ cup tomato sauce

Equipment

4-quart enameled or stainless steel casserole with cover ·
3-quart saucepan

Working time: 30 minutes

Cooking time: 2 hours

Serves: 4

1. Soak the lentils in water to cover overnight.
2. The next day, remove the excess fat from the duck and prick the skin all over with the tines of a fork. In the casserole render some of the fat and in it brown the duck pieces on all sides. Pour off all but 2 tablespoons fat and reserve another 2 tablespoons fat for the lentils. Add half the onions and the prosciutto to the casserole and cook briefly, stirring, until the onions turn golden. Add the wine, garlic, herbs, salt and pepper. Bring to the boil, then cover and cook at the simmer 1 hour.
3. Meanwhile in the saucepan heat the reserved duck fat and in it lightly brown the remaining onion, carrot, and celery. Moisten with 3 cups cold water and tomato sauce. Drain the lentils and add to the saucepan. Bring to the boil and simmer the lentils 45 minutes. Season.
4. Remove the duck from the casserole. Tilt the casserole and spoon off as much fat as possible. Boil down the cooking liquid to thicken. Return the duck to the casserole. Add the lentils and their cooking liquid. Cook, covered, 1 hour. Serve hot.

Note: Do not use quick-cooking lentils for this dish.

CASSOULET TOULOUSAIN

White beans with pork, pork sausage, and lamb in the style of Toulouse (France)

Cassoulet is to Languedoc as Bouillabaisse is to Provence. In fact they are the two most famous dishes of southern France. There are as many versions of cassoulet as there are people who cook it, and French gastronomes like nothing better than to sit around and discuss the relative merits of Tante Duval's recipe versus Madame Dupont's. It's like listening to Spaniards talk about paella, Moroccans arguing over couscous, or Texans quarreling over chili. Every cook has her own way, and if by chance she should give you her recipe be advised that her "secret" may well be left out.

Actually there are three basic kinds of cassoulet all made with pork: the classic version from Castelnaudary includes bacon and garlic sausage; the Toulouse variation adds pork, lamb, and preserved or fresh goose; and the variation from Carcassonne usually includes all of the above plus a partridge when in season. If you can obtain goose fat (see list of suppliers, page 333), you might want to add some of that, too, but *confit d'oie* (cooked and preserved goose) is almost impossible to find in America. If you make your own add it in step 5 with the link sausages. Use only one preserved leg or breast, cut into four or five pieces. A roasted fresh duck is not a good substitute for *confit d'oie*. I don't think a fresh duck contributes much, but if you do decide to throw one in be sure to prick it all over so that the fat runs out during roasting. You can use duck fat in cassoulet, by the way, in place of pork fat, goose fat, or lard.

Cassoulet is really a marvelous dish, rich and especially satisfying for winter lunch. Its deep golden crust is lovely to look at, especially when you know that inside there is a champagne colored sauce sparkling with bits of browned pork, pork sausage, and lamb. The ball of parsley, chopped bacon, and garlic sitting amidst the beans slowly transmits flavor through the dish and fills your kitchen with a fabulous aroma that builds anticipation for the cassoulet.

Ingredients

- ½ pound pork rind, cut into small pieces
- 2 pounds dried white beans
  - Bouquet garni: bay leaf, celery leaves, thyme, and parsley, tied together and wrapped in cheesecloth
- 1 clove garlic, peeled and slightly crushed
- 1 onion stuck with 2 cloves
  - Salt and freshly ground black pepper
- 2 pounds pork shoulder, cut into 1½-inch chunks

Continued

   1 pound lamb breast, cut into 1½-inch chunks
   ¼ cup rendered pork fat, goose fat, or lard
   1 cup chopped onion
   2 tablespoons tomato paste
      Bouquet garni: parsley, bay leaf, and thyme tied together
   1 pound garlic pork sausage such as *kielbasi*
         or *cotechino*, or substitute *cervelas*
   ½ pound pork sausage links
   3 tablespoons finely chopped parsley
   1 tablespoon finely chopped garlic
   ¼ cup finely chopped bacon
   ½ cup dry white wine
   ¾ cup soft white breadcrumbs

Equipment

Saucepan with cover for the beans · Large casserole
or saucepan with cover for the meats · Small skillet ·
Slotted spoon · Earthenware or stoneware bean pot
about 7 inches deep and 10 inches in diameter with a
5½–6-quart capacity

Working time: 60 minutes

Cooking time: 1¾ hours plus 3 hours the day before

Slow baking time: 2 to 3 hours (approximately)

Serves: 10 to 12

    1. The day before you plan to serve, simmer the pork rind in plenty of water for 3 hours, skimming often. Cool. Refrigerate the rind and the cooking liquid. Soak the beans in water to cover overnight.

    2. The following day, drain the beans and place in a saucepan. Add the pork rind and its cooking liquid. Add more water to cover. Bring to the boil. Add the bouquet garni wrapped in cheesecloth, the crushed garlic clove, and the onion stuck with cloves. Season with salt and pepper. Reduce the heat to the simmer and cook, covered, 30 minutes.

3. Meanwhile in a casserole or another saucepan, brown the pork and the lamb on all sides in 2 tablespoons fat. Remove the meats to a side dish. In the drippings soften the onion. Return the meat to the casserole. Add the tomato paste, bouquet garni, and season with salt and pepper. Moisten with 2 cups water. Cover and cook at a simmer 30 minutes.

4. Meanwhile prick the garlic sausage 4 or 5 times. Add to the beans after they have cooked 30 minutes. Continue cooking the beans, uncovered, 45 minutes longer, adding water if necessary. Cook until the beans are tender, but not splitting. Remove the sausage and set aside. Remove and discard the bouquet garni and the onion.

5. Prick the link sausages then brown in the skillet. Drain and add to the pork and the lamb. Continue cooking, covered, a further 30 minutes over very low heat, adding more water if necessary.

6. Preheat the oven to 325 degrees.

7. In the bean pot put all the cooked pork rind in 1 layer, cover with a layer of beans, then a layer of pork and lamb. Cut the garlic sausage into 1-inch pieces and place between the pork and lamb chunks. Add another layer of beans, then add the pork link sausages. Combine parsley, garlic, and chopped bacon, mixing into a compact ball and push into the middle of the beans and meat. Top with the remaining beans. Add wine to the meat cooking liquid, and by rapid boiling reduce to 1 cup. Separately boil the bean cooking liquid down to 1½ cups. Pour the meat cooking liquid over the beans and add just enough of bean cooking liquid to moisten them. Spread a layer of breadcrumbs on top and dribble over a little of the remaining goose or pork fat. Set the dish in the oven to bake ¾ hour or until a golden skin forms on the top of the beans. Gently stir up the skin that has formed. Sprinkle with another layer of breadcrumbs and return to the oven to bake until another golden layer appears—in about 30 minutes. Lower the oven heat to 275 degrees and continue to bake, stirring up every 30 minutes or whenever another layer forms. It is traditional to serve the dish after the seventh "stir" but two or three stirrings will do fine. Serve directly from the casserole.

GARBANZOS A LA CATALANA

Chick-peas with tomatoes, fresh sausage, and peppers (Spain)

This dish, extremely popular in homes in Barcelona, normally requires a fresh sausage which is a specialty of Catalonia. In the ingredients list I suggest some substitutes, but if you have a sausage-making machine you can make these sausages with ease. Grind ½ pound of pork with 2 to 3 ounces of pork fat, moisten the meat with a few tablespoons of white wine, salt, pepper, and pinches of cinnamon or nutmeg, powdered cloves, and crumbled thyme. Then force the seasoned meat into a casing and hang the sausage in an airy place for 24 hours. The sausage is cooked in boiling water and is eaten hot or cold.

Ingredients

    1½ cups dried chick-peas, picked over
     ¼ teaspoon baking soda (optional—
          see *hummus bi taheeni* page 124)
     ½ pound Catalonian sausage
          or fresh country-style pork sausage
      5 ounces slab bacon or lean salt pork
        Oil or lard
      1 cup chopped onion
      1 teaspoon finely chopped garlic
      1 cup diced sweet green pepper
      4 large red ripe tomatoes, peeled, seeded, and chopped
        Grated nutmeg or cinnamon
     ¼ teaspoon ground thyme
        Salt and freshly ground black pepper

Equipment

Saucepan with cover · Skillet · Wide earthen
or stoneware baking dish, about 13 inches wide
and 2 inches deep with cover or aluminum foil

Working time: 30 minutes

Cooking time: 2½ hours

Serves: 6

1. Pick over the chick-peas and soak overnight in water to cover. Drain, rinse well, and cook in simmering water, covered, about 1 hour.

2. Simmer the sausage in water 20 minutes or prick the bought sausages with the prongs of a fork and brown in a skillet. Drain off most of the fat and cut the sausage into 1-inch chunks; set aside.

3. Simmer the bacon or salt pork 10 minutes in water, drain, and rinse well.

4. In the sausage fat or in 1 tablespoon oil or lard, brown the bacon or salt pork, onion, garlic, and green pepper, stirring.

5. Add the tomatoes, nutmeg, thyme, salt and pepper to taste. Cook, covered, 10 minutes. Fold in the sausage slices.

6. Preheat the oven to 375 degrees.

7. Drain the chick-peas reserving 2 cups cooking liquid. Put the chick-peas in the baking dish. Spoon in the prepared tomato sauce. Moisten with the reserved cooking liquid. Season with salt and pepper to taste. Cover the dish and set in the oven to bake 1½ hours, stirring from time to time. Serve in wide soup plates.

Pasta, Couscous, and Other Mediterranean Farinaceous Foods

ONE of the most convincing theories of the evolution of human culture has to do with the cereal grains. Early man was a hunter. He led a nomadic life, moving about in pursuit of wild game. But when he became a farmer and began to cultivate crops he settled down and formed communities and in these communities the germ of his culture was born. The first crops were the grains, and even today they are the stuff which links men in all the corners of the earth. Wheat, rice, corn, barley, sorghum and rye—they are the great connecting crops of mankind.

Men have cultivated grain around the Mediterranean Sea since before recorded time. And wheat has always been and continues to be the great Mediterranean cereal crop. There is rice, too, and some of the other grains, but wheat is king, and bread the staple of Mediterranean life.

I've decided in this book not to give any recipes for breads. They are available elsewhere, and it seems to me, too, that almost any Mediterranean bread is now available commercially in the United States. But I felt it implausible to write a book about

Mediterranean food, and not dwell, for a time at least, on some of the great farinaceous foods. Hence this chapter with its notes on the making of pasta, the preparation of North African couscous and *briks*, and a few pastry dishes which did not fall easily into the other chapters devoted to flavorings, but which I wanted to include all the same.

PASTA

In 1972, when I was a free-lance food consultant, I helped Tony May and Francesca Baldeschi organize an Italian fortnight at the Rainbow Room in New York. Chefs, wines, and even some fresh ingredients were flown over for this orgy of Italian gluttony which included specialties of every region of Italy, served up on separate nights. We offered, too, 50 kinds of Italian pasta, everything from *pappardelle con la lepre* (with hare's sauce) *to pasta con le sarde* (with sardines and wild fennel), and some other extraordinary handmade pasta dishes such as *orecchiette* ("little ears"), *crespelli* (stuffed and fried crêpes), and *panzarotti* (large fried ravioli).

Though we offered fifty pasta dishes we did little more than scratch the surface. Whole books have been written about Italian pasta. There are literally hundreds of recipes, many of them never written down. It's said that every woman in Italy has her own way of preparing spaghetti, not to mention lasagne, fettuccine, ravioli, and the other classic pasta forms. On the road from Positano to Amalfi there's a trattoria that serves spaghetti cooked in a paper bag, and doubtless there are still more unusual pasta dishes yet to be ferretted out.

In other chapters of this book I give some pasta recipes: a walnut sauce called *aia* for green *tagliatelle*: three ways of making the olive-based spaghetti *puttanesca*; a herb oil sauce from Genoa; a rare and previously unpublished pesto from the town of Nervi; and a dish called *la gallina del Ghiottoni* in which the pasta is stuffed inside a chicken. These dishes appear separately because they are dominated by one or another of the Mediterranean flavorings which are the subject of this book. But there are a few pasta dishes I want to include too, simply because they are extraordinarily good. I offer five of them here, all rather unusual, and varying from *tagliatelle con burro rosso*, quick and simple to prepare, to *pasticcio di maccheroni alla Piedmontese*, an elaborate, complicated, time-consuming pasta extravaganza that rewards all the effort it demands. But before you embark on these recipes, you should give serious consideration to making your own pasta. It tastes better than the package varieties, and enables you to produce a wide range of forms which you can fill with homemade stuffings.

PASTA

Homemade noodle dough (Italy)

Ingredients

      1½ cups all-purpose flour
      ½ cup semolina flour (see note)
      1 teaspoon salt
      4 large eggs, lightly beaten
      1 teaspoon oil

Equipment

      Large pastry board · Rolling pin

Working time: 1 hour

Makes: About 1 pound pasta

Note: If semolina is unavailable use an additional ½ cup all-purpose flour.

    1. Make a mound of flour on the pastry board and press a hollow in the center to form a well. Add the salt, eggs, and oil. Using a fork, gradually mix the flour into the center. Use your hands to blend the mixture and knead until a ball of dough is formed. If the dough is crumbly, sprinkle it with a few drops of

water. Work the dough by pressing and pushing it with your fists; then turning it over and repeating this process. Sprinkle with more flour as needed. Continue to knead the dough for about 10 minutes or until it is very smooth, firm, and elastic. Cover with a towel and let stand 30 minutes.

2. Quarter the ball of dough. Roll out one of the portions into a large rectangle. The dough will stretch easily if you push it with the rolling pin, dust it often with flour, and lift it often in order to make half turns and keep the rectangular shape. When thin enough to be translucent set aside to dry 20 minutes. Meanwhile repeat the above process with the remaining quarters of dough.

3. To make *tagliatelle*: gently roll up the sheets of dough, like rolling up a rug, and cut into ½-inch-thick strips. Toss with flour while unravelling the strips and set aside in mounds, covered with a towel, until ready to cook.

4. Cook in boiling salted water 3 minutes or until the pasta is tender. Homemade pasta cooks in very little time. Drain and serve with butter and grated parmesan cheese or a special sauce.

BURRO ROSSO

Red butter sauce (Italy)

This is an Italian red butter sauce, just enough for the pound of *tagliatelle* you will have made from the previous recipe. It's also delicious on *agnolotti da vigilia* (see page 144).

Ingredients

½ pound butter
2 teaspoons tomato paste
4 tablespoons heavy cream
½ teaspoon crumbled sage leaves
1 teaspoon sweet paprika
Salt
4 tablespoons grated parmesan cheese
Bowl of grated parmesan cheese

Equipment

Small saucepan · Whisk

Cooking time: 2 to 3 minutes

Makes: 1½ cups sauce, enough for 1 pound *tagliatelle*

In a small saucepan melt the butter. Whisk in the tomato paste and cream. Add sage, paprika, a little salt to taste, and 4 tablespoons cheese. Heat but do not bring to the boil. Pour over freshly cooked pasta and serve with a bowl of grated parmesan cheese on the side.

AGNOLOTTI TOSCANI

Stuffed pasta with meat

This is a typical Tuscan stuffed-pasta dish in a superb recipe given to me by Paolo Zappi-Manzoni. If you have any leftover filling freeze it and use it as the stuffing for olives in *fritto misto* (page 63).

Ingredients

    1 recipe for pasta (page 141)
    3 1½-ounce veal scallops
    3 tablespoons butter
    1 teaspoon marrow from a beef bone
    4 ounces mortadella sausage, finely chopped
    1 egg, lightly beaten
    2 tablespoons grated parmesan cheese
       Grated nutmeg
       Salt and freshly ground black pepper
  ½ cup melted butter
       Bowl of grated parmesan cheese

Equipment

> Skillet · Mixing bowl · *Agnolotti* cutter 2 inches
> in diameter or a cookie cutter · Slotted spoon ·
> Large pot

Working time: 1½ hours

Cooking time: 10 minutes

Serves: 6 as a first course

1. Make the pasta.
2. Sauté the veal in butter until golden brown and cooked through. Remove and allow to cool. Add the marrow to the pan juices. Lower the heat and cook gently, mashing the marrow into the buttery juices. Scrape into a mixing bowl.
3. Finely chop the veal, mix with the mortadella, and chop together until pasty. Add to the mixing bowl. Stir in the egg and the cheese. Season with nutmeg, salt and pepper. Combine thoroughly.
4. Separate the dough into 4 parts. Roll out one part into a thin sheet measuring 11 by 17 inches. Drop small teaspoonsful of stuffing 2½ inches apart on one sheet; roll out a second ball of dough to the same size, cover the first sheet, and lightly press around each mound with your fingers. Dip the cutter into flour and cut into rounds. Press down around the edges to seal securely. Line up on a floured cloth and cover with a second cloth.
5. Drop the *agnolotti* into boiling salted water and cook for 3 to 5 minutes or until they rise to the surface. Test to see if they are tender. Drain and serve at once with melted butter and grated parmesan cheese.

AGNOLOTTI DA VIGILIA

Stuffed pasta without meat for Fridays (Italy)

Use the recipe for pasta dough on page 141. Make the *panzarotti* stuffing. Roll out the dough into 4 thin sheets 11 by 17 inches. Drop teaspoonsful of the stuffing 2 inches apart on two of the sheets and cover as directed for *panzarotti*. Do not brush with beaten egg. Use a 1½- or 2-inch *agnolotti* or cookie cutter to form discs. Allow to dry at least 30 minutes before cooking. Drop into boiling salted water and cook 3 to 5 minutes or until the *agnolotti* are tender and rise to the surface. Drain and serve with *burro rosso*.

PANZAROTTI

Fried stuffed ravioli with tomato-cheese sauce (Italy)

This is a very good recipe for an unusual pasta dish, given to me by Tony May, manager of the Rainbow Room in New York.

Usually, ravioli is boiled, but here it's fried in oil. And the pasta itself is different: there are no eggs in this dough—only flour, water, and oil.

Ingredients

2¼ cups all-purpose flour, preferably unbleached flour
⅓ cup olive oil or melted margarine
2 teaspoons salt
½ cup cooked Swiss chard or spinach
1 tablespoon butter
¼ cup chopped onion
1 cup ricotta cheese
2 egg yolks
Freshly ground black pepper
Grated nutmeg
¼ cup grated parmesan or pecorino cheese
1 egg, beaten
1 cup fresh or canned tomato sauce
3 tablespoons diced mozzarella cheese
½ teaspoon crumbled oregano
Cooking oil for deep frying
Bowl of grated parmesan cheese

Equipment

> Assorted mixing bowls   ·   Rolling pin   ·
> 2 small saucepans   ·   Deep fryer   ·   Slotted spoon   ·
> 1½- or 2-inch cookie cutter   ·   Pastry brush

Working time: 1½ hours

Cooking time: 10 minutes

Makes: 60 ravioli (approximately), enough for 6 as a first course

1. In a large bowl make a mound of flour and press a hollow in the center to form a well. Add oil and salt and enough water (about ⅓ cup) to make a firm dough. Knead as directed in step 1 in the recipe for pasta (page 141). Cover the dough and set aside while making the stuffing.

2. Finely chop the Swiss chard or the spinach. In a saucepan heat the butter and in it cook the onions until light brown. Add the chopped greens and cook together for 1 minute over low heat, stirring. Off heat add the ricotta, egg yolks, pepper, nutmeg, 2 tablespoons parmesan, and if necessary a little salt. Combine thoroughly.

3. Divide the dough in 4 parts. Roll one part into a thin sheet, 11 by 17 inches. Brush with beaten egg. Place ½ teaspoonful of stuffing on the dough in 3 evenly spaced rows, about 2 inches apart each way. Roll out the second ball of dough to the same size, brush with egg, and place over the filling, egg side down. Lightly press around each mound with your fingers. Dip the cookie cutter into flour and cut out discs of the mounds. Press down around the edges of each ravioli to seal securely. Line up on a floured cloth and cover with another cloth. Repeat with the remaining 2 balls of dough.

4. Heat the tomato sauce with the mozzarella cheese, oregano, and 2 tablespoons grated parmesan cheese. Season with black pepper and salt if necessary. Keep hot.

5. Heat the oil in a deep fryer to 375 degrees. Slip in the ravioli, a few at a time, making sure not to crowd the fryer, and cook 5 minutes or until brown and puffy on both sides. Serve hot

with the prepared tomato sauce. Pass the bowl of grated parmesan separately.

PASTA CON MOLLICA DI PANE
Pasta with breadcrumbs (Italy)

This is a real peasant pasta dish from Sicily.

Ingredients

- 1½ teaspoons finely chopped garlic
- ¼ cup olive oil
- 2 2-ounce tins anchovies, rinsed and drained
- 1½ cups fresh or canned tomato puree (not tomato paste) or 1 # 303 can whole tomatoes, pureed
- ⅓ cup finely chopped parsley
  Freshly ground black pepper
- ½ teaspoon crumbled oregano
- ¾ pound spaghetti
  Salt
- ⅓ cup fresh white breadcrumbs toasted in the oven with a few drops of olive oil

Equipment

Heavy skillet · Large pot

Working time: 10 minutes

Cooking time: 5 to 8 minutes

Serves: 4

1. Gently cook the garlic in olive oil until golden. Add the anchovies and mash to a puree with the back of a wooden spoon. Cook 1 minute. Stir in the tomatoes and parsley and cook, uncov-

ered, at the simmer 2 to 3 minutes. Season with pepper to taste.
Add the oregano.

2. Cook the spaghetti in boiling salted water until tender.
Drain. Toss with the hot sauce and sprinkle with the breadcrumbs. Serve at once.

PASTICCIO DI MACCHERONI ALLA PIEMONTESE

Piedmontese macaroni pie with chicken livers, sweetbreads,
quenelles, truffles, and mushrooms (Italy)

I have this recipe from my friend Simonetta Ponzone Lanza,
who remembered it from her childhood spent near Turin. The
cook at the Lanza family manoir used to make this dish, but her
particular version was never written down. Simonetta wanted
very much for her children to taste it, so one day the two of us sat
down, worked it out, and then spent two more days at my stove. I
should tell you that we didn't include cockscombs, premature and
unlaid chickens' eggs, or thin slices of beef tenderloin, all of
which were part of the original sauce. (Note that this dish is com-
posed of two sauces, a *ragù* and a brown sauce mixed together to
form the base of a *finanziera* sauce.)

Ingredients

Sweet pastry
 3 cups all-purpose flour, sifted
 ½ cup sugar
 8 tablespoons unsalted butter or lard, or a mixture
 2 egg yolks, lightly beaten
 ¼ cup ice water

Ragù
 2 tablespoons clarified butter or oil
 ½ pound ground beef
 ¼ cup chopped onion

1 slice bacon, diced
1 small clove garlic, peeled
1 celery rib, sliced
1 chopped carrot
¼ cup dried mushrooms, soaked in water until soft
1 cup dry white wine
1 cup beef stock
½ tablespoon tomato paste
   Salt and freshly ground black pepper

Finanziera sauce alla Piemontese
1 cup *ragù*
1 cup homemade or canned brown sauce
¼ pound fresh cultivated mushrooms
¼ pound wild mushrooms (optional)
9 tablespoons butter
¼ pound chicken hearts and kidneys, thinly sliced
3 or 4 fresh chicken livers, cut into small pieces
½ veal sweetbread (about ½ pound)
   Lemon juice
1 black truffle, finely diced (optional)
1 white truffle, finely diced (optional)
2 veal quenelles, canned or homemade
      or 10 ½-inch veal meatballs browned slowly in butter
¼ cup dry white wine
   Grated parmesan cheese

½ pound small elbow macaroni
1 egg beaten with 1 teaspoon water

Equipment

Large mixing bowl · Heavy-bottomed 3½-quart casserole
with cover · Fine mesh sieve · Skillet · Saucepan ·
8-inch spring-form mold, buttered · Slotted spoon ·
Pastry brush · Large pot and colander · Rolling pin

Working time: 2 hours

Cooking time: 3 hours 45 minutes

Baking time: 30 minutes or more

Serves: 6 to 8 as a first course

1. Make a pastry with flour and sugar and a little salt. Rub in the butter and/or lard. Mix in the egg yolks and enough ice water to form a ball of dough. Knead until smooth and wrap in waxed paper. Chill 3 hours.

2. Soak the veal sweetbread for 2 hours in cold water. Trim and cook for 20 minutes in simmering water that has been salted and acidulated with lemon juice. Rinse, drain, and dice.

3. To make the *ragú*, heat the clarified butter in a heavy casserole and in it lightly brown the beef. Mix in the onion, bacon, garlic, celery, carrot, and the mushrooms. Continue cooking 3 to 4 minutes, stirring often. Moisten with wine and reduce to a glaze over high heat.

4. Stir in the beef stock and the tomato paste and season with salt and pepper. Cook, over low heat, partially covered, skimming often to remove impurities that rise to the surface. Strain through a fine sieve pushing down to extract all the juices. Reduce to 1 cup if necessary.

5. To make the *finanziera* sauce, combine the *ragú* and the brown sauce in a large saucepan. Set aside.

6. In the skillet gently sauté the mushrooms for 10 minutes in 2 tablespoons butter. Remove and add to the combined sauce. Add 2 more tablespoons butter to the pan and in it gently sauté the chicken hearts and kidneys for 10 minutes. Add the chicken livers and continue cooking 5 minutes, stirring often to avoid forming hard surfaces. Remove, drain, and add to the combined sauce. Add 2 more tablespoons butter to the skillet and in it gently sauté the diced sweetbreads without browning. Season with salt and pepper. Add to the combined sauce. Fold the truffles and the veal quenelles into the sauce.

7. Discard the burned butter in the skillet; pour in the wine and cook over high heat, scraping up all the bits and pieces that adhere to the skillet. Reduce the wine to almost a glaze then scrape it into the combined sauce. Correct the seasoning of the

sauce. Set aside partially covered dotted with 1 tablespoon butter. Allow to cool slightly.

8. Cut the pastry into 2 parts one slightly larger than the other. Roll the larger one to a ¼-inch-thick circle about 13 inches in diameter. Fit it into the spring-form mold, leaving a ½-inch overhang. Chill the pastry.

9. Partially cook the macaroni in boiling salted water, drain, then rinse under cold running water and drain again. Mix with 2 tablespoons butter. Gently fold 2 to 3 tablespoons parmesan cheese and the macaroni into the sauce. Set aside and allow to cool.

10. Preheat the oven to 350 degrees.

11. Roll the remaining pastry to a 10-inch circle for use as a cover; trim. Use the pastry trimmings to make long narrow strips for a lattice design on the pastry cover. Chill the pastry cover and the strips.

12. Using a slotted spoon, transfer all the macaroni, assorted meats, mushrooms, and truffles to the pastry-lined mold. Keep the remaining sauce in the saucepan. Top with the pastry cover; press the edges together to seal.

13. Arrange the pastry strips lattice fashion on top. Brush the top with egg glaze and set the *pasticcio* in the oven to bake 30 to 45 minutes or until the crust is golden brown. Serve the *pasticcio* hot with the remaining sauce, reheated, and pass a bowl of parmesan cheese.

COUSCOUS

In Morocco, Algeria, and Tunisia couscous is the most famous and popular food. I have written extensively about it in my Moroccan cookbook (*Couscous and Other Good Food from Morocco*), and I refer interested readers there. In that book I also give 23 couscous recipes, everything from a classic Middle Atlas pumpkin couscous to a sophisticated couscous, with seven vegetables, in the manner of Fez, to the ultimate in Berber elegance, a couscous made of grilled barley shoots.

North African couscous is so popular that many countries have come up with versions of their own. There is *keskes* in Senegal, *cuscuz* in Brazil, and *cuscusu* in Trapani, Sicily for which the sauce is the local fish soup *ghiotta di pesci*. In Lebanon where they make a couscous of large semolina pellets cooked with onions and chicken they call it *mahgrabia* which means "from the Mahgreb"—Morocco, Algeria, and Tunisia.

One of the most important things about couscous is that the grains be light and separate and fluffy. You must avoid any instant couscous you may see in the store no matter what promises are made on the package. And even when you buy good imported couscous grain, forget the package instruction and follow my advice below. The steps may seem complicated, but really they're not, and the couscous will come out perfectly every time. Other than that you'll do well to buy a *couscousiere*, available now in most cooking equipment stores. It's not only extremely practical for cooking couscous, but you can use it to steam vegetables, fish, and meats.

HANDLING COUSCOUS GRAINS

These are the master instructions for handling couscous, to be followed when indicated in the two recipes in this book. Though they look complicated, the principle behind them is very simple: all the wetting, drying, raking, aerating, and steaming of semolina grains is done with the purpose of swelling them with as much water as possible without allowing them to become lumpy or soggy. But you must be careful: the smaller and fresher the couscous grain, the less water is needed.

1. *First washing and drying of couscous:* Wash the couscous in a large, shallow pan by pouring water over the grain in a ratio of 3 parts water to 1 part grain (that is, if the recipe calls for 2 cups of couscous, use 6 cups of water, and so on). Stir quickly with the hand and then drain off excess water through a sieve. Return the couscous grains to the pan, smooth them out, and leave them to swell for between 10 and 20 minutes. After roughly 10 minutes, begin with cupped wet hands to work the grains by lifting up handsful of grain, rubbing them gently, and letting them fall back into the pan. This process should break up any lumps that may have formed. Then rake the couscous with your fingers to circulate it and help the grains to swell. *Note:* Home-

made freshly rolled couscous is simply dampened and immediately steamed as directed in step 2.

2. *First steaming of the couscous.* Dampen a strip of cheese-cloth, dust it with flour, and twist into a strip the length of the circumference of the rim of the bottom part of the *couscousiere.* Use this to seal the perforated top. Check all sides for effective sealing: the top and bottom should fit snugly, so that steam rises only through the holes. *The perforated top should not touch the broth below.* Slowly dribble ¼ of the swollen couscous grains into the steamer, allowing them to form a soft mound. Steam 5 minutes and gently add the remaining couscous. When all the grains are in the steamer, lower heat to moderate and steam 20 minutes. Do not cover the couscous while it steams. *Note:* Each time you place the top of *couscousiere* on the pot in order to steam couscous, use cheesecloth to reseal the two containers.

3. *Second drying of the couscous.* Remove the top part of the *couscousiere.* Dump the couscous into the large, shallow pan and spread out with a wooden spoon. Sprinkle ½ to 1 cup cold water and 1 teaspoon salt over the grains. Separate and break up lumps by lifting and stirring the grains gently. Oil your hands lightly and rework the grains—this helps to keep each grain separate. (Some people oil the grains *before* steaming, but this results in a tougher texture.) Smooth the couscous out and allow it to dry for at least 10 minutes. If the couscous feels too dry, add another cup of water by handful sprinkles, raking the couscous well before each addition. If you are preparing couscous in advance, at this point let it dry then cover with a damp cloth. It can wait many hours. (*Very important note:* If the stew in the bottom of the *couscousiere* is fully cooked and perfectly seasoned and the sauce reduced to the correct amount prior to the final steaming of couscous grains, you should transfer the stew to a separate sauce-pan, keeping it warm, and perform the final steaming of the couscous over boiling water.)

4. If you want to serve right away, allow the couscous to dry for 10 minutes, then pile it back into the *couscousiere* top, being sure to reseal the two containers with cheesecloth, for its final steaming of 20 minutes. If you have prepared steps 1 through 3 in advance, 30 minutes before serving break up lumps of couscous

by working the grains lightly between your wet fingers. Steam the couscous in the *couscousiere* top for 20 minutes, as previously directed.

SEKSU TANJAOUI

Couscous in the style of Tangier (Morocco)

This is a good all-around North African couscous, tastier than anything you're likely to be served in any couscous joint in Paris. The couscous is made with lamb and pumpkin, carrots, turnips, zucchini, onions, and chick-peas. It's topped by a glazed dressing of almonds, raisins, and onions. The sauce is hot, spiced with lots of pepper, and ginger and saffron. The play of this spicy sauce against the sweet glazed topping is one of the many delights of this dish.

Ingredients

    1 cup dried chick-peas
        or 1 20-ounce can cooked chick-peas, drained
    4 cups couscous (1½ pounds)
 1½ pounds lamb neck or shank
    Salt
    2 rounded teaspoons freshly ground black pepper
    1 teaspoon ground ginger
 ⅛ teaspoon pulverized saffron
    3 onions, quartered
    2 sprigs each: parsley and fresh coriander,
        tied together with thread
    8 tablespoons unsalted butter
    1 large Spanish onion, quartered
        and thinly sliced lengthwise
    Ground cinnamon
 ½ cup black raisins
 ¼ cup sugar
    6 small carrots, scraped and quartered
    6 small turnips, scraped and quartered

1½ pounds pumpkin, peeled, cored,
and cut into 2-inch chunks
3–4 small zucchini, halved
Oil
1 cup whole, blanched almonds
2 tablespoons *smen* (page 201), or unsalted butter

Equipment

Saucepans · Large shallow pan · Sieve ·
Couscousiere or large stockpot fitted with a colander ·
Cheesecloth · Slotted spoon · Skillet · Large serving
dish

Working time: 45 minutes

Cooking time: 2½ hours

Serves: 6

1. Soak the dried chick-peas overnight.
2. The next day, cover the chick-peas with fresh, cold water
and cook, covered, 1 hour. Drain, cool, and remove the skins by
submerging the chick-peas in a bowl of cold water and gently
rubbing them between the fingers. The skins will rise to the top of
the water. Discard the skins and set the chick-peas aside. (If you
are using canned chick-peas, peel and set aside.)
3. To prepare the couscous, follow step 1 in the master instructions page 152.
4. To prepare the broth, place the lamb, 2 teaspoons salt,
pepper, ginger, saffron, quartered onions, herbs, and 5 tablespoons butter in the bottom of the *couscousiere*. Heat the butter
over low heat, swirling the pan once or twice to let the spices and
meat mix gently. When the butter is melted, cover with 3 quarts
water and bring to a boil. Add the drained chick-peas, cover, and
simmer 1 hour. (Canned chick-peas should not be added until 30
minutes before serving.)
5. Begin the preparation of the glazed topping. After the
lamb has cooked 1 hour, transfer 2 cups of the simmering lamb

broth to a saucepan. Add the Spanish onion, ½ teaspoon ground cinnamon, raisins, sugar, remaining butter, salt, and freshly ground black pepper to taste. Cook, covered, 1 hour, then remove the cover and continue cooking until the liquid has evaporated and the onions have a glazed appearance. This takes about 30 minutes. Set aside, uncovered.

6. Meanwhile add the carrots and turnips to the *couscousiere*. Follow steps 2 and 3 in the master instructions.

7. Thirty minutes before serving, add the pumpkin and the quartered zucchini (and the canned cooked chick-peas if using them) to the *couscousiere*. With wet hands break up any lumps of couscous by working the grains lightly between your fingers. Bring the broth to the boil, reseal the two containers with cheesecloth, and steam the couscous another 20 minutes.

8. Reheat the glazed onions and raisins. Heat the oil in the skillet and fry the almonds until golden brown. Drain and set aside.

9. Dump the couscous onto the serving dish and toss with the *smen* or butter. Use a fork to smooth out any lumps. Spread out and form a well in the center. Remove the lamb bone and discard, then cut the lamb into bite-size pieces. Place the lamb and vegetables in the well and cover with the onion-raisin glaze. Taste the broth for seasoning, then moisten the grain with it. Scatter the almonds on top just before serving. Serve hot.

KOUSKI BIL HOUT

Fish couscous with quince and raisins (Tunisia)

There's no question in my mind that Moroccan couscous is superior to that of Algeria and Tunisia, as is Moroccan food in general. However the Tunisians have developed a number of ways of making couscous with fish—a dish combination that is very rare in Morocco, and in fact is served only in the Atlantic city of Essaouira.

Basically there are two types of Tunisian fish couscous: one very spicy, with lots of *harissa* and *tabil*, and the other mellow and exotic made with quince, raisins, and a curious mixture called *bharat*.

Bharat (which you will need for this recipe) consists of two parts ground cinnamon to one part ground dried rose buds (obtainable at most good spice stores). *Bharat* is used frequently in sweet Tunisian *tagines*, such as a stew of lamb, chestnuts, apricots, chick-peas, and honey. In this recipe it contributes to the truly exotic taste of a fish stew, with quince and raisins poured over fluffy couscous grains.

This recipe is my adaptation from *La Cuisine Tunisienne* by Mohammed Kouki.

Ingredients

½ cup dried chick-peas or 1 cup canned
    cooked chick-peas, drained
2 pounds porgies or scup, cleaned and trimmed
    (keep heads and trimmings)
    Salt and freshly ground black pepper
⅓ cup olive or vegetable oil
1 pound tomatoes, chopped
1 onion, quartered
1 celery rib, chopped
1½ teaspoons sweet paprika
4 cups couscous
2 quince (1 pound) peeled, quartered,
    and sautéed in 2 tablespoons butter for 3 minutes
½ cup raisins
    Bharat (a mixture of 2 parts ground cinnamon
    with 1 part ground dried rose buds)
2 tablespoons unsalted butter at room temperature

Equipment

Saucepan · *Couscousiere* · Large shallow bowl ·
Sieve · Cheesecloth · Slotted spoon ·
Large serving dish

Working time: 20 minutes

Cooking time: 2 hours

Serves: 6

1. Cover the dried chick-peas with water and soak overnight.

2. The next day, drain the chick-peas and cook in fresh water to cover for 1 hour. (If using canned chick-peas, peel them and set aside.)

3. Slice the fish crosswise into 6 even portions. Rub the flesh with salt and pepper. Set aside.

4. Prepare the couscous by following step 1 (first washing and drying of the couscous) in the master instructions on page 152.

5. Heat the oil in the bottom of the *couscousiere*. Add tomatoes, onion, celery, and fish heads. Cook, stirring, 2 to 3 minutes. Add the paprika and 2 quarts water. Season with salt and pepper. Bring to the boil then reduce the heat and cook, covered, at the simmer 30 minutes.

6. Follow steps 2 and 3 (first steaming and second drying of the couscous) in the master instructions on page 153.

7. Meanwhile drain the chick-peas, cool, and remove the skins by submerging them in a bowl of cold water and gently rubbing them between the fingers. The skins will rise to the top of the water—discard them.

8. Strain the fish broth and return to the *couscousiere*. Bring to the boil. Add the chick-peas, sautéed quince, and the raisins. Continue cooking, covered, at the simmer for 30 minutes.

9. Twenty minutes before serving, add the fish and the drained, peeled canned chick-peas (if using them) to the broth. With wet hands break up any lumps of couscous by working the grains lightly between your fingers. Bring the broth to the boil, reseal the two containers with cheesecloth and steam the couscous another 20 minutes.

10. Rub 1 teaspoon *bharat* into the butter. Dump the couscous onto a large serving dish and toss with the spiced butter, using a fork to smooth out any lumps. Spread out and form a well in the center. With a perforated spoon lift out the fish (discarding any loose bones) and place in the well. Cover with the chick-peas, the raisins, and the quince. Readjust the seasoning of the broth. Strain some of the broth over the couscous to moisten it.

Decorate with lines of *bharat* and serve hot. Serve the remaining broth in a large sauceboat.

OTHER MEDITERRANEAN FARINACEOUS FOODS

There are numerous pastry dishes scattered in other chapters of this book: *tortino ripieno di scarole* and the Provençal pizza *pissaladière* under "olives"; *torta di cavolo*, and a cheese and herb pie from Corsica under "cheese," etc. All of them, from *klandt bil karmouss* (pastry leaves stuffed with figs) to *petits pâtés de Béziers* (little meat pastries with raisins from Languedoc) are, in their way, farinaceous: they are made of wheat flour and they contain a lot of starch. But there are several wheat, dough, and pastry dishes that I wanted to include, and just couldn't fit in elsewhere. I give them on the following pages: Tunisian *briks* or savory pastries; *lahm bi ajim*, a Middle Eastern version of pizza; *tabbouleh*, a cracked-wheat salad from Lebanon; and finally *tourte Tante Vivienne*, a chicken and sausage pie from Languedoc.

TUNISIAN BRIKS

The *brik* is the Tunisian equivalent of the pizza—a delicious pastry dish that can be prepared in innumerable ways, eaten any time of the day, and bought right out on the street. It consists of a strudel or phyllo-type dough filled with any one of a hundred stuffings, fast fried, served up hot, and eaten with the hands.

In Tunisia they call the pastry *malsouqua*, which is exactly the same as the Moroccan *warka*, and surprisingly close to Chinese spring roll skins. *Malsouqua* is rather difficult to make and unobtainable in the United States. But Greek phyllo leaves are a good substitute and if you use them your *briks* will be fine.

Here first is a master recipe for *briks* with a stuffing of onion, egg, and brains. At the end I suggest three alternate stuffings: *sweba* which is cooked seasoned ground meat; anchovies and onions; and ground cooked chicken and potatoes.

BRIKS BIL MOHK

Brain and egg turnovers (Tunisia)

Ingredients

¾ pound lamb, calf, or beef brains
    Salt and freshly ground black pepper
    Vinegar
2 tablespoons unsalted butter
¼ cup finely chopped onion
1 tablespoon finely chopped parsley
1 tablespoon grated parmesan cheese
2 phyllo leaves or 4 Chinese spring roll skins
4 eggs
    Oil for frying
    Lemon quarters

Equipment

2-quart saucepan · Deep skillet · Slotted spoon

Working time: 15 minutes

Cooking time: 25 minutes

Frying time: 5 minutes

Serves: 4

1. Soak the brains for 30 minutes in several changes of water. Remove the membranes then rinse and drain. In the saucepan bring 1½ quarts seasoned and acidulated water to the simmer. Slip in the brains, cover, and cook over low heat for 20 minutes. Drain, cool, and dice.

2. Melt the butter in the saucepan and cook the onion over low heat until soft but not browned. Add the brains, parsley, salt

and pepper to taste. Cook gently 10 minutes, stirring often. Stir in the cheese. Mix and mash, then separate into 4 equal parts.

3. Spread out the pastry leaves and cut them in half. Leave the spring roll skins whole. Fold each of the pastry leaves in half and place ¼ of the filling 2 inches away from one corner. Flatten the filling slightly to make a hollow in the center. Break an egg into the hollow. Fold over the pastry to cover the egg; dab the edges in the egg white, press the edges to adhere, and fold each rim over ½ inch for a secure closing, being careful not to break the egg inside. If you are using spring roll skins, fold in the left and right sides in order to make a square then proceed as directed above. Repeat with the 3 remaining pastry leaves.

4. Heat oil to the depth of 1 inch in a large deep skillet. When hot but not smoking slide in one *brik*. Lightly push it down into the oil then press one corner in order to make the *brik* swell. When golden brown on both sides transfer to paper towels to drain. Repeat with the 3 remaining *briks*. Serve hot with lemon quarters.

VARIATIONS

Sweba

Ground meat and egg turnovers

For each brik mix 2 tablespoons ground beef cooked with a little onion and parsley and seasoned with salt and pepper. Mix in 1 tablespoon grated parmesan cheese and a few drops of lemon juice. A sliced hard-boiled egg is used instead of a raw one.

Briks bil sthum

Anchovy and egg turnovers

For each brik: 6 fillets of anchovies and 1 tablespoon chopped onion cooked in butter then mixed with 1 tablespoon grated parmesan cheese, freshly ground black pepper, and topped with a raw egg.

Briks bil djej

Chicken and egg turnovers

Leftover cooked chicken and boiled potatoes ground together, seasoned with salt and freshly ground black pepper, and bound with a beaten egg. A sliced hard-boiled egg is used instead of a raw one.

LAHM BI AJIM

Meat pies (Lebanon)

Lahm bi ajim are like little pizzas and Mexican *quesadillas*—open tartlettes stuffed with meat. Filled with a mixture of ground lamb, onion, pine nuts, yogurt, and spices they make a delightful first course or hors d'oeuvre. First I give you the traditional dough recipe—the way the dish is made in Beirut. But frankly I find this dough a little heavy to eat with drinks, so I include a variation that uses a lighter cream cheese pastry. The stuffing, of course, remains the same.

Ingredients

Pastry
   1 package dry-active yeast
   ½ tablespoon sugar
   2½ cups all-purpose flour
   1½ teaspoons salt
   ¼ cup melted and cooled butter

Filling
   2 tablespoons butter
   ½ cup finely chopped onion
   1 pound ground lamb or beef
      Salt and freshly ground black pepper
   2 tablespoons chopped parsley
      Pinches of ground cloves, cinnamon, and grated nutmeg

⅓ cup pine nuts, toasted in the oven
½ cup unflavored yogurt
    A bowl of unflavored yogurt (optional)

Equipment

Mixing bowls · Skillet · 2 buttered baking sheets

Working time: 30 minutes

Cooking time: 25 minutes

Baking time: 15 minutes

Makes: 18 to 22 pies

1. In a small bowl soften the yeast with the sugar in 3 table-spoons lukewarm water. Let stand 2 to 3 minutes then stir until the yeast is completely dissolved. Stir the yeast into 1 cup luke-warm water in a large bowl. Gradually stir in the flour and salt until a soft dough is formed. Knead the dough well until it is completely smooth and elastic. You may find that you need to add more flour during this time. Place the dough in a greased bowl, cover with a towel, and set in a warm place, free of drafts, until the dough has doubled in bulk—about 2 hours.

2. To make the filling melt the butter in the skillet and in it cook the onions without browning until soft. Add the meat and continue cooking 3 to 4 minutes breaking up any lumps of meat with a fork. Add salt, pepper, and spices. Mix in the parsley and the pine nuts. Allow to cool then stir in the ½ cup unflavored yogurt.

3. Punch down the dough and turn out onto a workspace. Work in the melted butter, a tablespoon at a time, working well after each addition. Knead the dough until smooth, adding a little flour from time to time if necessary.

4. Preheat the oven to 450 degrees.

5. Twist off 18 to 22 equal-sized balls of dough. Flatten each into ⅛-inch-thick rounds. Gently press out the sides and mold the dough into tartlette shapes about 2½ inches in diameter. Fill each

with a heaping tablespoon of filling. As you work place each filled
tartlet on a buttered baking sheet. Set in the oven to bake 15 to 20
minutes. The tartlet dough will remain soft but will be cooked.
Serve hot and pass a bowl of unflavored yogurt if desired.

VARIATION

The above filling with cream cheese pastry is my favorite
way to serve these pies.

Ingredients

> ⅔ cup cream cheese
> ¼ pound unsalted butter
> 2 cups all-purpose flour
> 1 teaspoon salt

Equipment

> Mixing bowl · Rolling pin · Wax paper ·
> 2½-inch cutter · Buttered baking sheets

Working time: 10 minutes

Makes: 16 tarts

Blend the butter and the cream cheese together. Work in the
flour and the salt. Press to knead the dough in order to incorporate the flour evenly. Wrap in wax paper and chill 2 hours. Roll
out between sheets of wax paper and cut out 16 2½-inch rounds.
Make small rims to hold the filling. Fill the forms and bake in a
preheated 350-degree oven 30 minutes. Serve hot.

TABBOULEH

Cracked wheat salad (Lebanon)

Tabbouleh is a very popular Middle Eastern hors d'oeuvre
made with burghul or cracked wheat, one of the staples of the

region, and the most important component in the Syrian and Lebanese national dish, kibbe.

Ingredients

1 cup fine burghul (cracked wheat)
1 small onion, grated
3 scallions, finely chopped
2 small red ripe tomatoes, peeled, seeded, and chopped
2 tablespoons chopped fresh mint leaves
1 cup chopped Italian parsley
Salt and freshly ground black pepper
Scant ½ cup olive oil
½ cup freshly squeezed lemon juice
Small tender romaine lettuce leaves
12 black olives

Equipment

Large mixing bowl · Large sieve lined with cheesecloth · 6 salad plates

Working time: 15 minutes

Serves: 6

1. Soak the wheat in 1 quart cold water for 15 minutes; drain. Dump into a large sieve lined with cheesecloth and squeeze out the extra moisture. The wheat must feel dry. Dump into a mixing bowl, add the onion, scallions, tomatoes, mint leaves, parsley, salt and pepper to taste. Thoroughly blend the mixture using your hands. Mix the lemon juice and oil then pour over and toss using a fork. Correct the seasoning. Let stand 2 to 3 hours in a cool place before serving.

2. Line each salad plate with 2 or 3 lettuce leaves. Make 6 small cones (about ½ cup per person) of the wheat mixture; place on the lettuce leaves and decorate with black olives.

TOURTE TANTE VIVIENNE
Chicken and sausage pie from Languedoc (France)

"Tante Vivienne" is the pseudonym for a great and old friend of mine who is too modest to let me use her real name. I knew her well in Paris in the early 1960s but we lost touch until the last couple of years when she moved to an inherited family farm on the outskirts of the French coastal town of Sète. I can say truthfully that "Tante Vivienne" is one of the best French cooks I know, and that on the two occasions when I visited her this past year she taught me some of her culinary secrets. By some fortuitous stroke there is a direct link between Tangier and Sète. A Moroccan ship called the *Agadir* hauls tourists back and forth, and serves up the most bland food I ever hope to eat. But while my fellow passengers complained I remained serene. I had the comfort of knowing that I would soon be eating in the kitchen of "Tante Vivienne."

She taught me to make *crème d'ail, croquets de Languedoc, gasconnade*, and *poulet aux 40 gousses d'ail*, all dishes included in this book. She taught me many other things as well which someday I hope to publish in a book devoted exclusively to the marvelous food of Languedoc. And she taught me the following chicken and sausage pie, which I've served up at dinner parties time and again with great success.

To me *tourte Tante Vivienne* is some kind of ultimate in French country cooking—savory, strong in flavor, honest, everything that Mediterranean food should be. This is not the classic cooking of Versailles, but the peasant cooking of a coastal town: simple, rustic, filling, and robust.

Ingredients

　　Pastry: Make this twice
　3½　cups all-purpose flour
　1½　teaspoons salt
　　12　tablespoons unsalted butter, chilled
　　　　　and cut into small pieces

    5 tablespoons lard, chilled and cut into small pieces
    3 egg yolks, lightly beaten
    ¾ cup ice water (approximately)
    1 egg yolk beaten with 1 teaspoon water

Filling
    ½ pound fresh cultivated mushrooms
    8 tablespoons unsalted butter
    1 medium onion, finely chopped
      Freshly ground black pepper
    2 pounds ground pork (10 percent fat 90 percent lean)
    ½ teaspoon spiced salt (salt seasoned with white pepper, cinnamon, nutmeg, and cloves or mix salt with *quatre épices**)
    ½ teaspoon crumbled fresh thyme
    1 tablespoon cognac (optional)
    2 2½–3-pound broiler chickens
    ¼ pound thinly sliced bacon, cut into 1-inch squares, blanched
    2 tablespoons chopped fresh parsley

Equipment

Mixing bowls · Skillet · Two 10-inch tart molds or cake pans, buttered · Rolling pin · Pastry brush · Two 1½-inch pastry tubes or parchment paper funnels ·

Working time: 45 minutes

Baking time: 1½ hours

Makes: 2 *tourtes*, serves 10 to 12

1. To make the pastry, mix flour with the salt, rub in the chilled butter and lard. Mix in the egg yolks and ice water to form a ball of dough; knead until smooth. Wrap in wax paper and chill 2 to 3 hours.

* Spice Parisienne under the Spice Islands label.

2. Slice the mushrooms thinly. Heat 3 tablespoons butter in a skillet. Add the onions and gently cook them until soft. Add the mushrooms and continue cooking 5 to 6 minutes or until most of the liquid in the pan has evaporated and the mushrooms are cooked but not browned. Season with salt and pepper. Allow to cool.

3. Season the ground pork with spiced salt, thyme, black pepper, and if desired a splash of cognac. Mix thoroughly then fold in the mushroom-onion mixture. Set aside.

4. Quarter the chickens and remove all the bones. Rub the flesh with salt and pepper. In a heavy skillet heat the remaining 5 tablespoons butter and in it quickly brown the chicken quarters on both sides. Remove and allow to cool. Cut the chicken quarters into 1½-inch pieces.

5. Preheat the oven to 375 degrees.

6. Roll out ¼ of the dough into a circle a little larger than the tart mold. Line the mold, prick the bottom and spread ½ the pork mixture on the pastry, patting it down. Then add a layer of ½ the browned chicken and scatter ½ the bacon squares on top. Sprinkle with 1 tablespoon chopped parsley. Quickly roll out the second quarter of pastry, moisten around the edges, cover the *tourte*, and crimp to seal. Save all trimmings of pastry dough for the decoration. Repeat this step using the second tart mold, the remaining pastry dough, pork mixture, chicken, and bacon. Chill the *tourtes* at least 15 minutes.

7. Roll out the pastry trimmings into 10-inch strips and cut into ¼-inch-wide strips. Moisten with water and make a lattice design on top of each *tourte*. Make a small opening in the center of each *tourte* and insert in each a funnel to allow steam to escape during the baking. Brush the tops with egg yolk glaze and set the *tourtes* in the oven to bake 1½ hours.

8. Serve hot on large round serving dishes. Use a serrated knife to cut into serving wedges.

Herbs, Spices, and Aromatics

Look around an American kitchen. Rosemary, basil, thyme—all the herbs are there in a dried state, usually in a rack of neatly labeled uniform little jars.

But go around behind a house in Provence, Italy, or Greece. Somewhere near the kitchen door you'll find the herbs growing in little pots. No abominations like "dried parsley flakes" here. You're in the Mediterranean world where herbs and spices are important, not afterthoughts to "pep" up food.

Before getting into specific flavorings and some recipes that show what they can do, I think it might be a good idea to take a little Mediterranean tour, and see the picture as a whole.

In Andalusia the spicing is simple: cinnamon, paprika, saffron. Olive oil and garlic are vitally important. Next door in Catalonia the spicing becomes more intricate, with sharper contrasts and stronger flavors. Bitter orange peel, chocolate, and almonds are used to balance the spices.

In Languedoc goose fat and garlic are used to hold flavor in the main dishes and aniseed in the desserts. Provence, on the other hand, is a land of herbs, and here, perfumed waters are used.

In Italy herbs are king. Liguria is full of basil and marjoram which are used in numerous imaginative ways. Further south we find red pepper and the stronger flavored oregano. And in Sardinia there are traces of Spain—saffron in the rice, the pasta, and the soups.

The cuisines of Yugoslavia, Turkey, and the Middle East are all variants of Ottoman Empire food. The Yugoslavs use lots of caraway and paprika, an influence from Austro-Hungarian ties. All over the Levant we find cinnamon, allspice, and mint in rice, meats, and desserts, a heritage of the distinguished and wonderful cuisine of the Turks.

Egypt, Lebanon, Syria, and Palestine are strong on cinnamon, showing a preference for sweet spices and perfumed waters, too. But as we move toward Tunisia things begin to heat up: *tabil* and red hot *harissa* sauce. The Algerians use black pepper and cinnamon, the old formula of the Turks, then combine it with the red hot paprika of the Tunisians to create a synthesis between Maghreb and Levant.

Finally Morocco, truly a land of spices, with its *ras el hanout* —a mixture of more than twenty different exotic flavorings. The Moroccans go further with spices than any country except India. For their snail dish *boubouche* ("little slippers"), they combine crushed gum mastic, whole hot peppers, crinkled peels of sweet and bitter orange, crumbled mint leaves, verbena, thyme, anise, licorice, and caraway.

ANISEED

The best aniseed is the fragrant green variety from Spain with its strong warm flavor and licorice taste. It's used in cakes, breads, cookies, and spice drinks.

In Languedoc, in southwestern France, aniseed is used in rustic cakes like *le soleil d'anis*, often served on hot summer afternoons along with a glass of cold sparkling wine from Limoux.

The Syrians use aniseed to flavor their sugary spice drink, *miglee*, and include it in the making of fig jam, not only because of the refreshing association but because they believe that aniseed wards off the hatching of worm larvae in figs.

The Corsicans like cookies sweetened with aniseed-flavored sugar, and in Calabria *mostaccioli* cookies, made with flour and honey, are flavored with an anise liqueur called Sambuca. Sambuca is a popular after-dinner drink which Italians serve *con la* . *mosca.* Literally this means "with flies," an image for the coffee beans they float on top.

The Mediterranean is famous for its anise-flavored apéritifs. The Catalonians make one of the best anisettes in the world, *anís del mono.* The French produce *pastis,* a close relative of the forbidden absinthe. Greek *ouzo,* Turkish *raki,* and French *pastis* all turn milky when diluted with water. They are all quite powerful, should be drunk in small quantities, and are best when served with something to eat.

BASIL

The Greeks call basil *basileus,* which means "the royal herb." When I've asked Greek friends why they don't use it in their cooking they've told me it's best as defense against the "evil eye," and that's why there's a pot of basil on the door step of every Greek house.

Basil is only worthwhile fresh, so I suggest you grow it if you can. Plant it in late spring in pots or in a sunny spare plot in your garden. Harvest it in late summer, and you can indulge in an orgy of pesto and *pistou.*

Basil is very important in some parts of the Mediterranean, particularly in Liguria and Provence. It has a natural affinity with tomatoes and fresh cheese. Try *coccarda* (see page 94). This to me is real elegance—pure, simple, and superb.

The great aficionados of pesto are the Genoese. Their blend of fresh basil, pecorino cheese (best if it comes from Sardinia), olive oil, nuts, and garlic is a great and savory sauce. Pesto is served over egg pasta or in minestrone soup and finds its way into meat and fish dishes, too. One way of using it is to substitute it for snail butter on mussels. Sweet basil leaves mashed in a mortar with garlic, nuts, and butter cover steamed mussels set on half shells, then set under a broiler until bubbly hot.

This recipe for pesto comes from Nervi, a small town a little south of Genoa. In Nervi they make pesto with cream, creating a light, smooth avocado-green sauce that makes a good change from the usual recipe. It's even easier than the classic procedure, too, since it can be made in the blender in one operation. No need for the slow dripping in of olive oil as one pounds the basil and garlic. This, to me, is the best pesto recipe of all. Try it over fettuccine, trenette, semolina gnocchi, and broad lasagne noodles. Italian "lettuce leaved" basil is recommended for this dish; it is less spicy but much finer.

PESTO

Ligurian basil sauce from Nervi (Italy)

Ingredients

    2 cups fresh large basil leaves
    ½ cup olive oil
    ½ cup grated cheese (⅓ cup grated parmesan and
          2½ tablespoons grated pecorino
          or ½ cup grated parmesan)
    ¼ cup pine nuts
  2–3 small cloves garlic, peeled
      Salt
  2–3 tablespoons heavy cream
    1 pound spaghetti or *trenette* (fettuccine)
      Bowl of freshly grated parmesan

Equipment

Saucepan · Sieve · Electric blender

Working time: 5 minutes

Makes: 2 cups sauce, serves 6

1. Drop the basil leaves in simmering water; leave them 10 seconds then drain. This tenderizes the leaves. Squeeze gently to remove the water. Place the leaves in the blender. Add the olive oil, cheeses, pine nuts, garlic, and ½ cup water. Blend until very smooth. Salt to taste.
2. Cook the pasta in boiling salted water until al dente.

Meanwhile heat the pesto sauce without boiling in a saucepan. Stir in the cream. Pour the sauce over freshly cooked pasta, toss rapidly, and serve at once. Pass a bowl of grated parmesan at the table.

To Freeze Pesto: Follow the directions in Step 1, omitting the cheese, garlic, and salt. Pack into plastic cartons. Close tightly and freeze. Thaw completely before using; add the garlic, cheese and salt, heat, and stir in the cream as directed.

✿ ✿ ✿

Across the Italian border there is Provence. Here the specialty is *pistou*, a thick vegetable soup embellished with a spoonful of crushed basil and garlic mixed with oil called a *pommade*. I always thought *pistou* an overrated soup until I tasted this version from Marseilles. Claude Thomas, who gave me the recipe, told me the trick is to use a ratatouille as the base. The eggplant, tomatoes, and green pepper should cook down until they're in a juicy liquid state. Then, and only then, should you begin to make the soup.

PISTOU MARSEILLAISE

Vegetable soup with basil (France)

Ingredients

- ½ pound dried white beans
- ½ pound eggplant, peeled and cut into small chunks
  Salt
- ¼ cup olive oil
- 3 cups chopped onions
- 1 tablespoon chopped garlic
- ¾ pound small, firm zucchini (about 4 or 5), peeled and cut into small chunks
- 1 medium sweet green pepper (or 2 small elongated light-green Italian peppers), seeded, deribbed, and cut into small chunks

Continued

2½ cups peeled, seeded, and chopped tomatoes
3 quarts boiling water
1 cup diced carrots
⅔ cup diced celery ribs
1 cup string beans, cut small
1 cup wax beans, cut small
   Bouquet garni: 3 basil leaves, parsley sprigs, 1 bay leaf,
      and 2 sprigs thyme or ¼ teaspoon crumbled dried
      thyme, tied together
   Freshly ground black pepper
¼ teaspoon grated nutmeg
1 pound potatoes, peeled and diced
¾ cup elbow macaroni

Pommade
1 cup fresh large basil leaves, torn into small pieces
1–2 teaspoons finely chopped garlic
   About 1 cup olive oil
⅓ cup grated parmesan or gruyère cheese
   Salt and freshly ground black pepper
   Bowl of freshly grated parmesan or gruyère cheese

Equipment

Colander · Large soup pot with cover · Large mortar
or mixing bowl with wooden pestle

Working time: 1 hour

Cooking time: 3 hours (approximately)

Serves: 8 to 10

   1. Cover the beans by 1 inch with water. Allow to soak overnight.
   2. Salt the eggplant pieces for 15 minutes in the colander.
Rinse and squeeze gently to remove the bitter juices.
   3. Heat the oil in the soup pot. Add the onions and cook
them gently until soft. Add the garlic and cook, stirring, 2 min-

utes longer. Add the eggplant and cook, stirring, for 3 to 4 minutes. Add half the zucchini and cook 3 minutes more. Add the green pepper and cook 3 minutes longer, stirring often. Stir in the tomatoes and allow the mixture to simmer 5 minutes, stirring often. Cover the pot and cook at the simmer for about 30 minutes.

4. Pour the boiling water into the simmering mixture, stirring briskly. Drain the beans and add to the pot. Cook, covered, over gentle heat 1½ hours.

5. Add the carrots, celery, string and wax beans, bouquet garni, pepper, and nutmeg and continue to cook at the simmer for 20 minutes. Salt to taste.

6. Add the remaining zucchini and the potatoes and continue to cook 10 minutes longer. Stir in the macaroni and continue to cook at the simmer until tender.

7. Meanwhile make the *pommade*: Pound the basil leaves and garlic to a paste in a large mortar or bowl. Slowly add half the oil alternating with the cheese. Add the remaining olive oil, stirring, until the mixture is well blended and thickened. Season with salt and pepper. Scrape into a small serving bowl or serve directly from the mortar.

8. Correct the seasoning of the soup. Serve hot and pass a bowl of grated cheese and the *pommade*.

BAY LEAVES

Imported bay leaves from Turkey are milder than our California ones. In all the recipes in this book I used Mediterranean bay leaves—actually from our own laurel tree, which stands just outside our house. If you buy imported ones the proportions will always be right; if you use California bay leaves halve the amounts.

The French bouquet garni is the standard herb bouquet comprising a bay leaf, thyme, a few parsley sprigs, and sometimes a few celery leaves tied together and added to stocks, stews, soups, and pot-au-feu. In Provence a dried orange peel is added to daubes and bouillabaisse.

The Turks alternate bay leaves with skewered fish, then broil the fish kebabs over hot coals.

In this recipe for calf's liver you can enjoy bay leaves in a prominent role. Lamb, pork, or beef liver may be substituted and will be just as good.

FEGATO DI VITELLO CON FOGLIE DI LAURO

Calf's liver with laurel leaves (Italy)

Ingredients

  10 imported bay leaves
   1 pound calf's liver, cut into 1-inch cubes
      Salt and freshly ground black pepper
      Pinch of grated nutmeg
      Vegetable oil
   1 lemon, quartered

Equipment

Mortar and pestle · Mixing bowl · 4 long skewers

Working time: 5 minutes

Broiling time: 8 minutes (approximately)

Serves: 3 to 4

1. In a mortar pound 3 of the bay leaves until almost a powder. In a mixing bowl toss the liver cubes with the ground bay leaves, salt and pepper, grated nutmeg, and 3 tablespoons oil. Allow to stand 1 hour.
2. Cut the remaining 7 bay leaves into 1-inch pieces. Thread seasoned liver cubes alternately with bay leaves. Brush with oil. Broil quickly on all sides, 2 or 3 inches from a broiler flame until the first drops of light pink liquid ooze up. Serve at once with lemon quarters.

CAPERS

Capers are the small closed green flower buds of small wild shrubs that grow all around Mediterranean shores. The biggest and fleshiest grow in Sicily and as a result the Sicilians use them the most. They salt or pickle them and use them in salads, as a base for sauces for chicken and game, as additions to fish tarts, in tomato sauces, and on their famous pizzas.

Capers are much appreciated in Apulia, in southeastern Italy, where they're used inside meatballs. They're delicious on boiled green vegetables, especially string beans. Gently sauté a little chopped parsley and a spoonful of rinsed capers in a few tablespoons of butter for a minute or two. Then sprinkle them with lemon juice, season with salt and pepper, and pour the bubbling mixture over freshly boiled green beans.

Provence is noted for its use of capers, especially in the caper-olive-anchovy paste, *tapenade*. (See page 52 for one version.) *Tapenade* makes a delicious spread on small slices of toasted French bread.

Capers are popular in the Spanish Mediterranean island of Ibiza, too. A smooth sauce of sieved crushed capers, ground almonds, crushed garlic, and chopped parsley is poured over freshly fried pollock (*mero*).

CARAWAY SEEDS

The Tunisians use caraways a great deal in spice mixtures, in their famous hot red-pepper *harissa* sauce, and blended with garlic in salads and stews. The following salad of mashed zucchini is refreshing in late summer. You can use green and black olives as decoration or cubes of feta cheese.

SLATA KERA

Zucchini salad (Tunisia)

Ingredients

1½ pounds small firm zucchini (about 8 or 10), trimmed
1½ teaspoons chopped garlic
1½ teaspoons ground caraway seed
3–4 tablespoons olive oil
1 tablespoon vinegar
  Salt, freshly ground black pepper, and cayenne

Equipment

Vegetable steamer or *couscousiere* · Vegetable or
potato masher

Working time: 5 minutes

Cooking time: 20 minutes

Makes: 1¾ cups, *serves* 6

1. Steam the zucchini until tender. Mash to a puree.
2. Combine mashed zucchini with garlic, caraway, olive oil, vinegar, and seasonings; mix well. Chill before serving.

CORIANDER

Please remember that coriander is both an herb and a spice, that the taste of each is different, and that the one cannot be exchanged for the other.

Fresh coriander is available in Portuguese, Latin American, or Chinese markets under the names "cilantro" or "Chinese parsley," and you can easily grow it fresh by simply planting the seeds.

There is no substitute for the special flavor of the coriander herb. It's one of the most important ingredients in Moroccan food and, to a lesser degree, the food of Algeria, Tunisia, and the Middle East. The Palestinians serve fresh fava beans with a dusting of chopped fresh green coriander and garlic.

The following recipe is adapted from *Grandes Recettes de la Cuisine Algerienne* by Youcef Fehri. Slow simmering is the key to success with this dish, best prepared in an earthen or stoneware dish. To avoid breaking the dish set it over asbestos or a trivet, or cook it slowly in the oven.

H'MAM M'DOUZANE

Squab with coriander and spices (Algeria)

Ingredients

> 4 ready-to-cook squab
> Salt and freshly ground black pepper
> ⅛ teaspoon ground saffron
> 1 teaspoon ground aniseed
> ⅓ cup vegetable oil
> 1 tablespoon chopped fresh coriander
> 2 tablespoons finely chopped scallions
> Juice of 1 lemon

Equipment

> A shallow earthenware or stoneware dish with cover or a heatproof serving skillet with fitted cover · An asbestos pad to protect the earthenware dish (optional) · Tongs

Working time: 10 minutes

Cooking time: 45 minutes

Serves: 4

1. Quarter the squab. Rub all over with a mixture of salt, pepper, saffron, aniseed, and some of the oil.
2. Heat the remaining oil in the dish and in it slowly brown the squab pieces on both sides. This takes 10 to 15 minutes. Add

1½ cups water, ½ tablespoon coriander, and 1 tablespoon scallions. Cook, covered, at the simmer ½ hour, turning the pieces often to cook evenly.

3. Uncover the dish and allow the cooking juices to reduce to a thick gravy, about ¾ cup. Sprinkle with the remaining coriander, scallions, and lemon juice. Serve at once.

*   *   *

Ground coriander seeds (the spice) form the base for a delicious paste for Moroccan roasted lamb. For a 10-pound forequarter blend 1½ tablespoons ground coriander seeds with 1 tablespoon chopped garlic, 2 teaspoons ground cumin, 1 teaspoon paprika, and 5½ tablespoons softened butter. Rub the forequarter with salt and pepper then spread with this paste before roasting.

CUMIN

Cumin seeds smell like old hay, but when they're ground in a mortar a marvelous aroma is released. The mixture of cumin, coriander, and garlic is very popular in Morocco, Cypress, and Greece. The Cypriot ham, *loutsa*, is a boned pork loin rubbed with salt, pepper, garlic, lemon, coriander, and cumin, baked in the oven and served cold in thin slices. Cumin, along with coriander and garlic, is the essential flavoring in the spicy Greek sausage, *soutzoukakia*.

In Morocco when you order *mechoui* you will be served a crusty roasted lamb, a small bowl of ground cumin, and a bowl of salt. The lamb, still very hot, should be eaten with the fingers— you dip the morsels of meat into the cumin and salt. And all across North Africa from Cairo to Tangier, shelled hard-boiled eggs sprinkled with cumin and salt is a popular street snack.

Autumn is the time to eat freshly killed quail, and the Egyptians have a special way of flavoring them. They blend cumin, ground coriander, grated onions, and chopped parsley, then rub the mixture into the quail flesh before grilling over hot coals.

Claudia Roden, in her excellent *A Book of Middle Eastern Food*, describes her mother's recipe for *dukkah*, an Egyptian spice mixture served with bread and olive oil as a breakfast treat. The *dukkah* contains sesame seeds, hazelnuts, coriander seeds, and cumin seeds all roasted and pounded together well.

Algerians use cumin in many of their stews. A particularly interesting one is made of thin slices of a leg of lamb rubbed with ground cumin, dusted with breadcrumbs and grated cheese, then rolled in beaten eggs and fried in oil. Afterwards the meat is simmered in a cumin, cinnamon, pepper flavored onion sauce.

FENNEL

Fennel can appear in two separate forms—seed or bulb. You can discover the way its mild licorice flavor can excite the palate by slicing a bulb into thin strips, soaking them in ice water until crisp, then serving them with lemon juice and salt.

Loup au fenouil is a particularly delicious dish. Long straw-colored dried fennel stalks are set alight under a broiled bass giving it a lovely aroma and imparting a delicate taste. It's excellent with a *sauce beurre blanc.* You can always tuck a few fennel seeds into the cavity of a fresh fish or give it a splashing of pastis. It's not a substitute for burning fennel stalks, but it does give a good taste.

The Italians use fennel a great deal. In Tuscany, they put it into a delicious sausage called *finocchiona*, which has a subtle licorice flavor. The bulbs, too, are popular, and in Tunisia, which has many Italian dishes because of historic ties, you will find things like stuffed fennel bulbs (see page 111).

Fennel greens grow wild in America and are available in Italian markets around March 19, the day of the Sicilian feast of St. Joseph. A popular St. Joseph's day dish is *pasta con le sarde* which should be made with the very aromatic wild fennel, though farmers' fennel will get you by.

Sarda, the soft fresh cheese of Sardinia, makes a good sandwich with boiled wild fennel—the two are pressed into a pocket of bread, then browned in a hot stove.

FENUGREEK

Fenugreek has little taste until it is heated; then it tastes like burnt sugar and smells like celery. It's very hard and must be softened by soaking in hot water. When it's dry, it's pounded into powder.

The Arab name for it is *helba*—the same word used for the Israeli spice dip brought to Israel by the Yemenite Jews. *Helba* sauce is made of fenugreek, pureed tomatoes, garlic, lots of hot peppers, ground coriander, cardamom, and caraway seeds.

Moroccan Berber men encourage their wives to eat bread spiced with fenugreek because they believe it makes them plump. The spice is also used in *pastourma*, the Turkish and Greek spiced dried beef that looks like bacon.

HARISSA

Harissa sauce is useful for perking up black or green olives or for spicing up a side sauce for couscous. This Tunisian hot pepper sauce is easy to make or it can be purchased in cans or bottles. It's used in Tunisia in *tagines*, in salads, and as an accompanying sauce for brochettes.

The Indonesian spice mixture, sambal oelek, makes a respectable substitute.

HARISSA

Hot pepper sauce (Tunisia)

Ingredients

> 2 tablespoons crushed red pepper flakes,
>   or ¼ cup dried chili peppers
> 1 clove garlic, peeled
> ½ teaspoon caraway seeds
> ¼ teaspoon ground cumin
> 1 roasted pimento, chopped, or 1 tomato, peeled, seeded,
>   and chopped
> Salt
> Olive oil

Equipment

> Mortar and pestle or electric blender   ·   Small clean jar with fitted lid

Working time: 5 minutes

Makes: 3 tablespoons

1. Grind or pound the peppers in the mortar or electric blender.
2. Add the garlic, spices, pimento or tomato, and salt. Crush or whirl until well blended.
3. Scrape into a clean jar, cover with a layer of olive oil, cover tightly, and refrigerate until needed.

HERB MIXTURES

The French are awfully good at making up bundles of herbs and aromatics to throw into stews and soups—everything from the simplest bundle of thyme, bay leaf, and parsley which makes the classic bouquet garni to the more elaborate mixtures of Provence, Corsica, and Roussillon which perfume the dishes of these regions.

I have a friend from Provence who is always mixing thyme with a crumbled bay leaf, some fennel seeds, and peppercorns, then putting the mixture up in olive oil for a few weeks before spreading it on grilled meats.

The Corsicans mix thyme, rosemary, perennial savory, oregano, marjoram, and parsley in equal amounts to scent their stews and such charcuteries as their fresh grilled sausage, *figatelli*.

Beurre Montpellier is a useful herb butter. Use a tablespoon on broiled fish or pile around a cold poached fish for a buffet dinner. Elizabeth David says it's good with *oeufs en cocotte*.

BEURRE MONTPELLIER
Green Butter of Languedoc (France)

Ingredients

- ¼ pound butter, softened to room temperature
- ½ cup cooked chopped spinach
- 1 bunch watercress, stemmed, parboiled, drained, and chopped, making about 3 tablespoons
- 1 tablespoon finely chopped parsley
- 1 teaspoon mixed dried herbs, or 2 teaspoons fresh herbs, chopped
- 2 hard-boiled eggs, peeled and chopped
- 2 teaspoons lemon juice
  Freshly ground black pepper
- 6 anchovy fillets, rinsed, drained, and mashed
- 1 tablespoon capers, rinsed and drained
- 2 tablespoons olive oil

Equipment

Electric blender · Mixing bowl

Working time: 10 minutes

Makes: 1⅛ cups (approximately)

1. Cut the butter into small pieces. Set aside.
2. Place spinach and watercress in a corner of a clean towel and squeeze out any excess moisture. Place in a blender jar with remaining ingredients. Whirl until completely smooth.
3. Scrape into a bowl. Blend with the butter and pack into small earthen or stoneware jar. It will keep a few days, covered, in the refrigerator. Serve the butter at room temperature.

FILETS DE SOLE
À LA FAÇON PROVENÇALE

Poached fish fillets with herbal oil (France)

Ingredients

>   ½ onion, sliced
>   Salt and 8 black peppercorns
>   Bouquet garni: 1 imported bay leaf, 4 sprigs parsley,
>   a few sprigs thyme (or ½ teaspoon dried), a few
>   fennel branches, tied together
>   ½ cup dry white wine
>   2 1½-pound fish fillets suitable for poaching: flounder,
>   dab, lemon or gray sole; dover or blackback
>   ⅔ cup olive oil
>   3 tablespoons chopped mixed fresh herbs: parsley, fennel
>   leaves, thyme, marjoram, and a hint of rosemary
>   2 lemons, quartered

Equipment

>   Wide pan for poaching fish, buttered   ·   Small saucepan   ·
>   Slotted spatula

Working time: 10 minutes

Poaching time: 10 to 12 minutes

Serves: 4

1. Preheat the oven to 350 degrees.
2. Put the onion, salt, peppercorns, and bouquet garni in the poaching pan. Add the wine and enough water to half fill the pan. Bring to a boil.
3. Lower the heat, slip in the fish, cover with a sheet of

buttered waxed paper, and set in the oven to poach, 10 to 12 minutes.

4. Meanwhile, gently heat the oil in a saucepan with the mixed fresh herbs. Off heat, allow to steep 10 minutes. Season with salt and pepper.

5. Remove the fish fillets using a slotted spatula and place on a serving dish. Reserve the fish poaching liquid for soups or sauces. Sprinkle the fish with lemon juice. Spoon over the herb-flavored oil and decorate with lemon quarters. Serve tepid or cool.

JUNIPER BERRIES

Juniper berries have to be well crushed if you're going to use them in stuffing or sauces. Otherwise the little shells will get stuck between your teeth. Robert Landry in his book *Les Soleils de la Cuisine* says that the Turks marinate lamb with juniper berries and oregano to give it the taste of venison. (The French like to marinate lamb in a wine mixture which includes a small amount of juniper, too.)

Juniper stalks can be used in smoking or grilling, as in the Spanish chorizo. Corsican black birds fatten themselves on juniper berries, thus readying themselves for the famous *pâté de merles*. Corsican black birds have particularly tender flesh but the secret of the pâté is in the flavoring—cognac, madeira, and myrthe liqueur seasoned with juniper berries and nutmeg, and enriched with truffles.

MARJORAM, OREGANO, ZA'ATAR

These three are so close in spirit they can easily be spoken of together. All three grow wild on the mountain slopes of Mediterranean shores and are used a great deal in Mediterranean cookery. The Greeks sprinkle marjoram or oregano on skewered lamb, or dust cubes of feta cheese with it, then decorate the cheese with olives moistened with olive oil and lemon. In Morocco *za'atar*, which is a sort of hybrid of oregano and marjoram, is used with zucchini and as an herbal drink after a heavy meal.

Moroccans mix marjoram with sweetened milk and the Algerians make a marjoram-flavored zucchini soup. It's an essential herb in Roman egg and lemon *brodetto* (see page 291), and in Liguria one always finds a few leaves of marjoram in such cheese and vegetable tarts as the famous *torta Pasqualina*.

MILOUKIA

Miloukia, a green leafy vegetable not unlike spinach, has been eaten almost daily in Egypt since the time of the Pharaohs. Like okra it gives a viscous texture to soups. Dry miloukia leaves are available in Middle Eastern food stores—2 ounces is equivalent to a pound of the fresh herb.

A soup broth made from rabbit, goose, chicken, meat or duck, and chopped miloukia is popular in Egypt, Syria, Lebanon, and Palestine. A Lebanese friend told me that it's best to add miloukia slowly and then shake rather than stir the pot. In Lebanese homes this soup is served like an Indian curry dinner, with bowls of boiled rice, pieces of the meat or chicken or rabbit which made the broth, and chopped vegetables on the side. Often a *taklia*, a mixture of green coriander or mint and garlic, is sauteed in butter and added to the soup just before it's served. Sometimes hot chilies are added too.

In Palestinian homes cooked finely chopped miloukia leaves are surrounded with bowls of chopped onions in vinegar, toasted bread cubes, rice, and chicken or meat.

MINT

Mint is so easy to grow you often see pots of it outside the kitchens of American homes. If you buy a fresh bunch of mint, leave a few leaves on the stalks, then push them about one inch into fresh soil and keep them moist. Soon your "cuttings" will root and from then on you'll have fresh mint whenever you need it. Mint is essential to Moroccan tea, which will help with "tourist tummy" if you get it.

The Romans have enjoyed mint-flavored zucchini since ancient times, and the Greeks make a beef broth memorable because of the addition of mint. Yogurt and fresh mint make a refreshing combination and are eaten a great deal in the Levant.

Dried pulverized mint is much used in Tunisia and gives

surprisingly good flavor to salads and *tagines*. Here is a delicious recipe I learned from a Tunisian cook in Kairouan.

TAGINE NANA

Lamb and mint tagine *in the style of Kairouan (Tunisia)*

Note that while in Morocco a *tagine* is a stew, in Tunisia it is something quite different—first prepared as a stew and then baked with the addition of beaten eggs and grated cheese, resulting in a firm molded dish similar to a custard pie.

Ingredients

  1   pound boneless lean lamb, cut into 1-inch cubes
      Salt and freshly ground black pepper
  2   tablespoons vegetable oil
  1   cup chopped onion
  4   medium red ripe tomatoes, peeled, seeded, and chopped
1½   teaspoons sweet paprika
1½   teaspoons *tabil* (see page 202)
  1   teaspoon freshly ground black pepper
  6   eggs, lightly beaten
½   cup breadcrumbs
¼   cup grated parmesan or gruyère cheese
1½   tablespoons pulverized dried mint leaves
      Clarified butter

Equipment

Small heavy casserole with cover   ·   Shallow 1-quart ovenproof serving dish   ·   Mixing bowl and whisk

Working time: 15 minutes

Cooking time: 1½ hours

Serves: 4

1. Trim the lamb of excess fat. Season the chunks with salt and pepper. Heat the oil in the casserole and brown the lamb with the chopped onions. Stir in the tomatoes, paprika, *tabil*, and ground black pepper. Cover tightly, set over low heat to simmer 1 hour, adding a little water if needed.

2. Transfer the lamb to an ovenproof serving dish, cover and keep moist. Reduce the cooking juices to ½ cup and let cool.

3. Preheat the oven to 350 degrees.

4. Beat the eggs to a froth, add the cooled cooking juices, the breadcrumbs, grated cheese, and mint. Season with very little salt and pepper. Pour the egg mixture over the lamb. Set on the middle shelf of the oven to bake 15 minutes.

5. Raise the oven heat to the highest setting, remove the dish, dribble over the clarified butter, and return the dish to the highest shelf in the oven. Bake 10 minutes. Serve hot cut into wedges.

SLATA TOONSIA

Mixed salad (Tunisia)

The same cook taught me this Tunisian mixed salad, similar to the Lebanese appetizer or *mezze* called *fatouche*. *Fatouche* means, literally, "moistened bread," but in the *mezze* form it consists of a cubed salad of lettuce, onion, tomatoes, cucumbers, and bread moistened with lemon juice and oil, the whole then flavored with mint. I think *Slata Toonsia* is more interesting because of the addition of peppers and green apples.

Ingredients

    1 cup red ripe tomatoes, peeled, seeded, and diced
    1 cup chopped onion
    1 cup sweet green peppers, seeded, deribbed, and diced
    1 tablespoon finely chopped hot green chili pepper, seeded
    1 cup raw green apple, peeled, cored, and diced
 1½ tablespoons vinegar

Continued

4½ tablespoons olive or salad oil
1 tablespoon pulverized dried mint leaves
Salt and freshly ground black pepper

Equipment

Glass serving bowl

Working time: 10 minutes

Serves: 4 to 6

Combine tomatoes, onion, peppers, and apple in the serving bowl. Add vinegar and oil and toss well. Sprinkle with pulverized mint, salt, and pepper. Mix thoroughly. Serve at room temperature.

MYRTLE

Myrtle, with an aroma close to rosemary and juniper, is used a lot on the Mediterranean islands of Sardinia, Corsica, and Crete. It's good as a flavoring for lamb, and the Sardinians are fond of it with small birds. But the flavor of myrtle is quite strong so rather than adding it directly the Sardinians wait until the birds are roasted, then, still hot, place them under a bed of myrtle leaves to absorb the aroma. They do the same with small roasted pig, but feel free to stuff the leaves directly into a wild boar, since that creature has a strong flavor of its own.

Corsican *pâté de merles* is flavored with a liqueur made from myrtle called myrthe.

On the island of Korčula in Yugoslavia there is a specialty of fish smoked over myrtle branches for 14 days, then wrapped in cabbage leaves and cooked in oil with garlic, lemon, parsley, and vinegar.

ORANGE FLOWER WATER

In North Africa orange flower water is often made in the home. Arabs invented the distilling process, and their alambic stills are pretty much the same as the sort of distilling apparatus you might find in a modern chemistry laboratory.

Orange flower water is used to flavor cakes and cookies in Provence and in Lebanon. It is used to flavor almond pastries in the Maghreb—even the pastry dough wrapped around the almond paste. The Algerians perfume meatballs with it, and in Morocco it's used to perfume the water with which you rinse your hands after a grant *diffa*.

PAPRIKA

The Yugoslavs use lots of paprika, because of the Austro-Hungarian influence on their cuisine, and it's used a lot, too, in the Maghreb.

A popular north Adriatic Yugoslav dish is *Slavonski ćevap*—skewered meat first marinated under a layer of sliced onion, a few blueberries, white wine, and plenty of paprika, then threaded onto skewers with tomato and green peppers, wrapped in caul fat and roasted over hot coals.

Paprika appears frequently in Algerian, Moroccan, and Tunisian salads, as well as in a marinade of cumin, coriander, garlic, and lemon juice called *chermoula* and used for fish dishes.

PARSLEY

Flat leaf parsley is most used around the Mediterranean, and of course it's an essential herb in a bouquet garni. Try to use it fresh—I can't think of anything much worse than "dried parsley flakes."

In Languedoc, in southwestern France, a shoulder of lamb is prepared with a *persillade*—a mixture of chopped parsley, shallots, and breadcrumbs pressed against the meat before browning —and served up with a wild mushroom sauté. Deep fried parsley makes a good accompaniment for steaks. Wash it, dry it well, dip it in boiling oil, drain it, and serve at once.

Italian *salsa verde* is based on parsley, and served with boiled fish or meat. The Greeks have a parsley sauce bound with lemon and eggs, and the Spanish make one that goes beautifully with fried fish.

MERO A LA CHICLANERA

Fried halibut or pollock with parsley sauce (Spain)

Ingredients

¾ cup roughly chopped parsley
½ teaspoon chopped garlic
   Juice of ½ lemon
   Salt and freshly ground black pepper
4 1-inch-thick halibut or pollock steaks
   Flour seasoned with salt and pepper for dredging
½ cup olive or vegetable oil
2 tablespoons chopped onion
1 tablespoon flour

Equipment

Electric blender · Large skillet

Working time: 10 minutes

Cooking time: 8 minutes

Serves: 4

1. Place the parsley and the garlic in the blender jar. Add ¼ cup water. Whirl until smooth. Thin with another ¼ cup water. Add lemon juice, salt and pepper. Set aside.

2. Dip the fish steaks into seasoned flour and shake off any excess. Fry in hot oil until nicely browned on both sides. When cooked remove to a warmed serving dish. Pour off half the oil. Cook the onion in the remaining oil and pan drippings until soft and golden. Add the flour and cook until light brown, stirring. Add the parsley mixture. Cook, stirring, 2 minutes. Pour over the fish and serve at once.

PIMENTÓN

This is the Spanish paprika so beloved by the Andalusians. The peasants of Almería are famous for their light *pimentón*-flavored dark red fish soup made with fresh anchovies, firm, white-flesh fish, sardines, fried onions, tomatoes, garlic, and cumin.

The Spanish call second-quality *pimentón "arena"* or *"sand."* *Pimentón* is a little stronger than Hungarian paprika, and is essential in the justly famous Andalusian boiled meat casserole, *cocido.*

COCIDO A LA ANDALUZA

Boiled meat and vegetables with pumpkin and pimentón *sauce*
(Spain)

Ingredients

    1½ cups (about ½ pound) dried chick-peas
    2 pounds rump or chuck roast
    1 5-ounce slab salt pork
    3 pounds beef bones, cracked
    1 onion, chopped
    8 small potatoes, peeled
    ½-pound wedge of fresh pumpkin, peeled
        and cut into 3 pieces
    ½ pound chorizo sausage links
        Herbs: 2 sprigs parsley, 2 leeks, 1 celery rib
        and 1 bay leaf
    1 pound fresh green beans
    1 tomato, peeled, seeded, and chopped
    2 large cloves garlic, peeled
    1 heaping teaspoon *pimentón* (Spanish paprika
        or substitute strong not sharp Hungarian paprika)
        Freshly ground black pepper and salt
    1½ cups soup noodles

Equipment

> Large soup pot · Slotted spoon · Small saucepan ·
> Electric blender

Working time: 30 minutes

Cooking time: 2¾ to 3 hours

Serves: 6

1. Cover the chick-peas with cold water. Soak overnight then drain. Soak the salt pork 2 hours in cold water; drain.
2. In a soup pot bring about 4½ quarts water to a boil. Add the meat, salt pork, beef bones, and onion. Cook at the simmer 1 hour, skimming the surface often to remove the scum that rises to the surface.
3. Add the chick-peas to the pot and cook 1 hour longer.
4. Add the potatoes, pumpkin, chorizo, and assorted herbs. Cook, covered, 30 minutes or until the potatoes and the pumpkin pieces are tender. Transfer the meat, potatoes, and chick-peas to a deep heatproof serving dish. Discard the salt pork, bones, and herbs. Taste the cooking liquid and readjust the seasoning. Moisten the meat with 2 cups cooking liquid. Set the pumpkin pieces aside. Keep the meat hot in a warm oven.
5. Cook the green beans in salted water until tender. Meanwhile blend the pumpkin with the tomato, garlic, *pimentón* or paprika, and 2 cups cooking liquid in an electric blender. Correct the seasoning. Put 2 cups of this sauce in a sauceboat and keep warm. Reserve the remaining sauce for the soup.
6. Bring the cooking liquid to the boil and cook the soup noodles in it until just tender. Stir in the remaining pumpkin sauce. Serve the soup as a first course. Pile the string beans in the center of the meat dish, serve as a main course, passing the sauce separately.

Note: Leftover cooking liquid from a *cocido* makes an excellent Spanish garlic soup for 2. Heat the soup in a large skillet. Separately fry 6 slices of French-style bread in oil until golden on both sides. Place 3 slices in each soup plate. Add 1 teaspoon finely chopped garlic to the simmering soup. Cook 5 minutes. Poach 4 eggs in the soup then transfer to soup plates and serve at once.

ROSEMARY

In Tunisia there's an interesting rosemary variant called *kilil* which is extremely aromatic. It's used in a regional dish of lamb cubes rubbed with paprika, then steamed over a bunch of *kilil* in the top of a couscousiere. The broth below is full of onions, and seasoned with cinnamon, pepper, and salt. Later couscous is added to the top and steamed through the *kilil*, too.

Rosemary has such a powerful aroma you needn't eat it to get the point. It penetrates everything that is cooked with it, and the Italians use it a great deal, tucking great bouquets of it under roasts of lamb, veal, or pork.

In Abruzzi, in central Italy, there's a famous lamb dish made with rosemary and chili peppers. The people there also like to rub lamb with a rosemary and honey paste before putting it in to roast. In Tuscany there's a popular chestnut flour cake, flavored with rosemary, pine nuts, and sultanas and served with a generous helping of ricotta cheese, and in Rome there's a superb way of serving rosemary-flavored rib steaks.

COSTATA DI MANZO ALLA ROMANA

Rib steaks in the style of Rome (Italy)

Ingredients

> 2 boned rib steaks, 1 inch thick
> 1 tablespoon finely chopped fresh rosemary,
>   or ½ tablespoon dried
> 2 cloves garlic, peeled and chopped
> ½ cup olive oil
> ¼ teaspoon freshly ground black pepper
>   Salt
>   Lemon quarters

Equipment

> Cleaver · Wax paper · Mortar and pestle ·
> Wide shallow dish

Working time: 5 minutes

Broiling time: 8 minutes (approximately)

Serves: 4 to 5

1. The day before serving pound the slices of meat between sheets of wax paper until somewhat thinner. In a mortar pound the rosemary and the garlic to a paste. Stir in the olive oil and season with pepper and a little salt. Marinate the meat overnight in the oil mixture, turning the meat once or twice.

2. Remove the meat and pat dry with paper towels. Broil 4 minutes on each side or until done to taste. Place on a warmed serving dish, sprinkle with lemon juice and serve at once.

ROSES

Dried roses are used to make rose water and the various spice mixtures in the Maghreb. *Bharat,* a mixture of 2 parts ground cinnamon to 1 part ground dried roses, is widely used in Tunisian cooking. (See page 156 for couscous with quince and fish.)

Neset Eren, in her book *The Art of Turkish Cooking,* exclaims over the qualities of rose jam, which, she says, makes a delicious sauce over vanilla ice cream. Rose water gives puddings and cakes a delicious exotic flavor, and appears in recipes throughout the Arab world.

SAFFRON

Saffron is used to flavor and color bread, rice, fish soups, pasta (in Sardinia where there's a strong Spanish influence), Milanaise risotto, Spanish paella, Provençal bouillabaisse, and Moroccan couscous.

Saffron, the dried stigmas of *crocus sativus*, should be set on a flat dish over a pan of boiling water. When the stigmas become brittle they should be pounded to a fine powder. This is the best way to get the full use of every thread of saffron—the world's most expensive spice.

In Tunisia there's a *tagine* with "bananas": really cooked mashed potatoes mixed with ground meat and grated cheese, then combined with chopped hard-boiled eggs and seasoned with salt and pepper. Saffron is used to make the mixture yellow, then it's formed into banana shape, and cooked in boiling oil.

In Languedoc and Périgord *le mourtairol* is a beef, chicken, ham, and vegetable casserole simmered for many hours. Some of the cooking juices are removed, cooked until creamy with saffron and a loaf of toasted French bread, then dolloped by the spoonful back into bowls of the soup.

Paella is the most famous saffron dish, and rightly so. There are as many ways to make it as there are Spanish cooks, but the common ingredient is always the saffron which permeates paella and gives it its distinctive taste.

The history of paella is long and complicated indeed. It was invented in southern Spain, and in its early form was not made with chicken, pork, sausage, or seafood, but with rabbit, snails, and freshwater eels. It was traditionally made outdoors over an open fire, and rather than being accompanied by salad, it was eaten while chewing on a raw wild scallion.

PAELLA

(Spain)

Ingredients

- ¾ cup olive oil
- 1 cup grated onion
- ½ pound boneless pork shoulder cut into 1-inch cubes
- 1 3-pound chicken, cut into 8 pieces
- 1 teaspoon finely chopped garlic
- 2 cups peeled, seeded, and chopped tomatoes
- 2 bay leaves

Continued

    4 sprigs fresh parsley
      Salt and freshly ground black pepper
  ½ teaspoon pulverized saffron
  ¼ pound sweet green peppers, seeded, deribbed,
      and cut lengthwise into thin strips
  ¼ pound green beans, trimmed and cut into 1-inch lengths,
      or 9 ounces frozen artichoke hearts, thawed
  12 mussels, well scrubbed
  ½ pound small clams, scrubbed and soaked in cold water
      30 minutes to eliminate sand
  3 cups raw imported Spanish or Italian rice
  1 7-ounce jar roasted red peppers, drained
      and cut into thin strips
  ½ pound shelled and deveined shrimp
  ¼ pound fully cooked chorizo sausage, skinned
      and thinly sliced
  2 lemons, quartered

Equipment

Large heavy casserole with tight-fitting cover · Pot for
steaming mussels and clams · A very large skillet
or paella pan measuring 15 to 16 inches across

Working time: 1 hour

Cooking time: 1 hour 20 minutes

Serves: 8

    1. In the large casserole heat ⅓ cup olive oil and in it cook
½ cup grated onion for 2 minutes, stirring. Add the pork and
chicken and sauté for 5 minutes, stirring. Then add the garlic, tomatoes, herbs, salt, pepper, and saffron. Cover and cook over
medium heat about 25 minutes, stirring from time to time.
    2. Meanwhile steam the mussels and clams in 1 cup water
until they open, about 5 minutes. Discard any that do not open.
Reserve the mussels, clams, and cooking liquor and discard the
shells. Strain the liquor.

3. Add the green peppers and green beans or artichokes to the casserole. Cook, covered, 5 to 10 minutes longer.

4. Meanwhile heat the remaining olive oil in the paella pan and cook the remaining ½ cup grated onion 1 minute. Add the rice and cook, stirring until all the grains are coated, 8 to 10 minutes.

5. Add the mussel and clam liquor plus 7 cups water to the casserole. Bring to the boil. Slowly pour the bubbling sauce over the rice. Then slide the remaining contents of the casserole evenly over the sizzling rice. Add the red peppers, shrimp, chorizo slices, mussels, and clams. Stir once. Cook, uncovered, over brisk heat until the liquid is absorbed and the rice is tender, about 20 minutes. Rotate and shake the pan from time to time to cook the rice evenly. Allow the contents to rest 5 minutes before serving. Serve directly from the pan with the lemon wedges.

SAGE

Sage, like myrtle and rosemary is a strong herb, and needs careful handling. See page 11 for *acqua cotta,* a vegetable soup cooked atop a bed of sage.

In Yugoslavia sage is added to fish, pasta dishes, marinades, and sparingly to pastries. The Tuscans say that their famous *fagioli all'uccelletto,* with a seasoning of sage, garlic, and tomato makes white beans taste like small game.

SESAME SEEDS

Tahini or sesame paste, an emulsion of sesame seeds and oil, is much used in the Middle East. Before you use it be sure to stir the mixture in the can until it's well blended and smooth.

The simple tahini cream sauce, the base of many dishes such as *hummus, baba ghanoush,* and a sauce for cold poached fish, makes a delightful dip when mixed with lots of chopped parsley.

Combine 1 cup of well-mixed tahini with 1 teaspoon finely chopped garlic and ½ teaspoon salt. Beat well then stir in enough cold water (about ⅔ cup) to make a thick sauce. Thin it with lemon juice, still stirring and you'll have a flavorful sauce for grilled foods, cooked cold vegetables, and fish.

Sesame seeds are used in halvah, the famous Turkish sweet. The Moroccans toast them and sprinkle them over sweet *tagines*, and the Israelis use them to coat chicken.

OAF SUM SUM

Fried chicken with sesame seeds (Israel)

Ingredients

> 4 leg and thigh pieces of chicken, halved
> Salt and freshly ground black pepper
> 1 egg, lightly beaten
> ⅔ cup all-purpose flour
> 1 cup sesame seeds
> 2 teaspoons paprika
> Oil for frying

Equipment

> Shallow bowl · Paper or plastic bag · Skillet and tongs · Baking sheet

Working time: 10 minutes

Cooking time: 30 minutes (approximately)

Serves: 4

1. Preheat the oven to 350 degrees.
2. Rub the chicken pieces with salt and pepper. Beat the egg with ½ cup water in a shallow bowl. Combine flour, sesame seeds, paprika, and salt to taste in a plastic bag, mixing well. Place the chicken pieces, 2 or 3 at a time, in the egg mixture then in the plastic bag. Close and shake until the chicken is nicely coated with the sesame seed mixture. Remove to a dish. Repeat with the remaining pieces of chicken.
3. In hot but not smoking oil brown the chicken pieces on both sides. Transfer to a baking sheet, set on the middle shelf

of the preheated oven to finish the cooking in about 20 minutes. Serve hot.

SMEN

Smen is a cooked salted butter much used in Morocco. A variant is *sahmeh*, a reddish-purple colored butter with a strong taste popular in the Levant.

The most famous of all Palestinian dishes is *mousakhan*, always served on a big dish. The broth of a boiled chicken is used to moisten *pita* bread. When the bread is mushy lots of sliced cooked onions are strewn on top plus black pepper and cinnamon. Pieces of the chicken are then laid on, *sahmeh* is spooned over, and the whole thing is then sent to the oven to bake. *Mousakhan* is clearly related to *trid*, the prophet's favorite dish. (See my book, *Couscous and Other Good Food from Morocco*.)

SMEN

Herb-flavored butter (Morocco)

Ingredients

> Salt
> ¼ cup dried oregano leaves or a combination
>   of oregano and marjoram
> ½ pound very fresh unsalted butter

Equipment

> Saucepan · Sieve · Shallow bowl · Sterile
> glass jar with tight-fitting cover

Working time: 5 minutes

Cooking time: 10 minutes

Ripening time: 15 to 30 days

1. Boil a small handful of salt and the oregano leaves in ¾ quart water for 5 minutes. Strain into a bowl and allow to cool.

2. When the blackened "oregano water" has cooled to the point where it will no longer melt butter, add the butter, cut into pieces, and knead until it has the consistency of mashed potatoes, pressing the mixture again and again against the bottom of the bowl so that every bit has been thoroughly washed. Drain the butter and then squeeze to extract excess water. Knead into a ball, place in the glass jar, and cover tightly.

3. Store in a cool place (not the refrigerator) for at least 15 days before using. Once it has been opened, store in the refrigerator, where it will keep 1 month.

SPICE MIXTURES

La kama is used in Tangier, as opposed to *ras el hanout*—the favorite mixture of the rest of Morocco. To make *la kama* combine:

        1 tablespoon each: ground ginger, ground black pepper,
            and ground turmeric
    ½ tablespoon ground cinnamon
        1 teaspoon grated nutmeg

        Use in *tagines, harira* soups, etc.

Tabil is the favorite spice mixture of Tunisia. It is used a great deal to season meat dishes, stuffings, and sautéed vegetables. To make *tabil* combine:

    2½ teaspoons finely chopped garlic
    2½ teaspoons finely ground caraway seeds
      2 teaspoons finely ground coriander seeds
    2½ teaspoons crushed red pepper flakes

        Here are two dishes that require *tabil*, a famous Tunisian lamb and spinach *tagine*, and a delicious dish of brains and eggs.

TAGINE SEBNAKH

Lamb and spinach tagine *(Tunisia)*

Ingredients

> 1 pound boneless lean lamb, cut into 1-inch cubes
> Salt and freshly ground black pepper
> 2 tablespoons vegetable oil
> 1 cup chopped onion
> 2 ripe tomatoes, peeled, seeded, and chopped
> 1 tablespoon *tabil* (see above)
> 1½ cups water
> 6 eggs
> ¼ cup breadcrumbs
> ¼ cup grated parmesan cheese
> 1 cup chopped cooked spinach
> 2 tablespoons clarified butter

Equipment

> Small heavy casserole with cover · Shallow 1-quart
> ovenproof serving dish · Mixing bowl

Working time: 15 minutes

Cooking time: 1½ hours

Serves: 4

1. Season the lamb with salt and pepper. In the casserole brown the lamb in hot oil with the chopped onion. Add the tomatoes, *tabil*, and 1½ cups water. Bring to a boil. Simmer, covered, about 1 hour or until the lamb is very tender.

2. Transfer the lamb to an ovenproof serving dish, cover, and keep moist. Reduce the cooking juices to ½ cup and let the cooking juices cool.

3. Preheat the oven to 350 degrees.

4. Beat the eggs to a froth, add the breadcrumbs, grated cheese, and spinach. Stir the cooled cooking liquid into the eggs and season with pepper and very little salt. Pour the egg mixture over the lamb. Cover the dish with foil and bake on the middle shelf of the oven for 15 minutes. Raise the oven heat to the highest setting, remove the foil cover, and dribble the clarified butter over all. Set on highest shelf and bake 10 minutes. Serve at once cut into wedges.

AIJJA

Brains and eggs in tomato sauce (Tunisia)

Ingredients

½ pound calf, lamb, or beef brains
Salt and freshly ground black pepper
Vinegar
¼ cup olive oil
2 cups fresh or canned tomato sauce
½ tablespoon *tabil* (see page 202)
¼ teaspoon ground caraway seeds
½ teaspoon harissa (see page 182)
1¾ teaspoons sweet red paprika
3–4 cloves garlic, peeled and chopped
1 medium sweet green pepper, or 3 small elongated light-green Italian peppers, seeded, deribbed, and cut into 1-inch pieces
4 fresh eggs

Equipment

Enameled or stainless steel saucepan with cover · Skillet with cover

Working time: 20 minutes

Cooking time: 30 minutes

Serves: 4

1. Soak the brains for 30 minutes in several changes of water. Remove the membranes then rinse and drain. In the saucepan bring 1½ quarts seasoned and acidulated water to the simmer. Slip in the brains, cover, and cook over low heat for 20 minutes. Drain. Cool and cut into bite-size pieces.

2. Heat the oil in the skillet. Add the tomato sauce, spices, garlic, and green peppers. Cook, uncovered, over low heat 10 minutes. Add the brains. Break whole eggs into the simmering sauce. Poach, covered, until the eggs are just set, basting the tops of them once or twice with the sauce. Serve at once.

VARIATION

One pound tiny well-flavored meatballs previously fried in oil may replace the brains.

SUMAC

Sumac is sour and is sometimes used in the Levant in place of lemon juice over shish kebabs. Mixed with thyme it's called *zather* (not to be confused with the oregano hybrid, *za'atar*). *Zather* is good with *labni* (see page 212), and the Syrians add it to fried onions to turn them a lovely yellow mustard shade.

If you obtain *sumac* in grain form, soak it in water, strain it, then press the mixture. Use it like lemon juice over tomato and cucumber salads and meat.

THYME

Thyme is one of the herbs in the traditional bouquet garni. In Libya it's used with laurel leaves to season freshly killed gazelle. In Provence it's mixed with a pinch of cayenne to flavor meat brochettes. It gives a strong robust flavor to stews and thick soups.

Thyme grows wild on stoney ground and mountain slopes. The bees of Mt. Hymettus feast on purple flowering thyme, and thus the wonderful flavor of this most famous honey of Greece.

WHITE ITALIAN TRUFFLES

White Italian truffles are an aromatic, important in certain luxurious Italian dishes. They're found in Morocco, too, but the Moroccan ones are much inferior, and really not comparable to the Italian. Really the color of putty, white Italian truffles, even in a very small quantity, can completely change the taste of a dish. Found in the hills of Piedmont, and the oak forests of Umbria and Tuscany, they may be eaten raw in salads, stuffed into quails, slivered and added to chicken *cacciatora*, omeletes, canapés, and baked potatoes.

To make a delicious sauce for tagliatelle mix ¼ cup cream, ⅔ cup grated parmesan cheese, the liquor from a ½ ounce tin of white truffles, salt, pepper, and the truffles neatly sliced. Toss the sauce with a pound of cooked pasta. It will serve 6.

Perhaps the best use of white truffles is in a risotto. Risottos are creamy rice dishes, served in place of pasta as a first course. They can be topped with shellfish, meat, game, herbs, sausages, or cheese (there is a famous risotto made of four cheeses—parmesan, fontina, bel paese, and provolone). The principle behind a risotto is to get the rice creamy and tender by slowly swelling it with small additions of hot stock. Risottos must be carefully tended—you must keep the stock simmering as you cook the rice, stirring every so often to keep it from sticking, and being careful that it doesn't boil. At the moment the rice has absorbed some stock, you add a little more.

RISOTTO CON TARTUFI BIANCHI

Risotto with white truffles (Italy)

Ingredients

> 2 quarts chicken stock
> ½ cup unsalted butter

    1 small onion, finely chopped
  1¾ cups imported Italian Arborio rice
   ¼ cup grated parmesan cheese
    1 1-ounce tin natural white truffles, sliced

Equipment

    2 large saucepans

Working and cooking time: 40 minutes (approximately)

Serves: 6 to 8

1. Heat the chicken stock and keep at a low simmer.
2. In a second saucepan melt half the butter, add the onion and sauté until golden. Stir in the rice and sauté, stirring, until well coated. Then stir in 1 cup of hot stock and cook, stirring, until all the stock is absorbed before adding another cup of simmering stock. Do not let the rice become too dry, but cook until creamy and tender.
3. Just before serving stir in the grated cheese and remaining butter. Mix well. Correct the seasoning. Serve at once with the sliced truffles on top.

Yogurt

YOGURT is a Turkish word, and though it's eaten now all over the world, it probably comes from the Middle East. The Indians use it in great quantity, of course, and over the last several decades it has become hugely popular as a health food in Western Europe and the United States. I still think the Bulgarians make the best tasting yogurt in the world—I'd go a long way to find some Bulgarian yogurt culture to start a batch for myself at home.

In the Middle East yogurt is made with cow's milk, goat's milk, sheep's milk, or even the milk of a camel. Cow's milk seems best, though a Greek might argue on behalf of the quality of his sheep's-milk yogurt, called *proveio*.

The Turks have infinite uses for it, and most of the great Mediterranean yogurt dishes have origins in Turkish cuisine. Besides serving it plain, or mixed with fruit preserves, yogurt is marvelous as a cooking medium, a sauce thickener, a cooling agent, and a drink.

The Turks serve it often with their pilaf, made of cooked lamb, fried onions, raisins or currants, pine nuts, tomatoes, and garlic. They use it as a sauce on eggplant slices fried in batter or in a hot soup made with mint, garlic, onions, lamb, and rice. They mix it with sugar and then pour it on fresh fruits and berries, or concoct it in a dessert called *maourtini*—an orange-flavored cake in which the yogurt substitutes for milk, covered in turn with hot syrup and decorated with pistachios, strawberries, and whipped cream.

There are all sorts of stories about the origins of yogurt, most of them having to do with astonished Middle Eastern nomads who find the milk in their goatskins curdled to a delicious substance when they return to their tents at the end of a hot summer day. *Voilà!* Yogurt, the great health food, is born, and thus begins the great tradition of preserving fresh milk in a curdled state—a tradition that has brought us the glories of cheese.

Today most people buy their yogurt in the supermarket, or else make it themselves in a yogurt-making machine. The supermarket varieties cost too much, especially if you're a big yogurt eater like me. And as for the machines, they're quite all right, but the truth is that you can make yogurt yourself without any special equipment and for a fraction of the supermarket cost. The only thing you have to remember is to keep the yogurt culture alive. I've told my children many times: "Eat as much yogurt as you want, but *never* eat the last one in the fridge."

If they do it's no great tragedy. I simply buy another jar of commercial yogurt, or another packet of dry yogurt culture. Theoretically (though I don't advise it) it's *possible* to make a lifetime supply, 25,000 batches, a generation a day for 70 years, using the same culture you used the first time.

Here's how to make your own yogurt, the simplest, least expensive way, and on the following pages I've put together a group of recipes in which yogurt is the prime ingredient and the key. Some are very simple, like *Labni,* the fresh Lebanese cheese, or *tarator,* a delicious Yugoslav yogurt and cucumber soup. Others are more complicated like *shish barak bi laban* a fine Lebanese dish of lamb dumplings and *kibbe* in a tasty yogurt sauce. And another, *laban oummo,* a modern-day version of the classic, legendary "baby lamb cooked in its mother's milk."

YOGURT
Homemade Yogurt

Ingredients

1 quart milk, whole or skimmed
¼ cup commercial yogurt

Equipment

Heavy saucepan · Large bowl · Towels
or heavy flannel cloth

Cooking time: 5 minutes

Jelling time: 6 hours (approximately)

Makes: 4 cups

1. Simmer the milk for five minutes, stirring often. Cool to about 110 degrees or until a few drops of milk on the inside of the wrist feel warm. Stir the yogurt into the milk then pour into a large bowl. Cover and wrap in towels. This helps the culture to ferment the milk. Place in the warmest part of the kitchen. Do not disturb for 6 hours.

2. Uncover the bowl. Cover the bowl with cellophane wrap and set in the refrigerator to chill completely. The yogurt will keep fresh for a few days.

3. To make more yogurt use some of your homemade yogurt as a starter.

LABNI

Fresh cheese made from yogurt (Lebanon)

Ingredients

2 cups yogurt
½ teaspoon salt

Equipment

Muslin sack or several layers of cheesecloth made into a bag ·
Large bowl

Working time: 5 minutes

Dripping time: 24 hours

Makes: ½ cup

Combine yogurt and salt. Pour into a muslin sack, tie up, and
suspend over a large bowl. Let drain overnight. The bowl will
catch the dripping liquid. In the morning discard the water. Un-
wrap the cheese and use as a spread on *pita* or form into small
balls and serve with olive oil and chopped fresh mint or with
black olives.

MAHAMMARA LABNI

Fresh cheese with dill and pimento (Lebanon)

Ingredients

½ cup *labni* (see recipe above)
    Salt and freshly ground black pepper
1 tablespoon chopped fresh dill
1 roasted pimento, chopped
    Sweet paprika
8 melba toasts

Equipment

   Mixing bowl

Working time: 5 minutes

   Combine *libni*, salt, pepper, dill and pimento, mixing well,
Spread on melba toast and sprinkle with paprika. Serve with
cocktails.

YOGURT ÇORBASI

Yogurt soup (Turkey)

Ingredients

   ¼ cup raw rice
   5 cups rich chicken or beef stock
   1 tablespoon cornstarch
   2 cups unflavored yogurt
   2 egg yolks, beaten
   2 tablespoons chopped fresh mint
 1–2 tablespoons butter

Equipment

   2 saucepans · Whisk

Working time: 5 minutes

Cooking time: 25 minutes

Serves: 4 to 6

   1. Cook the rice in the stock 20 minutes.
   2. In a second saucepan make a smooth paste with the cornstarch and a little yogurt. Add the remaining yogurt and beat
until smooth. Add the egg yolks and a few spoonsful hot stock.
Set over low heat and bring to the boil, stirring constantly.

3. Pour the yogurt mixture into the simmering stock and continue to cook, stirring, 2 minutes. If the soup is too thick thin with a little water. Just before serving sprinkle with chopped mint and dribble over some melted butter.

TARATOR

Yogurt and cucumber soup (Yugoslavia)

The combination of yogurt and cucumbers is popular through all the Middle East. In Turkey they make a soup, *cacik*, without the walnuts and mint but with a good sprinkling of chopped fresh dill. In Greek *tavernas* you will be served *tzatziki*, a thick cucumber and yogurt dip.

In Yugoslavia I've eaten an excellent variation on *tarator*— the soup was spiked with raw chopped hot green pepper instead of chopped mint.

Ingredients

    ½ cup walnut halves
    3 large cloves garlic, peeled
    2 tablespoons olive oil
    4 cups unflavored yogurt
    2 firm cucumbers, peeled and seeded
      Salt and freshly ground black pepper
      Chopped mint

Equipment

Mortar and pestle · Mixing bowl · Grater (optional)

Working time: 5 to 10 minutes

Serves: 4

In a mortar pound the walnuts with the garlic until pasty; then start adding the oil, drop by drop, stirring constantly. Dump the yogurt into a large mixing bowl and beat until liquid. Beat in the walnut-garlic paste. Dice or grate the cucumbers; drain, then fold into the yogurt soup. Season with salt and pepper. Chill well. Garnish with chopped mint if desired.

FISTUQUIA

Green beans with yogurt and taklia (Middle East)

Ingredients

 2¾–3 cups (approximately ¾ pound) Italian green beans, cut into 1-inch lengths, or 2 packages frozen Italian-style green beans
  Salt
 1 tablespoon cornstarch
 1 egg
 1½ cups unflavored yogurt, beaten until thin and smooth
 1 cup cooked rice

Taklia

 1 teaspoon finely chopped garlic
 1 tablespoon oil
 1½ tablespoons chopped fresh mint leaves or fresh coriander

Equipment

 2 saucepans · Small skillet

Working time: 10 minutes

Cooking time: 20 minutes

Serves: 4 to 6

 1. Cook the beans in boiling salted water 15 minutes or until tender; drain and keep hot.
 2. Meanwhile in another saucepan using a wooden spoon beat the cornstarch and the egg into the yogurt. Set over medium

heat, bring to the boil and cook, stirring constantly, until thick and creamy. Add salt to taste.

3. Fold in the rice and the hot beans.

4. To make the *taklia*, fry the garlic in oil 1 minute; add ¾ tablespoon mint, fry, stirring 30 seconds, and pour over the yogurt. Simmer gently, stirring, 2 to 3 minutes to blend flavors. Turn out onto a serving dish, sprinkle with remaining chopped mint. Serve lukewarm or cool.

ÇILBIR

Poached eggs with yogurt (Turkey)

I think this is a fascinating way to serve poached eggs, unusual and delicious, particularly good as a light supper late at night.

Ingredients

    1 cup unflavored yogurt
    1 small clove garlic, chopped
      Salt
    4 large eggs
    1 tablespoon vinegar
      Freshly ground black pepper
    2 tablespoons unsalted butter
    1 teaspoon sharp paprika

Equipment

    4 ovenproof ramekins · Wide saucepan · Small saucepan

Working time: 5 minutes

Cooking time: 5 minutes

Serves: 2 or 4

1. Heat the oven to 300 degrees.

2. Combine yogurt, garlic, and salt. Put equal amounts in each ramekin and set them in oven to heat up gently.

3. Meanwhile poach the eggs in acidulated water. Drain and set 1 egg in each ramekin. Sprinkle with salt and pepper to taste. Keep hot in the oven.

4. Quickly melt the butter in the small pan. Stir in the paprika to make the butter a bright red color. Dribble the butter over each egg, leaving the paprika powder behind in the saucepan. Serve at once.

V A R I A T I O N

Substitute fried chopped onions for the garlic.

S H I S H   B A R A K   B I   L A B A N

Lamb dumplings and kibbe in yogurt sauce (Lebanon)

Ingredients

Dumplings (see note)
2 cups all-purpose flour, sifted
1 teaspoon salt
1 tablespoon clarified butter or oil
⅔ cup warm water (approximately)
10 ounces ground lamb or beef
½ cup finely chopped onion
½ teaspoon Lebanese spice mixture:
    2 good pinches cayenne, 2 good pinches ground
    cinnamon, and 1 good pinch grated nutmeg
2 tablespoons butter
¼ cup pine nuts

Kibbe

1 pound boned lamb cut from the leg, ground twice
1 medium onion, finely chopped
Salt and freshly ground black pepper
1 cup fine burghul
2 ice cubes

Continued

Yogurt sauce

   2 quarts (double recipe) homemade yogurt (see page 211)
   1 tablespoon cornstarch
   1 egg

Taklia

   2 teaspoons finely chopped garlic
   2 tablespoons butter, melted
   3 tablespoons finely chopped fresh coriander or mint

Equipment

   2 baking trays · Rolling pin · Skillet ·
   5-quart enameled casserole · Whisk ·
   Electric beater on stand with dough hook attachment
   (optional) · Meat grinder

Working time: 2 hours

Cooking time: 30 minutes

Serves: 6

1. First make 36 dumplings: Mix the flour with the salt on a flat workspace and make a well in the center. Slowly work in the melted clarified butter or oil and enough warm water to make a soft ball of dough. Add more water if necessary. Knead the dough until it forms a smooth ball. Allow to rest 30 minutes under an inverted bowl.

2. Meanwhile prepare the stuffing: Brown the meat with the onions and spices in butter. Season with salt. Use a fork to break up the lumps of meat. Stir in the pine nuts and toss with the meat over high heat until lightly toasted. Allow to cool.

3. Knead the dough again until very elastic. Separate into 4 parts and roll each into ⅛-inch-thick sheets. Cut into 2-inch squares. Place 1 teaspoon stuffing in the center of each square, fold to form a triangle and press the edges to adhere firmly. Set aside to dry 1 hour.

4. Make the kibbe: Grind the ground lamb with the onions and season with salt and pepper. Wet the burghul with water, drain, and squeeze out all the moisture. Mix into the meat and knead well. Traditionally the kibbe is pounded in a mortar until smooth. I use an electric beater with a dough hook attachment. Knead the kibbe 10 minutes at medium speed. During the final part of the kneading, add 1 or 2 ice cubes. After the kibbe has been thoroughly kneaded form into 18 walnut-size balls. Set aside in a cool place.

5. Make the sauce: In the large casserole using a wooden spoon beat the 8 cups yogurt until thin and smooth. Dilute the cornstarch in a little cold water. Whisk the cornstarch and the egg into the yogurt. Slowly bring to the boil, stirring constantly.

6. Drop the dumplings and the kibbe into the yogurt (there is enough room!) and allow to cook at the simmer 20 to 25 minutes. Season with salt and pepper.

7. Meanwhile make the *taklia*: sauté the garlic and the coriander or mint in melted butter for 1 minute. Stir into the yogurt mixture just before serving. Serve in a large deep serving dish with rice pilaf as an accompaniment. This dish can be served hot, tepid, or cold.

Note: You may substitute 1½ 12-ounce packages of frozen ravioli for the homemade dumplings.

Raw kibbe is delicious mixed with chopped fresh mint and oil as a sandwich filling.

BOSANSKE CUFTE

Bosnian meatballs with yogurt (Yugoslavia)

This is a recipe that has its origins in Turkey. It is similar to a Turkish dish called *kadin budu* (fried meat balls with caraway seasoning)—not surprising since there are many Moslems living in Bosnia, and Turkey has long been an influence.

Ingredients

>   1 pound ground beef
>   1 onion, chopped
>   4 eggs
>   ½ cup dry breadcrumbs
>   Salt and freshly ground black pepper
>   Flour
>   3 tablespoons butter
>   1½ cups yogurt, beaten until smooth
>   1½ tablespoons caraway seeds, finely ground
>   in an electric blender

Equipment

Skillet · 12-inch buttered baking dish · Mixing bowl

Working time: 10 minutes

Cooking time: 1 hour

Serves: 4

1. Preheat the oven to 350 degrees.

2. Combine the beef, onion, 1 lightly beaten egg, breadcrumbs, and salt and pepper. Blend thoroughly and shape into 12 small balls. Roll in flour and brown in butter. Drain then place in the prepared baking dish. Set in the oven to bake 30 minutes.

3. Thoroughly beat the 3 remaining eggs and slowly stir the yogurt into them. Add the caraway seeds. Season with salt and pepper. Pour over the meatballs and continue to bake until the egg-yogurt mixture is set.

MOUSSAKA

Baked meat and eggplant casserole with yogurt sauce (Greece)

Impossible to write a Mediterranean cookbook without including a recipe for Greek moussaka. The yogurt sauce, from Sarah Scoville, is in my opinion the best way to make the dish.

Be sure not to confuse Greek moussaka with the Arab dish called *musakkáa*. The latter is simply a stew of eggplants, tomatoes, and chick-peas.

Ingredients

> 2 pounds eggplant
> Salt
> 1–1½ pounds ground beef
> 5 tablespoons butter
> 1 onion, grated and drained
> ½ cup tomato puree or 3 red ripe tomatoes, peeled, seeded, and chopped
> 2–3 tablespoons chopped parsley
> 1 teaspoon chopped garlic
> Freshly ground black pepper
> 2 pinches of ground cinnamon
> Oil for frying
> 3 eggs
> 2 cups unflavored yogurt, beaten until smooth
> About ¾ cup grated cheese such as kefalotiri or parmesan or gruyère
> Grated nutmeg

Equipment

> Colander · Large skillet · Slotted spoon · Saucepan · 10-by-14-by-2-inch baking dish, buttered

Working time: 30 minutes

Cooking time: ¾ hour

Serves: 6 to 8

1. Peel the eggplants and cut into ½-inch rounds. Salt them and leave to drain in the colander 30 minutes.

2. Brown the meat in 4 tablespoons butter with the onion. Add the tomato puree, parsley, garlic, salt and pepper to taste, and the cinnamon. Simmer gently until all the liquid evaporates. Allow to cool.

3. Rinse the eggplant slices, squeeze gently, and pat dry with paper towels. Heat the oil in a skillet and fry the eggplant slices until brown on both sides. Drain and set aside.

4. Thoroughly beat the 3 eggs. Slowly stir in the yogurt. Mix in the cheese. Season with salt, pepper, and grated nutmeg.

5. Preheat the oven to 375 degrees.

6. Arrange half the eggplant slices in 1 layer on the bottom of a buttered oven dish. Cover with a layer of cooked meat and a final layer of eggplant. Pour the sauce over the top and dot with butter. Set in the oven to bake ¾ hour until the top is swollen and golden brown.

LABAN OUMMO

Lamb cooked in its mother's milk (Lebanon)

This is one of those legendary Middle Eastern dishes, comparable in a way to the famous delicacy "squid cooked in its own ink." T. E. Lawrence mentions eating it in Arabia, and there are variations in other countries, too. Among the most interesting, a dish called *caldariello*, which Waverly Root found in the Apulia region of Italy. There cut up lamb is cooked in a fat-bellied cauldron (hence the name *caldariello*) along with olive oil, onion, parsley, wild fennel, and sheep's milk.

Years ago in southern Yugoslavia I tasted a dish which I've never found in any book. An infant lamb was cooked in sheep's milk, and served with raw green onions on the side. It was rather good.

I think *laban oummo* is much tastier. Probably because yogurt replaces the classic "mother sheep's milk."

Ingredients

        2 pounds boned leg of lamb, cut into 1-inch pieces
        1 cup chopped onions
           Salt and freshly ground white pepper
        1 tablespoon cornstarch
        1 egg
     1½ cups unflavored yogurt
        1 tablespoon butter
           Taklia: 2 cloves garlic, crushed to a paste with a little
              salt and 1 tablespoon fresh mint, chopped or substitute
              1½ teaspoon crumbled dried mint leaves

Equipment

     Whisk · 4-quart heavy casserole with cover ·
     1½-quart heavy bottomed saucepan · Skillet

Working time: 10 minutes

Cooking time: 1½ hours

Serves: 4 to 6

1. Place the lamb and the onion in a heavy casserole. Add ½ cup water, 1 teaspoon salt and ¼ teaspoon pepper and cook, covered, for about 1 hour, or until the meat is very tender.

2. In a saucepan, whisk the cornstarch and the egg into a little yogurt, beating until smooth. Stir in the remaining yogurt. Bring to the boil over medium heat, stirring constantly. Lower the heat and continue to cook, stirring, until the yogurt is thick and creamy. Fold in the meat, onion, and cooking juices. Continue to cook for a few minutes to blend flavors.

3. Make the *taklia:* Heat 1 tablespoon butter in a skillet and in it sauté the garlic and the mint for 1 minute. Stir into the yogurt mixture. Readjust the seasoning and serve very hot with rice pilaf.

Cheese

THE proverbial Mediterranean picnic (for which all of us urban Americans forever long) takes place beneath an olive tree overlooking some wondrous unspoiled lagoon, and consists of a fullbodied "honest peasant" wine, a crusty "honest peasant" loaf of bread and, of course, a tangy hard or pungent creamy "honest peasant" cheese. It's a beautiful image that evokes our nostalgia for the sensuous life most of us crave. And sometimes, if we're lucky, on a vacation, or bumming around Europe when we're young, we actually bring it to life. It's a great cliché, and like all clichés it holds a lot of truth. That picnic, so elegant in its simplicity, is much in the style of Mediterranean life.

Honest peasant wine and honest peasant bread are easy to come by on Mediterranean shores. But to tourists cheese is often a problem. Aside from the famous Italian varieties—gorgonzola, bel paese, provolone, fresh mozzarella, pecorino sardo and the great and glorious parmesan—the Mediterranean is not famous for its cheese. The great French brands, the bries and roqueforts, the English stiltons, and cheshires, the Dutch edams and goudas and the Swiss gruyères and appenzellers are produced far away. Still the Mediterranean does have its cheeses, many of them fine indeed. And I think it might be well to take a *tour d'horizon* and look at them one by one.

The Mediterranean countries produce a wide range of soft fresh cheese. In North Africa you'll often see a country-made goat's cheese, moist and formed into a cake resting on palm leaves in a basket. When you buy it you must specify whether you want it strong or mild. It's very good with olives, or stuffed into pastry leaves and fried, and in Tunisia, where they call it *gouta*, it's actually cooked in meat stews or tagines (see *tagine bil gouta*, page 240).

The Italians make ricotta which is not unlike our own fresh white cheeses in texture, though with a taste all its own. (It's difficult to make substitutions for it, unless the other ingredients in the recipe have strong flavors.) The Italians eat ricotta fresh on bread for breakfast, and use it to stuff ravioli or in dishes like *gnocchi di spinaci* (see recipe, page 242). Mascarpone is like our cream cheese mixed with sour cream, and is sold in Italy in little muslin bags. It's delicious mixed with strawberries and raspberries or scooped on top of other fresh fruits.

The Corsican broccio is much like ricotta except a bit more salty. Elizabeth David suggests it be beaten up with eggs, a little chopped wild mint, and made into a flat, round, oil-fried omelet. The Corsicans mix it with raisins and use as a stuffing for guinea hen, or mix it with herbs as a stuffing for floured fried artichoke bottoms.

Looking around the Mediterranean at other soft fresh cheeses we musn't forget the Greek mezithra, or the yogurt-based cheeses of the Middle East (see *labni*, page 212). In Yugoslavia and Turkey the soft fresh cheese is kajmak. When it's young and white its flavor is mild but as it ages it turns pungent and it becomes the color of straw. For the Yugoslav breakfast specialty *gibanica* (see recipe, page 228), I've worked up a substitute for aged kajmak combining feta and American white cheese.

In both Malta and Sardinia the country people make a similar tasting soft fresh goat cheese, for which they each have their respective uses. In Sardinia they make an Easter peasant dish called *pardulas* in which the cheese is stuffed into pastry along with sugar, lemon, eggs, and saffron, then baked and served up hot covered with country heather honey. The Maltese, on the other hand, use their fresh goat's cheese in their so-called Widow's Soup, with eggs, herbs, vegetables, and broth.

Of the firmer fresh Mediterranean cheeses the buffalo-milk based mozzarella is probably the most famous. An excellent American imitation is now available, sold by Italian grocers directly from the keg. Mozzarella, when very fresh, is delicious uncooked. Try a salad of fresh mozzarella, sliced tomatoes, and fresh basil (see *coccarda*, page 94).

In terms of fame Greek feta runs a close second to mozzarella. This white semisoft crumbly salty goat's milk cheese is much used in cooking and is excellent in salads or with olives. It's imported from Greece in tubs and kept moist in milk whey; try not to buy it dry.

I have three Greek recipes that call for feta (*stifado, garidhes à la murkolimano,* and *tiropitakia*), and since it is so readily available in the U.S. I suggest it as a substitute in many recipes for other more exotic semisoft cheeses. It can be used with herbs as a stuffing for roast pig, or as a thickening agent as in the Greek vegetable stew *giovetsi*. There are numerous ways to use it in salads—I particularly recall one, served on the island of Mykonos, which included anchovies, Kalamata olives, tomatoes, and grilled green peppers.

The Egyptian cow's milk cheese, domiati, is also preserved in salt milk whey brine, as is the Turkish tulim made from the milk of sheep. Tulim, though, is not sold from the tub, but from small sheepskin bags. The Spanish manchego (which I heartily recommend when well aged) is firmer than these others and can be sliced.

All the cheeses we've looked at so far fall into the fresh or perishable category. The Mediterranean has its share of fine ripened cheeses, too. The soft French banon is justifiably well known. It's made from goat's milk, cured in brandy, and ripened in grape or chestnut leaves.

In Italy the semisoft ripened bel paese is smooth and mild, and delightful to eat with fruit. The Cypriot haloumi gets better and better as it ages, and can be put to good use with mint as a stuffing for ravioli.

Of the firm ripe Italian cheeses the sausage-shaped provolone is the best known, and can be purchased either mild or sharp. But don't forget about the round caciocavallo. Both are soft and smooth when they're young, and both can be steamed and eaten hot. Greek kasseri is rather similar in flavor and grain, and can be fried because of its high melting point.

This brings us finally to the king of Mediterranean cheeses, the unsurpassable parmesan. There are lots of imitations, and though some of them are passable it's best to shop for the real thing. Look for the words *parmigiano reggiano* on the rind, and check for the traditional straw color and moist feeling of the grain. Don't grate parmesan until you're ready to use it.

When parmesan is young it is soft and has a wonderful nutty flavor. As it ages it becomes very hard, and then it's ready for grating. True parmesan never becomes stringy when it's cooked, which is one reason it turns up in so many recipes.

Pecorino romano and pecorino sardo are two other Italian hard-ripened cheeses. Romano is sharper than parmesan, and more aggressive, while sardo is even more pungent. In Nuoro, the capital town of Sardinia, there's a special sort of dry crumbly bread as thin as a communion wafer, called *o pan carasau*. It's dipped into warm water, then served with a sauce of eggs and grated sardo cheese. An extraordinary dish, I think, which is called *pillonca*.

Finally on the Mediterranean there is a so-called mold cheese—the blue-green veined gorgonzola. It's used in the delicious *gnocchi di spinaci*.

In this brief summary I've not been able to mention all the Mediterranean cheeses, but I hope I've given some notion of their great variety and usefulness in cookery. Although aside from the Italian cheeses only the Greek feta and the French banon bear great names, there's no question that the "honest peasant" cheese is alive and well on Mediterranean shores.

GIBANICA

Cheese pie (Yugoslavia)

This is a good hearty breakfast dish, but I definitely recommend that you eat it with buttermilk, yogurt, or a glass of plum brandy. Otherwise you may find it too heavy.

Traditionally it's made with kajmak—a cheese made in

Yugoslav homes. I've worked out a good substitute: a combination of half crumbled feta and half cottage cheese.

Gibanica is very close to the Turkish *borek* and the Greek *tiropitakia* (see following recipe). The main difference is in the filling: the Greeks add dill, marjoram, or parsley. Also, the Greeks usually dispense with the Yugoslav béchamel approach, and bind their filling with eggs and cream.

In the southern part of Yugoslavia they make a variation on *gibanica*, adding fried leeks to the pie filling.

Ingredients

      8 ounces (1 cup) pot, farmer, cottage, or cream cheese
      8 ounces (1 cup) crumbled feta cheese
      2 tablespoons butter
      3 tablespoons flour
      2 cups hot milk
      Pinch of grated nutmeg
      Freshly ground white pepper
      2 eggs
      1 pound phyllo leaves
      ½ cup melted butter or a mixture of oil and butter
      2 quarts buttermilk, well chilled

Equipment

    Food mill · Saucepan · Whisk · Mixing bowl ·
    Pastry brush · 11-by-10-by-2-inch baking dish, buttered

Working time: 15 minutes

Baking time: 45 minutes

Serves: 10 to 12

1. Push the cheeses through a food mill. Melt the butter in a saucepan. Add the flour and cook, stirring, 2 minutes without browning. Off heat whisk in the hot milk. Bring to the boil, stirring, and cook until thick and smooth. Remove from the heat.

Add the strained cheeses, nutmeg, and pepper, mixing well to combine. Gradually beat in the eggs. The mixture should be thick and creamy. Readjust seasoning.

2. Preheat the oven to 350 degrees.

3. Line the baking dish with half the phyllo and brush each evenly with a little melted butter. Spread ⅓ the cheese filling over the surface of the pastry. Top with 3 buttered pastry leaves. Repeat twice ending with a covering of buttered phyllo. Pour over any remaining melted butter. Bake for about 45 minutes or until golden brown.

4. Cut into 2-inch squares just before serving. Serve warm with glasses of chilled buttermilk.

Note: Equal quantities of unflavored yogurt and cold water beaten until creamy and smooth and seasoned with salt may be substituted for the buttermilk.

TIROPITAKIA

Cheese triangles with dill or fresh marjoram (Greece)

Ingredients

    8 ounces feta cheese, crumbled
        and pushed through a food mill
    ¾ cup creamed cottage cheese
    2 eggs
    1 egg yolk
    3 tablespoons finely chopped dill or fresh marjoram
      Freshly ground black pepper
    ½ pound phyllo pastry (about 12 sheets)
    ½ cup melted butter

Equipment

    Mixing bowl · Pastry brush · 2 greased baking sheets ·
    Damp towel

Working time: 45 minutes

Baking time: 25 minutes

Makes: 36 triangles (approximately)

1. In a mixing bowl combine the cheeses, mixing well. Add the eggs and the egg yolk and blend in completely. Mix in the dill and season lightly with ground black pepper.

2. Spread a phyllo leaf in front of you, keeping the other leaves under a damp towel. Cut vertically into 3 equal parts. Brush the surface with melted butter. Fold each phyllo leaf in 3 lengthwise. Place approximately 1 tablespoon filling on each piece, 1 inch from the bottom. Fold the left hand corner over the filling so as to make a triangle. Fold the triangle straight up, then fold upward to the left and continue folding as you would a flag until you reach the end and have a neat triangle. Tuck in any loose ends and brush with butter. Keep covered in the refrigerator until you are ready to bake.

3. Preheat the oven to 400 degrees. Bake the triangles until golden, turning once. Serve hot or warm.

MOZZARELLA IN CARROZZA

Cheese sandwiches (Italy)

This is a delicious Italian snack, the Roman version of a *croque monsieur.* Mozzarella is familiar to all pizza lovers as a soft white buffalo milk cheese.

Here it is firm and holds its shape sandwiched between bread slices and fried.

Another Roman specialty, popular in the old section of the city, is *crostini di mozzarella alla Romana.* Slices of mozzarella cheese are placed over sliced Italian bread then heated in the oven. A spoonful of anchovy paste is spread on top and the *crostini* are returned to the oven to bake for a couple of minutes.

Ingredients

    8 thin slices of crustless stale white bread
          each 3 inches square
  ⅔ cup milk
    4 ounces mozzarella cheese: 4 slices 2½ by 2½ by ¼ inches
    1 large egg, beaten
       Salt and freshly ground black pepper
       Breadcrumbs
       Oil
       Lemon wedges

Equipment

    Shallow bowls · Skillet and spatula

Working time: 10 minutes

Frying time: 4 minutes for each sandwich

Serves: 4

1. Dip the bread slices in milk and let drain on a wide plate.
2. Sandwich each slice of cheese between 2 bread slices, pressing down firmly around the edges so that they adhere.
3. Season the eggs with salt and pepper. Dip the sandwiches in eggs, and coat them with breadcrumbs.
4. Heat enough oil to the depth of ½ inch in the skillet and fry the sandwiches until golden on both sides. Drain on paper towels and serve hot with lemon wedges.

Note: Slices of prosciutto can be added to the sandwiches.

SALATIT MICHOTETA

Cheese salad (Middle East)

Claudia Rodin describes a similar recipe in her fine book on Middle Eastern food. She recommends that it be served with *ful medames*—an Egyptian brown bean dish.*

Ingredients

>   1 small cucumber
>   ½ cup (4 ounces) small-curd cottage cheese or ricotta
>   ½ cup (4 ounces) crumbled feta cheese
>   ¼ cup grated and drained onion
>   1 tablespoon minced green pepper
>   ¼ cup lemon juice
>   ¼ cup olive oil
>   Salt and freshly ground black pepper
>   Sprigs of fresh mint

Equipment

Grater   ·   Small shallow serving dish

Working time: 10 minutes

Makes: 1½ cups, serves 4

1. Peel the cucumber, halve lengthwise, score with tines of a fork, sprinkle with salt, and let stand ½ hour.
2. Combine the cheeses with the grated onion, green pepper, lemon juice, and oil; mix thoroughly. Season with pepper and a little salt. Drain, rinse, and cut the cucumber into small cubes. Mix into the cheese mixture. Place in a shallow serving dish and decorate with a ring of mint sprigs. Let stand in a cool place 30 minutes before serving.

* Available in cans from Middle Eastern shops.

GARIDHES A LA TURKOLIMANO

*Shrimp in tomato sauce with feta cheese
in the style of Turkolimano (Greece)*

Turkolimano is an area about 20 minutes out of Athens where one is inevitably taken to eat fresh fish. There's a street along the harbor filled with seafood restaurants, some of them rather touristy, others extremely chic. (Of course they all look the same—fashionability depends on where the countesses and film stars choose to dine.) They make a big production at these places of letting you choose your own fish, but no matter what you order you receive *garidhes*, too. With good reason—the dish is superb.

Ingredients

½ cup chopped onion
3 tablespoons olive oil
1 clove garlic, chopped
2 cups fresh or canned tomato sauce or a mixture of
     fresh tomato sauce, tomato paste, and water
¼ cup dry white wine
¼ cup chopped parsley
Salt and freshly ground black pepper
Pinch of cayenne
1½–2 pounds raw shrimp (about 50)
1 cup crumbled feta cheese

Equipment

Large enameled skillet · Shallow baking dish preferably enameled or earthenware

Working time: 20 minutes

Cooking time: 35 minutes

Serves: 4

1. Preheat the oven to 450 degrees.

2. In a skillet cook the onions in olive oil until soft and golden. Add the garlic, tomato sauce, wine, half the parsley, salt, pepper, and cayenne. Cook at the simmer, uncovered, 15 minutes, stirring often. The tomato sauce should be rather thick.

3. Meanwhile peel and devein the shrimp. Add to the sauce and cook 5 minutes. Place the cheese in the baking dish, cover with the shrimp and tomato sauce, set in the oven to bake 10 minutes. Sprinkle with remaining parsley and serve very hot.

LA GALLINA DEL GHIOTTONI

"Box" chicken or chicken with cheese sauce (Italy)

This is an interesting dish from northern Italy in which a poached chicken is stuffed with pasta and cheese sauce. More cheese sauce is then poured on top and the "box" is baked in the oven.

Ingredients

    1 3½–4-pound chicken, ready to cook
    1 sliced onion
    1 chopped carrot
    1 celery rib
      Bouquet garni: parsley sprigs, bay leaf,
        and thyme, tied together
      Salt and freshly ground black pepper
    3 tablespoons butter
    3 tablespoons flour
    2 cups boiling milk
    1 cup grated gruyère cheese
      Pinch of grated nutmeg
  1½ cups ziti

Equipment

Soup pot with cover · Assorted saucepans · Colander · Whisk · Buttered baking/serving dish

Working time: 25 minutes

Cooking time: 1 hour

Serves: 4

1. Place the chicken in the soup pot and add boiling water to cover, onion, carrot, celery, bouquet garni, and salt and pepper. Bring to a boil and cook, covered, at the simmer for 45 minutes or until the chicken is just tender.

2. Melt the butter in a saucepan, stir in the flour, and cook, stirring, over gentle heat 2 minutes. Off heat add the boiling milk, beating briskly with a whisk until smooth. Cook, stirring, 5 minutes. The sauce will be thin, do not worry. Stir in ½ cup grated cheese and season with salt, pepper, and nutmeg. Divide the sauce in half and set both aside.

3. Cook the *ziti* in boiling salted water until al dente, or just tender. Drain, rinse under cold running water, and drain again. Fold the *ziti* into half the cheese sauce.

4. Preheat the oven to 425 degrees.

5. Remove the chicken. Use the cooking liquid for some other purpose. When the chicken is cool enough to handle, lift off the breasts, each in one piece. Discard the breast bones. Place the chicken on its back in the buttered baking dish. Stuff with *ziti* and cover with the breast meat. Fold the remaining cheese into the remaining sauce. Correct the seasoning. Coat the chicken completely with the sauce and set in the hot oven to brown for 15 to 20 minutes. Serve hot.

POULET AU FROMAGE

Chicken with cream cheese and tarragon (France)

Ingredients

- 1 3-pound chicken, ready to roast plus the liver
- 4 tablespoons unsalted butter
- ¼ pound cream cheese
  Salt and freshly ground black pepper
- 3 sprigs fresh tarragon, chopped
- 2–3 tablespoons heavy cream
- 1 tablespoon chopped parsley

Equipment

Flameproof roasting pan

Working time: 10 minutes

Roasting time: 1 hour

Serves: 4 to 5

1. Preheat the oven to 350 degrees.
2. Chop the chicken liver. Mash it with 2 tablespoons butter and the cheese, season with salt and pepper and mix well to make a paste. Blend in half the chopped tarragon. This is the stuffing.
3. Rub the outside of the chicken with salt and pepper and the remaining 2 tablespoons butter. Stuff the chicken, truss, and set in the oven to roast 1 hour, turning often and basting with the pan juices.
4. Remove the chicken to a carving board. Discard the fat. Scrape out the stuffing and add it to the pan juices. Boil down and scrape up the bits and pieces in the pan using a wooden spoon or whisk. Add the cream, parsley, and the remaining tarragon. Cook, stirring, for 1 more minute. Correct the seasoning. Carve the chicken, pour the sauce over, and serve hot.

SFIRYA

Chicken tagine with potato-cheese croquettes (Algeria)

This is an Algerian family dish, an unusual approach to a typical North African *tagine*. In Morocco *tagines* or stews are often decorated with hard-boiled eggs, while in Tunisia they are spread with a blanket of cheese and beaten eggs. In a *sfirya* the cheese and eggs are bound together with potatoes to make embellishing croquettes.

Ingredients

1 3½-pound chicken, cut up
2 tablespoons clarified butter or *smen* (see page 201)
2 onions, grated and drained
½ teaspoon ground cinnamon
¼ teaspoon cayenne
1 clove garlic, peeled and chopped
1 can cooked chick-peas, drained and rinsed
1 cup water
Salt and freshly ground black pepper

Croquettes

2 pounds potatoes, peeled and quartered
Salt
2 eggs
⅔ cup grated gruyère cheese
¼ cup grated onion
2 tablespoons chopped parsley
Pinch of grated nutmeg
Freshly ground black pepper
Flour for dredging
Oil for frying

Equipment

4-quart heavy casserole with tight-fitting cover · Saucepan · Potato ricer or food mill · Skillet · Slotted spoon

Working time: 30 minutes

Cooking time: 1 hour

Serves: 6

1. In the casserole, sauté the chicken pieces in hot butter or *smen* until golden brown on all sides. Add the onion, spices, and garlic. Cook, covered, 5 minutes. Add the chick-peas and the water. Season with salt and a little black pepper. Bring to the boil and cook at the simmer, covered, 1 hour.

2. Meanwhile cook the potatoes in boiling salted water until tender. Drain, push through a ricer, and allow to cool. Combine with eggs, cheese, onion, parsley, nutmeg, salt, and black pepper. Form into 2-inch rounds, dust with flour, and fry in 4 to 5 tablespoons hot oil until golden brown.

3. Arrange the chicken in a deep bowl. Readjust the seasoning of the sauce and pour over the chicken. Surround with the hot cheese croquettes and serve at once.

STIFADO

Beef stew with onions and cheese (Greece)

Ingredients

> 3 pounds top round of beef, cut into 1½-inch cubes
> Salt and freshly ground black pepper
> 3 cloves garlic, peeled and chopped
> 1 bay leaf, crumbled
> 2-inch cinnamon stick
> 3 tablespoons red wine vinegar
> ½ cup red wine
> 24 small white onions
> 3 tablespoons butter
> 1 cup fresh or canned tomato sauce
> ½ teaspoon sugar
> 1 cup crumbled feta cheese

Equipment

> 4-quart earthenware, stainless steel, or enameled iron
> casserole with tight-fitting cover

Working time: 20 minutes

Cooking time: 2½ to 3 hours

Serves: 5 to 6

1. Preheat the oven to 325 degrees.
2. In the casserole combine the meat, salt, pepper, garlic, bay leaf, and cinnamon. Cover tightly and cook over low heat 10 minutes.
3. Add the wine vinegar and the wine. Cover tightly and place in oven to bake 1½ hours.
4. Trim the onions and make a small cross at the root end of each one. Drop into boiling water. Drain after 2 minutes and peel. In a skillet briefly sauté the onions in butter until glazed.
5. Add the tomato sauce, sugar, and the onions to the casserole. Return to the oven to bake 1 hour longer or until the meat is tender.
6. Five minutes before serving stir in the crumbled cheese. Serve hot.

TAGINE BIL GOUTA

Lamb and cheese tagine *(Tunisia)*

In North Africa when a cook wants a glazed egg or onion surface on her *tagine* she places an unglazed earthen plate on top of the stew pot then piles on hot coals. The French too have a utensil, called a *douha*, with a special place for coals. But if you lack these things and need to obtain a glaze just leave the *tagine* for 10 to 15 minutes on the highest shelf of a very hot oven.

Ingredients

> 1 pound boneless lean lamb cut into 1-inch cubes
> Salt and freshly ground black pepper
> 2 tablespoons vegetable oil
> 1 cup chopped onion
> ½ teaspoon *tabil* (see page 202)
> 6 eggs
> 2 tablespoons grated parmesan cheese
> 3 tablespoons breadcrumbs
> Pinch of pulverized saffron
> 1 cup crumbled feta cheese

Equipment

> Small heavy casserole with cover   ·   Shallow 1-quart
> ovenproof serving dish   ·   Mixing bowl

Working time: 15 minutes

Cooking time: 1½ hours

Serves: 4

1. Season the lamb with salt and pepper. In the casserole brown the lamb in hot oil with the chopped onion. Add the *tabil* and enough water to cover. Bring to a boil. Simmer, covered, about 1 hour or until very tender. Transfer the lamb to ovenproof serving dish, cover and keep moist. By way of boiling, reduce the cooking juices to ½ cup. Cool the sauce. Spoon off 3 tablespoons fat and set aside.

2. Preheat the oven to 350 degrees.

3. Beat the eggs to a froth with the grated cheese and the breadcrumbs. Stir the cooled sauce into the eggs and season with pepper. Add the saffron. Pour the egg mixture over the lamb. Scatter the cheese on top. Cover the dish with foil and bake on the middle shelf of the oven for 15 minutes. Raise the heat to the highest setting, remove the foil cover, and dribble the reserved oily cooking juices over all. Bake on the upper shelf of the oven

for 10 minutes or until the eggs are completely set and the cheese has melted and browned slightly. Serve at once, cut into wedges.

Note: Be careful about salting this dish, the cheese is quite salty.

GNOCCHI DE SPINACI AL GORGONZOLA

Spinach and cheese dumplings with gorgonzola sauce
(Northern Italy)

These spinach dumplings are absolutely delicious and extremely easy to make. They're lighter than most *gnocchi* because they require so little flour, but this gives them a tendency to fall apart. An Italian friend told me it's wise to roll the *gnocchi* the day before, then chill them overnight. That way they remain firm when they hit the simmering water.

Ingredients

    3 10-ounce packages frozen spinach leaves, thawed
    1 pound fresh ricotta cheese
    2 egg yolks, beaten
    2 whole eggs, beaten
    ¼ teaspoon grated nutmeg
       Salt and freshly ground black pepper
    4 tablespoons grated parmesan cheese
  3–4 tablespoons flour
    2 ounces gorgonzola cheese
    1 cup heavy cream
       Bowl of grated parmesan cheese

Equipment

Enameled or stainless steel saucepan · Food mill ·
Large and small mixing bowl · Floured cloth
set on a tray · Wide saucepan · Slotted spoon

Working time: 25 minutes

Cooking time: 10 minutes

Serves: 6 to 8 as a first course

1. Cook the spinach 3 to 4 minutes in the saucepan; drain well. Chop the spinach very fine. Push the ricotta cheese through the finest blade of a food mill into a large mixing bowl; pour off any liquid. Add the spinach, eggs, nutmeg, salt, pepper, and grated cheese; mixing thoroughly. Add enough flour to make the mixture hold together.

2. With well-floured hands shape the mixture into balls the size of large cherries. Place on a floured cloth and keep cold until ready to cook. Can be prepared one day in advance to this point.

3. To make the sauce: In a small mixing bowl set over a pan of simmering water melt the cheese. Stir in the cream. Keep hot.

4. Drop a dozen *gnocchi* at a time into a wide pan filled with boiling salted water. Cook 1 to 2 minutes or until they rise to the surface. Remove with a slotted spoon, drain well, and place in a buttered hot serving dish. Cover and keep warm until all the *gnocchi* are cooked. Spoon the sauce over the *gnocchi* and serve at once. Pass a bowl of grated parmesan cheese.

TORTA DI CAVOLO

Cabbage, cheese, and sausage pie (Italy)

Torta di cavolo is just one of many types of Genoese *tortas*, of which the most famous is the Easter pie, *torta Pasqualina*, stuffed with artichoke hearts, eggs, and ricotta cheese. There are *tortas* made with pumpkin squash, Swiss chard, and eggs, or mushrooms, ricotta, and anchovies. But *Torta di cavolo*, lined as it is with mortadella sausage, and filled with cheese, braised cabbage, and ground pork, is perhaps the most original of them all.

Ingredients

> *Pastry*
> 2¼ cups all-purpose flour
>   Salt
>   5 tablespoons butter, chilled and cut into small pieces
>   2 tablespoons lard or shortening, chilled
>   and cut into small pieces
>   1 egg
>   Ice water
>   1 egg beaten with 1 teaspoon water
>
> *Filling*
>   2 pounds green cabbage, quartered and cored
>   ½ cup chopped onion
>   4 tablespoons butter
>   2 tablespoons oil
>   ½ pound ground pork
>   ½ cup peeled, seeded, and chopped tomatoes,
>   or 1 tablespoon tomato paste and ½ cup water
>   2 tablespoons chopped parsley
>   1 teaspoon chopped fresh marjoram, or ½ teaspoon dried
>   ½ teaspoon finely chopped garlic
>   Freshly ground black pepper
> 3½ tablespoons flour
>   2 cups boiling milk
>   Grated nutmeg
>   1 cup ricotta, or fresh white cheese
>   ⅓ cup grated parmesan cheese
>   6 slices (about 5 ounces) mortadella sausage

Equipment

> Mixing bowl · Kettle · Large skillet · Saucepan ·
> Rolling pin · 10-inch tart mold · 1½-inch pastry
> tube or parchment paper funnel

Working time: 1 hour 20 minutes

Baking time: 1 hour

Serves: 6

1. To make the pastry, mix the flour with a little salt, rub in the chilled butter and lard. Mix in the egg and enough ice water to form a ball of dough. Knead until smooth. Wrap in wax paper and chill 2 to 3 hours.

2. Boil the cabbage leaves in salted water. Drain, separate the leaves, rinse under cold running water, squeeze dry, and chop roughly. In a skillet sauté the onion in 2 tablespoons butter and 2 tablespoons oil until soft and golden. Add the ground pork. Stir and break up any lumps with a fork and brown the meat.

3. Add the tomatoes, herbs, and garlic. Season with salt and pepper. Cook, uncovered, 5 minutes over medium heat. Add the cabbage, mixing well, and cook over high heat until all the liquid in the pan has evaporated and the cabbage begins to brown slightly. Correct the seasoning. Cool.

4. Melt 2 tablespoons butter in a small saucepan, stir in 3½ tablespoons flour. Off heat whisk in boiling milk. Cook, stirring, until thick and smooth. Add salt, pepper, and grated nutmeg. Allow to cool. Add the ricotta and the grated parmesan, mixing well.

5. Preheat the oven to 350 degrees.

6. Roll out half the dough into a circle a little larger than the tart mold. Line the mold, prick the bottom with the tines of a fork, and spread half the mortadella slices on the pastry. Spread the cabbage-meat mixture on top, patting it down. Then add the cheese sauce. Place the remaining slices of mortadella on top. Quickly roll out the second half of pastry, moisten around the edges, cover the pie, and crimp to seal. Save all trimmings of pastry for the decoration. Chill 10 minutes.

7. Roll out the trimmings into 10-inch strips and cut ¼-inch-wide strips. Moisten with water and make a lattice design on top of the pie. Make a small opening in the center and insert a funnel to allow steam to escape. Brush the top with beaten egg and set in the oven to bake 1 hour. Serve hot or warm.

TOURTE CORSE

Corsican cheese and herb pie (France)

This recipe is a Mediterranean improvisation. A friend served it to me last year in Languedoc. She told me it was Corsican and gave me the recipe. Actually it seemed much like the Greek spinach and cheese tart (*spanakopitta*) except with Swiss chard, and lots of fresh wild herbs—a Corsican touch.

Ingredients

    1 pound fresh spinach, washed and shredded
        or 10-ounce package frozen leaf spinach,
        completely thawed
    2 large bunches Swiss chard leaves, removed
        from the stalks, washed, and shredded
    ¼ pound fresh sorrel leaves, washed and shredded
        (optional)
    ½ cup olive oil
    1 tablespoon each: fresh chopped basil leaves, rosemary,
        parsley, thyme, and oregano or marjoram,
        or substitute 1 teaspoon each dried herbs
    2 cloves garlic, peeled
 1½ cups chopped onion
    ½ cup chopped scallions
      Salt and freshly ground black pepper
      Grated nutmeg
    2 cups (1 pound) broccio or ricotta cheese
    ¼ cup grated parmesan cheese
    2 eggs, lightly beaten
    ½ pound (12 sheets) phyllo leaves
    ½ cup melted butter

Equipment

Electric blender · Enameled or stainless steel saucepan ·
Enameled or stainless steel skillet · 10-inch tart mold,
buttered

Working time: 50 minutes

Baking time: 40 minutes

Serves: 6 to 8

1. Place the spinach, Swiss chard, and sorrel in the saucepan.
Cover and cook until wilted. Drain thoroughly.

2. Place 2 tablespoons oil, the mixed herbs, and the garlic in
the blender jar; whirl until pasty. Heat the remaining oil in the
skillet over medium heat and cook the onions and the scallions
until soft, stirring frequently. Add the herb paste, and cook, stirring, 1 minute. Stir in the spinach, Swiss chard, and sorrel. Cook,
stirring, over medium heat, for about 5 minutes or until most of
the liquid in the skillet has evaporated. Cool. Season with salt,
pepper, and grated nutmeg.

3. Combine the contents of the skillet with the cheeses and
the beaten eggs, mixing well. Readjust the seasoning. Cool.

4. Preheat the oven to 400 degrees.

5. Unroll the pastry leaves, keeping them under a damp
towel to prevent them from drying out. Butter the tart mold and in
it arrange half the pastry leaves, one on top of the other so that
they overlap the edges, quickly brushing melted butter between
every other layer. Spread out the prepared mixture in one even
layer over the pastry base, then cover with the remaining leaves
except one, brushing melted butter in between. Fold the overlapping leaves up and cover with the remaining leaf and fold it
neatly under the pie (like tucking in sheets). Brush the top with
butter and set in the oven to bake 40 minutes or until the pastry is
golden brown and crisp. Slide onto a serving plate, cut into
wedges, and serve hot.

FRITTURA DE RICOTTA PASQUALINA
Easter ricotta cheese fritters (Italy)

These Tuscan cheese fritters are usually served along with broccoli fritters and spinach fritters. Or better yet, they can be added to a *fritto misto* (see page 63).

To make a dessert variation simply add a few ground *amaretti* (Italian macaroons).

Ingredients

1 cup ricotta cheese
½ cup all-purpose flour
2½ teaspoons double-acting baking powder
1 egg
Pinch of grated lemon peel
¼ teaspoon salt
Pinch of freshly ground black pepper
2–3 tablespoons grappa, marc de Provence, or cognac
Oil for frying

Equipment

Mixing bowl · Deep skillet or deep-fat fryer ·
Slotted spoon

Working time: 5 minutes

Frying time: 12 minutes (30 seconds for each fritter)

Makes: 25

1. In a bowl combine ricotta, flour, baking powder, egg, lemon rind, salt, pepper, and grappa, mixing well. Cover with a towel and let stand 1 hour.

2. Fill the skillet to a depth of 1½ inches with oil and heat

to about 375 degrees on a fat thermometer. Fry the cheese balls, one at a time, until golden brown, being very careful to keep the temperature constant. Drain on paper towels. Serve hot or warm.

PEYNIRLI KABAK
Zucchini stuffed with cheese (Turkey)

Ingredients

    4 zucchini, each about 4½ inches long
      Salt
    1 cup feta cheese, drained and crumbled
    ⅓ cup grated gruyère cheese
    2 tablespoons flour
    1 tablespoon chopped fresh dill
    1 teaspoon crushed garlic
      Freshly ground black pepper
      Breadcrumbs
      Butter
    1 tablespoon paprika butter (see note)

Equipment

    4-quart saucepan · Mixing bowl ·
    9-by-12-inch heatproof serving dish, buttered

Working time: 10 minutes

Cooking time: 20 minutes

Serves: 8 as a first course

1. Wash the zucchini. Drop into boiling salted water and cook at the simmer 15 minutes or until just tender. Drain and allow to cool.

2. Mix the cheeses with the flour, dill, garlic, pepper, and very little salt. Slice the zucchini in half lengthwise and scoop out

the seeds. Arrange cut side up in the serving dish. Sprinkle the shells with pepper and very little salt. Fill with the cheese mixture. Dust lightly with breadcrumbs and dot with butter. Glaze under a hot broiler until the cheese is sizzling. Dribble a tablespoon of paprika butter on top. Serve hot.

Note: To make paprika butter: melt 1½ to 2 tablespoons butter in a small saucepan. Stir in ¼ teaspoon sharp paprika. Spoon off the clear red-hued butter and discard the butter sediment and the paprika.

FIGUES FRAÎCHES AU FROMAGE

Figs and creamed cheese (France)

Ingredients

   12 freshly picked black figs
    3 tablespoons light honey
      Juice of 1 lemon
    1 cup whipped or creamed cottage cheese
    3 tablespoons heavy cream

Equipment

Shallow glass serving dish · Small bowl · Sieve

Working time: 10 minutes

Serves: 4

1. Peel and slice the figs; put them in a shallow serving dish. Dilute the honey with lemon juice. Spoon over the figs. Let stand 1 hour.
2. Meanwhile sieve the cheese and beat in the cream. Serve chilled with the honeyed figs.

$\mathcal{N}uts$

IMAGINE a Mediterranean dinner in which each course is flavored with a different kind of nut. We could begin with *looz shorba*, a thick creamy Middle Eastern almond soup. The main course would be *kafta snobar*, a Lebanese dish of lamb patties sprinkled with toasted pine nuts, accompanied by braised green peppers stuffed with rice and pistachios in the style of the Turks. Afterwards, a walnut and fennel salad from France. And the dessert would be *bruciate briachi*—an Italian dessert of "burnt" (baked and shelled) chestnuts strewn with sugar, hot rum, and flamed.

Personally I wouldn't serve such a dinner except to make the point that the people around the Mediterranean have been highly imaginative with nuts. In Corsica they make a polenta with chestnut flour, and in Tuscany chestnut flour is combined with rosemary and pine nuts to make an interesting cake called *castagnaccio*. Israel, France, and Italy all claim the nut and raisin sauce served over boiled tongue, and the Milanaise have concocted their own version with pine nuts, cream, cinnamon, and sugar which they pour over boiled beef.

In Turkey they take sheets of strudel dough, sprinkle them with sugar and fried pistachios, roll them up like rugs, twist them into coils, and fry them in butter.

Almond paste or marzipan is used in all sorts of Mediterranean desserts and over baked fish in Morocco. And in Tunisia there's a pine nut cream called *aatrichiya* which is made with toasted ground pine nuts, almonds, sugar, and milk, and perfumed with geranium-scented water.

The Spanish, in the great tradition of the Moorish empire, use almonds with fish, chicken, meats, and eggs. In *huevos a la gitanella* the eggs are baked with a fried paste of garlic, almonds, and bread and seasoned with cumin, saffron, and nutmeg.

And while we're looking at various dishes, here's one called *Le saussoun* from Escudier and Fuller's *The Wonderful Food of Provence*, acquired they write, from the collection of the Abbé Deschamps of Roquebrune-sur-Argens. It's a spread for bread made from pounded almonds, anchovies, fennel, mint leaves, water, and oil.

The possibilities, you see, are endless, and the point, I think, is well made. Around the Mediterranean they don't just eat nuts, serve them up as snacks, nibble them with drinks. They *cook* with them, integrate them into their cuisines, and the results can be extremely good.

I hope the recipes that follow demonstrate in highly edible terms some of the possibilities of nuts and demolish the widely held notion that in cookery Mediterranean nuts are used mainly for desserts.

LA SALADE DE FENOUIL AUX NOIX

Walnut and fennel salad (France)

Ingredients

> 3–4 small fennel bulbs
> 1 tablespoon strong mustard
> 3 tablespoons freshly squeezed lemon juice
> 3 tablespoons heavy cream
> Salt and freshly ground black pepper
> ½ cup coarsely chopped shelled walnuts
> 1 tablespoon finely chopped herbs: parsley and/or tarragon

Equipment

Mixing bowl · 4-cup shallow serving dish

Working time: 10 minutes

Serves: 5 to 6 as a first course

1. Remove the fennel tops and cut away the hard outer stalks. Trim the base; then slice crosswise into very thin slices. Chill in a bowl of ice water; drain.

2. Combine mustard with lemon juice and cream. Season with salt and pepper. Place the fennel slices in the serving dish; pour over the dressing, scatter the walnuts on top, and sprinkle with herbs.

LOOZ SHORBA

Almond soup (Middle East)

If you really love almonds you might prefer this soup to the Spanish *gazpacho ajo blanco* (page 9). Here the almond taste is strong and rich while the Spanish soup is dominated by garlic.

Ingredients

    2 tablespoons butter
    ½ cup chopped onions
    2 tablespoons flour
    1 quart boiling chicken stock
    ½ cup ground blanched almonds
    ½ cup heavy cream
      Salt and freshly ground white pepper

Equipment

2 saucepans

Working time: 10 minutes

Cooking time: 25 minutes

Serves: 4 to 5

  Melt the butter in a saucepan, add the onions, and cook until soft but not browned. Stir in the flour. When blended add the boiling stock, stirring briskly. Allow to simmer a few minutes. Stir in the ground almonds. Cook at the simmer 20 minutes. Stir in cream and allow to heat through. Season with salt and pepper to taste. Serve hot.

SARDE A BECCAFICU

Sicilian sardines stuffed with nuts and raisins (Italy)

  In Sicily they like to stuff fish with raisins, pine nuts, and breadcrumbs, and even, sometimes, anchovies. This type of cooking clearly derives from the Middle East, and was brought to Sicily in the tenth century by the Saracens.

Ingredients

  12 fresh large sardines or smelts
    Salt and freshly ground black pepper
  ¼ cup soft white breadcrumbs moistened with a little
     olive oil
   2 tablespoons pine nuts or blanched almonds, chopped
   3 tablespoons yellow raisins, soaked in water
    Juice of ½ lemon
    Salt and freshly ground black pepper
 5–6 imported bay leaves
    Olive oil
  12 green olives, rinsed, pitted, and halved
    Lemon wedges

Equipment

  6-by-9-inch oiled baking dish

Working time: 15 to 20 minutes

Baking time: 30 minutes

Serves: 3 to 4

1. Preheat the oven to 375 degrees.
2. Cut off the heads and tails from each of the sardines. Slit the belly lengthwise and remove the backbone. Sprinkle the flesh with salt and pepper.
3. Mix the breadcrumbs with the nuts and raisins, season with salt and pepper.
4. Lay 6 sardines on their backs, spread a spoonful of stuffing over the insides and cover each with the remaining sardines, insides together. Arrange overlapping in the baking dish. Slip a bay leaf between each pair of stuffed sardines. Sprinkle with oil and bake 30 minutes. Garnish the dish with olives. Serve tepid or warm with lemon wedges.

GAMBAS A LA MENORQUINA

Shrimp in tomato sauce with almonds and pine nuts
(Spain)

Ingredients

 ⅓ cup olive oil
 1 cup chopped onion
 3 cups fresh or canned tomatoes, peeled, seeded, and chopped
 ½ cup ground blanched almonds
 ⅓ cup pine nuts
 4 cloves garlic, peeled and chopped
 2 tablespoons chopped parsley
 ¼ teaspoon cayenne, or more to taste
  Salt
 2 cups shelled cooked small shrimp

Equipment

   Electric blender   ·   Skillet

Working time: 10 minutes

Cooking time: 30 minutes

Serves: 3 to 4

   1. Heat the oil in the skillet and in it cook the onion until soft and golden. Add the tomatoes. Cook, uncovered, 15 to 20 minutes, stirring often.
   2. In a blender grind the almonds, pine nuts, garlic, parsley, and 3 tablespoons water to a paste. Stir into the tomato sauce. Cook, stirring, 5 minutes. If the sauce is very thick thin with ¾ to 1 cup water. Season with cayenne and salt.
   3. Fold in the shrimp. Allow to heat through. Serve on a bed of boiled rice.

Note: Small fresh fish such as whitings or fresh fillets of fish can be covered with the above sauce and baked in a 325-degree oven 20 to 30 minutes.

ÇERKEZ TAVUǦU
Circassian chicken (Turkey)

   Perhaps the most famous cold buffet food of Turkey, *Çerkez tavuğu* is said to have been Ataturk's favorite dish. Cold chicken is served with a sauce of ground walnuts and almonds moistened with a rich chicken stock. It's similar to another Turkish nut sauce called *tarator* (not to be confused with the Yugoslav soup *tarator*) made of ground walnuts moistened with oil and vinegar, then poured over cold boiled shellfish.

Ingredients

 2 whole chicken breasts, split
 2 small onions
 1 carrot, sliced
 1 celery rib, chopped
 1 bay leaf
 2 sprigs parsley
  Salt
 6 black peppercorns
 2 cups shelled whole walnuts
 ¾ cup whole blanched almonds or hazelnuts
  Cayenne
 2 tablespoons peanut oil
 ¼ teaspoon paprika

Equipment

Wide saucepan · Baking sheet · Electric blender ·
Sieve · Small saucepan

Working time: 20 minutes

Cooking time: 30 minutes

Serves: 8 as part of a buffet

 1. Simmer the chicken breasts until tender in water to cover flavored with 1 quartered onion, carrot, celery, herbs, salt, and black peppercorns. Allow to cool in the cooking liquid.

 2. Meanwhile lightly toast the nuts in a preheated 300-degree oven. Pulverize the nuts in a blender. Add the remaining onion, quartered, and a little of the cooking stock; whirl until smooth. Then slowly add enough strained cooking stock (about 1 cup) to make a creamy sauce. Season with salt and cayenne.

 3. Bone and cut the chicken into small serving pieces. Arrange on a serving dish. Coat completely with the walnut-almond sauce. Chill.

 4. Just before serving, dribble heated paprika-tinted oil over the surface making a design. Serve cold.

DJEJ BIL LOOZ (TARFAYA)

Chicken with almonds (Morocco)

In Morocco there're two ways to combine chicken with almonds. In one, called *kdra touimyia*, the almonds are boiled in stock for a long time until they're buttery soft. In this version they're fried in oil until crunchy and golden brown, then sprinkled on top of the prepared chicken just before the dish is served.

Ingredients

         Salt
     7   cloves garlic, peeled
     1   3½-pound chicken, quartered
     2   tablespoons chopped parsley
         Olive oil
     ⅛   teaspoon pulverized saffron
     ½   teaspoon freshly ground black pepper
     1   cup chopped onion
     ¾   cup whole blanched almonds
         Oil
     4   hard-boiled eggs

Equipment

     Mortar and pestle   ·   3½-quart casserole with cover   ·
     Skillet   ·   Slotted spoon

Working time: 15 minutes

Cooking time: 1 hour

Serves: 4

1. The day before you plan to serve, purify the chicken quarters. Make a paste with 1 tablespoon salt and 3 crushed gar-

lic cloves. Rub all over the chicken. Rinse well then pat dry with paper towels. In a mortar combine remaining garlic with parsley, pounding to a paste. Moisten with 2 tablespoons olive oil and add saffron and pepper. Rub this mixture into the flesh of the chicken. Cover and refrigerate overnight.

2. Heat ¼ cup oil in the casserole and in it cook the onion until soft and golden. Add the chicken. Sauté slowly until golden brown on both sides. Add 1 cup water and bring to a boil. Cover and simmer gently ¾ hour. Turn and baste the chicken quarters often. (You may need to add water during the cooking.)

3. In a skillet fry the almonds in 1 tablespoon oil until golden brown. Drain on paper towels.

4. To serve, cover the chicken with almonds, decorate with halved hard-boiled eggs, and serve hot.

PAVO RELLEÑO A LA MENORQUINA

Stuffed roast turkey with pine nuts and raisins (Spain)

In Spain turkeys and roasting capons are often stuffed with sausage, bread, eggs, almonds or pine nuts, raisins, sherry, and even, sometimes, with dried prunes, chestnuts, and Serrano ham. The classic way to make this dish is to stuff the bird and then hang it for a day wrapped in caul fat.

Ingredients

    1 7-pound young turkey, with liver
      Salt and freshly ground black pepper
  3–4 tablespoons oil
    1 cup chopped onion
    ¾ pound ground pork
    ¾ cup soft breadcrumbs
    ½ cup dry sherry
    ⅓ cup toasted pine nuts, chopped

Continued

    ½ cup raisins
       Ground cinnamon
    2 medium green apples
       Butter, oil, or a sheet of caul fat

Equipment

    Skillet   ·   Mixing bowl   ·   Roasting pan with rack   ·
    Bulb baster (optional)   ·   Kitchen twine and needle
    or skewers

Working time: 30 minutes

Roasting time: 2½ hours (approximately)

Serves: 8

    1. Season the turkey with salt and pepper. Heat the oil in the
skillet; cook the liver 5 minutes and remove to a side dish. Add
more oil to the skillet and gently sauté the onions until soft. Add
the pork; sauté 10 minutes, stirring often.
    2. Soak the breadcrumbs in sherry, then mix with the pine
nuts and raisins. Add cinnamon. Mix in the onion-pork mixture.
Finely chop the liver and add to the stuffing, blending well. Season to taste with salt and pepper. If the pork seems too under-
cooked to taste, fry a tablespoon of the mixture in oil for a few
minutes then readjust the seasoning.
    3. Preheat the oven to 325 degrees.
    4. Stuff the turkey, stick 1 apple into the neck cavity, and
sew up the opening. Stuff the body cavity with the pork mixture.
Stick the other apple at the bottom end and sew up the second
opening. Rub with butter or oil, or wrap in a sheet of caul fat.
Place breast side down on a rack set in a roasting pan. Roast for
approximately 2 hours or until the turkey is tender and golden
brown, basting often with the pan juices. Turn the turkey over
after it has cooked 1¼ hours. If using caul fat you will need to
remove a great deal of fat during cooking time. Do so every 15
minutes to avoid accumulating an excess of fat around the turkey.
Let stand 15 minutes before carving.

KAFTA SNOBAR

Lamb patties with pine nuts (Lebanon)

Adapted from *The Art of Lebanese Cooking* by George Rayess.

Ingredients

 ⅓ cup *labni* (see page 212)
 2 tablespoons tahini (sesame seed paste)
 Juice of 1 lemon
 1 clove garlic, peeled and crushed with ½ teaspoon salt
 ¾ pound lean lamb or veal, ground 3 times
 Salt
 ½ teaspoon freshly ground black pepper
 ¼ cup grated onion
 2 tablespoons chopped parsley
 1 teaspoon chopped fresh mint
 Flour for dredging
 2 tablespoons butter
 2 tablespoons oil
 ⅓ cup toasted pine nuts

Equipment

 Mixing bowls · Skillet · Meat grinder (optional)

Working time: 15 minutes

Cooking time: 10 minutes

Serves: 4

 1. Combine *labni*, tahini, lemon juice, and crushed garlic in a mixing bowl. Blend thoroughly.
 2. Separately combine ground meat, 1 teaspoon salt, pepper, onion, parsley, and mint. Push through a meat grinder or blend

thoroughly. Form into patties 2 inches in diameter. Dust with flour and fry in a mixture of butter and oil.

3. Pour off all but 3 tablespoons pan drippings. Add the *labni* paste and heat, stirring. Season with salt and pepper to taste. Pour over the meat patties, sprinkle with toasted pine nuts, and serve at once.

SALSA ROMESCO

Almond and hot pepper sauce from Catalonia (Spain)

This strong rich spicy sauce reminds me of the Mexican sauce *cascabel*. It's very good on broiled and poached fish, hot or cold shellfish, and broiled meat.

The Spanish seem to adore almonds. They use them in soups, fish dishes, with meats and in desserts. In Valencia there's a fresh-water eel dish called *all i pebre*, in which the eels are actually cooked in a similar almond-paprika-tomato-garlic-hot pepper combination.

Ingredients

  1 dried hot pepper
  ½ cup shelled whole almonds
  1 teaspoon finely chopped garlic
  1 teaspoon paprika
  2–3 broiled tomatoes, peeled, seeded, and mashed,
        making ⅔ cup
  Salt
  ½ cup olive oil
  2–3 tablespoons wine vinegar

Equipment

  Electric blender · Small bowl · Baking sheet

Working time: 10 minutes

Makes: 1¼ cups

1. Soak the hot pepper in water until soft.
2. Blanch the almonds and slip off their skins. Toast on a baking sheet in the oven until golden brown. Grind finely in the blender and set aside.
3. Discard the hot pepper seeds. Grind pepper, garlic, paprika, tomatoes, and a little salt in the blender until smooth. Gradually add the olive oil, still blending, to make a sauce the consistency of light cream. Add vinegar to taste. Pour into a small serving bowl and fold in the almonds.

A I A

Ligurian walnut sauce for green pasta or meatless agnolotti (Italy)

Sometimes called "nut pesto" or *salsa di noci* these two versions of Ligurian walnut sauce for pasta are delicious and very easy to produce. I happen to prefer the *pasta con salsa di noci* because it's lighter, but the first version is more traditional. The cream is my own addition—in Liguria they use buttermilk cheese.

Ingredients

> 1½ pounds *tagliatelle verdi*
>   or 1 pound *agnolotti da vigilia* (see page 144)
> ¾ cup shelled chopped walnuts
> ¼ cup pine nuts
> 1 small clove garlic, peeled
> ¼ teaspoon ground dried marjoram
> 2 tablespoons olive oil
> ¼ cup melted butter
> 1 cup light cream
> ½ teaspoon meat extract such as Bovril or Liebig
>   Freshly ground black pepper
> ⅓ cup grated parmesan cheese
>   Salt

Equipment

    Electric blender · 1½-quart saucepan

Working time: 10 minutes

Cooking time: 5 to 10 minutes

Makes: 1¾ cups sauce, serves 6 to 8 as a first course

    1. Make the pasta.
    2. While the pasta is drying prepare the sauce. Grind the nuts in a blender until coarse. Remove half the nuts and set aside. Add garlic, marjoram, and oil to the remaining nuts in the blender. Whirl until the ingredients are creamy. Transfer to a saucepan, stir in the melted butter and the cream and cook, stirring, over medium heat until hot but not boiling. Add the meat extract, freshly ground black pepper, and grated cheese. Reduce the heat to low and cook, stirring, for 1 minute. Fold in the reserved coarse ground nuts, taste for seasoning and readjust.
    3. Cook the pasta in boiling salted water. Drain the pasta and pour the sauce over it. Pass a pepper mill and more freshly grated cheese.

PASTA CON SALSA DI NOCI

Pasta with walnut sauce (Italy)

Ingredients

    ½ cup shelled walnut meats
    ½ teaspoon meat extract such as Bovril or Liebig
    ½ cup heavy cream
    ½ pound pasta such as *tagliatelle* or fettuccine
       Grated parmesan cheese
       Pepper

Equipment

Saucepan · Large pot · Slotted spoon

Working time: 5 minutes

Cooking time: 10 minutes

Serves: 3 as a first course

1. Finely chop the walnuts. Mix the meat extract into the cream and heat gently. Stir in the walnuts. Season with freshly ground black pepper and a little salt. Keep hot.

2. Cook the pasta in boiling salted water. Drain and pour the prepared sauce over. Pass a bowl of freshly grated cheese and a pepper mill.

ROZ SNOBAR

Rice pilaf with pine nuts (Syria)

Ingredients

1 cup finely chopped onions
4 tablespoons clarified butter or oil
1 pound lean lamb, cut into small pieces
Salt and freshly ground black pepper
¼ teaspoon ground allspice
1½ cups long-grain rice
3 cups hot beef stock
⅓ cup pine nuts, toasted or browned in oil

Equipment

Saucepan with tight-fitting cover · Skillet with tight-fitting cover

Working time: 10 minutes

Cooking time: 50 minutes

Serves: 5 to 6

    1. In a saucepan sauté the onions in 2 tablespoons butter or oil until soft and golden. Add the meat and brown it on all sides. Sprinkle with salt, pepper, and allspice. Moisten with 1 cup stock. Cook, covered, for 30 minutes or until the meat is tender.

    2. In a skillet fry the rice in the remaining butter or oil, stirring, until well coated on all sides. Add the meat, pan juices and the remaining beef stock to the skillet. Bring to the boil. Cover and cook at the simmer for about 20 minutes. Just before serving toss with a fork and sprinkle with toasted pine nuts.

ACELGAS CON PIÑONES

Swiss chard with pine nuts (Spain)

Ingredients

    2 pounds fresh Swiss chard, tender young beet tops, or spinach
    4 thick slices bacon, diced
    2 tablespoons olive oil
    1 clove garlic, peeled and crushed
  ½ cup pine nuts
    2 tablespoons yellow raisins plumped in hot water
       Salt and freshly ground black pepper

Equipment

Basin · Enameled or stainless steel saucepan with tight-fitting cover · Enameled or stainless steel skillet

Working time: 20 minutes

Cooking time: 15 minutes

Serves: 4

1. Remove the chard leaves from the stalks. Wash the leaves in 2 or 3 changes of cold water. Discard the stalks and any wilted or tough leaves. Place in the saucepan; cover and cook, stirring once or twice, over medium heat until tender. Drain and chop roughly.

2. Sauté the bacon until crisp in the skillet. Pour off almost all the fat. Add the olive oil and garlic clove and cook 1 minute. Discard the garlic clove. Add the pine nuts and sauté briefly. Add the Swiss chard and the raisins and toss well. Season with pepper and a little salt. Serve hot.

ISTARSKE FRITULE

Istrian hazelnut fritters (Yugoslavia)

Ingredients

- 1½ cups all-purpose flour
- 1½ tablespoons baking powder
- Pinch of salt
- 2 tablespoons sugar
- ¼ teaspoon ground cloves
- ½ teaspoon grated nutmeg
- 1 tablespoon grated orange rind
- 2 eggs
- ¾ cup toasted ground hazelnuts (3½ ounces)
- ¾ cup dry white wine
- 2 tablespoons cherry brandy
- Oil for deep frying
- Confectioners' sugar

Equipment

Sifter · Mixing bowl · Fat thermometer ·
Slotted spoon · Deep skillet

Working time: 10 minutes

Frying time: 15 to 20 minutes

Makes: 40 to 45 serving 8

1. Sift together the flour, baking powder, salt, and sugar. Add the spices, grated orange rind, eggs, hazelnuts, wine, and brandy. Mix thoroughly until a soft smooth batter is obtained. Cover and allow to stand 2 hours.

2. In the skillet heat the oil to 350 degrees on a fat thermometer. Drop the batter by teaspoonsful into the hot oil a few at a time. Fry until puffy and golden brown. Remove and sprinkle with confectioners' sugar. Serve hot or warm.

POUDING AU NOUGAT

Nougat pudding with chocolate sauce (France)

The best nougat is made with honey, sweet almonds, and egg whites.

Ingredients

    ½ pound nougat
    2 cups milk
    ½ vanilla bean or 1 teaspoon vanilla extract
    6 eggs
      Pinch of salt
    ½ cup sugar

Chocolate sauce

    4 squares sweet cooking chocolate
    ½ cup water
    2 tablespoons unsalted butter
    1 teaspoon vanilla extract
  2–3 tablespoons heavy cream

Equipment

    Electric blender · Saucepan · 2 mixing bowls ·
    Electric beater · 1½-quart mold, buttered ·
    Shallow baking pan

Working time: 20 minutes

Baking time: 1 hour

Serves: 6

1. To be prepared 1 day in advance: Finely grind the nougat in the blender. Dump into mixing bowl. Heat the milk in the saucepan with the vanilla bean; allow to steep 10 minutes, remove the vanilla bean and pour the milk over the nougat.

2. Preheat the oven to 350 degrees.

3. In another mixing bowl beat the eggs with the salt. Gradually add the sugar, beating well. Beat until pale yellow and thick. Stir in the nougat. Pour into a buttered mold. Place in a pan of hot water and set in the oven to bake 1 hour or until a knife inserted comes out clean. Allow to cool completely then refrigerate overnight.

4. To make the chocolate sauce: melt the chocolate with the water in a small saucepan. Add the butter and the vanilla. Stir over gentle heat until the butter is melted. Stir in the cream. Keep warm until ready to serve. Makes about 1 cup sauce.

5. Just before serving turn out the mold onto a shallow serving dish. Pass the sauce separately.

SOUFFLÉ DOLCE DI AMARETTI
Almond macaroon soufflé (Northern Italy)

Here's a good soufflé using the famous Italian *amaretti di Saronno*, vanilla-flavored almond macaroons. It's flavored, too, with Amaretto, liqueur distilled from bitter almonds. If you can't find amaretto use Noyau de Poissy a similar French liqueur, or a few drops of *bitter* almond extract.*

This soufflé is delicious with hot chocolate sauce.

Ingredients

        3 tablespoons all-purpose flour
        ¾ cup milk
        ½ cup sugar
        4 egg yolks
        ⅓ cup crumbled Italian almond macaroons
        ½ teaspoon vanilla extract
        2 tablespoons Amaretto or Noyau de Poissy
        6 egg whites
          Pinch of salt
          Confectioners' sugar

Equipment

        Heavy enameled saucepan · Whisk ·
        Large bowl for beating egg whites preferably one with a
        copper lining · Buttered and sugared 6-cup soufflé mold

Working time: 15 minutes

Baking time: 30 to 35 minutes

Serves: 4

1. In a heavy saucepan beat the flour with 3 tablespoons milk until smooth. Beat in remaining milk and sugar. Cook, stirring, until the mixture boils. Beat vigorously over medium heat until thick and smooth. Allow to cool.

2. Beat in the egg yolks, one by one. Then add the macaroons, the vanilla extract and the liqueur.

3. Preheat the oven to 400 degrees.

---

* Bitter almond extract is available from H. Roth & Sons. See supplier listing.

4. Stiffly beat the egg whites with a pinch of salt. Stir ¼ of the beaten whites into the base to lighten it. Then fold in the remaining whites. Transfer to the prepared soufflé mold and bake 30 to 35 minutes. After 10 minutes lower the oven heat to 350 degrees. Remove when puffy and golden brown, about 20 minutes more, dust with confectioners' sugar, and serve at once.

CROQUETS DE LANGUEDOC

Hazelnut crisps from Languedoc, France

The secret to the crispness of these lovely light cookies is not to overwork the batter after the flour is in.

Ingredients

>   5 tablespoons unsalted butter, softened
>   1 cup sugar
>   ½ cup egg whites (about 4 egg whites)
>   ¾ cup ground hazelnuts
>   2 teaspoons grated orange rind
>   ⅔ cup cake flour

Equipment

> Mixing bowl · 3 buttered baking sheets ·
> Pastry bag fitted with a large round tube · Spatula ·
> Wire racks

Working time: 10 minutes

Baking time: 10 minutes

Makes: 45 crisps

1. Preheat the oven to 425 degrees.
2. Place the butter and the sugar in the mixing bowl; beat until creamy. Beat in the egg whites. Fold in the ground nuts and the grated orange rind. Using a rubber spatula gently stir in the

flour 2 tablespoons at a time. Pack into a pastry bag. Drop small rounds of batter onto the greased baking sheets, leaving 3 inches between each round. Using a knife dipped in cold water flatten each into a thin oval shape. Bake until the edges are golden brown—about 10 minutes.

3. Use a spatula to detach the crisps and allow to cool on wire racks. Store in an airtight tin.

POLVORONES
Almond cookies (Spain)

Ingredients

>   ⅓ cup ground blanched almonds
>   ¾ cup sugar
>   1½ teaspoons ground cinnamon
>   Pinch of salt
>   ½ cup lard, softened to room temperature
>   3½ cups all-purpose flour
>   Confectioners' sugar

Equipment

> Mixing bowl · Rolling pin · 2-inch oval or
> round cooky cutter · 2 baking sheets, heavily floured ·
> 3 dozen 3-inch squares of tissue paper

Working time: 20 minutes

Baking time: 25 minutes (approximately)

Makes: 2½ to 3 dozen cookies

1. Preheat oven to 325 degrees.
2. In a mixing bowl combine the almonds with the sugar, cinnamon, and a pinch of salt. Cream the lard with the sugar mixture until well blended and smooth. Slowly work in the flour, cup by cup, until a very stiff dough is obtained, adding a few

drops of water if the dough remains crumbly. Turn out onto a floured workspace and knead the dough 2 to 3 minutes until smooth.

3. Roll out the dough to a large rectangle 10 by 15 inches and cut out rounds or ovals. Gather the trimmings and reroll the dough and cut out more cookies. Arrange on baking sheets. Bake until just firm but not brown. Cool then roll in confectioners' sugar and wrap in tissue squares twirling two ends to close securely. Store in cardboard boxes or tins if desired.

KARIDOPITTA

Honey walnut cake (Greece)

The Greeks make all sorts of wonderful cakes with nuts—*kadaif, baklava,* and this *karidopitta* which is very easy to make and *very* sweet.

Ingredients

>   1¼ cups sugar
>   ¾ cup honey
>   1¼ teaspoons ground cinnamon
>   Juice of ½ lemon
>   1¾ cups chopped walnuts
>   1½ cups all-purpose flour, sifted
>   1 teaspoon double-acting baking powder
>   4 tablespoons sweet butter, softened to room temperature
>   4 eggs, separated

Equipment

>   Electric beater · Saucepan · 8-or 9-inch square cake pan, buttered · Mixing bowls

Working time: 25 minutes

Baking time: 45 to 50 minutes

Serves: 8

1. To make the syrup: cook ¾ cup sugar and ¾ cup water in a small saucepan, stirring. Bring to the boil. Simmer 5 minutes. Stir in the honey, ¼ teaspoon ground cinnamon, and the juice of ½ lemon. Cook at the simmer 5 minutes longer. Allow to cool completely.

2. Preheat the oven to 350 degrees.

3. Combine 1¼ cups nuts, remaining cinnamon, flour, and baking powder. Set aside. Cream remaining ½ cup sugar with butter until light and fluffy. Add egg yolks, one at a time, beating well after each addition. Beat in the walnut mixture. Separately beat the egg whites until stiff. Gently fold the egg whites into the walnut mixture. Put the mixture into the prepared cake pan. Sprinkle the top with the remaining ½ cup chopped walnuts. Set in the oven to bake until the cake tests done.

4. Remove the cake from the oven. Cut into diamond shapes in the cakepan. Pour cool syrup over the hot cake. Cover and allow to stand overnight before serving.

HORCHATA

Earth almond drink (Spain)

Horchata is one of my favorite drinks, served all over southern Spain, and in an ice cream parlor on Avenue d'Espagne in Tangier. Much like Middle Eastern *sharbat* (a refreshing drink made of almonds and milk), *horchata* is made from so-called earth almonds, actually pieces of papyrus root. Earth almonds are called *chufa* in Spain, and taste something like aromatic chestnuts. According to one of my books there are references to them in ancient hieroglyphic inscriptions.

I don't think you'll be able to find earth almonds very easily, but if you do, here's how to make *horchata*. Wash and then blanch ½ pound of them for 5 minutes in boiling water, combine with another ½ pound that have been dry-pan grilled, and pound them to a paste in a heavy mortar. Let the paste sit overnight, add a quart of water, a cup of sugar cane syrup, stir, strain and chill until ready to serve.

Honey

"You can rely on the honey, Fraülein
Buddenbrook; it is a pure nature product—
one knows what one is eating."
—From *Buddenbrooks* by Thomas Mann

I'VE never forgotten that line from *Buddenbrooks,* and it seems
especially poignant to me now in this day of chemical food
additives.

Though bees are busy making honey all over the world I
think they do their best work around the Mediterranean. Of
course the secret of great honey is the flowers from which the
bees gather the nectar: sage, lavender, pine, orange blossoms,
eucalyptus, heather, acacia (mimosa), rosemary, and thyme.

The best French honey is from Narbonne and is flavored
with rosemary. Thyme flavors the famous Mount Hymettus honey
of Greece. The honey of Sardinia is reputed to be so strong that
they "soften" it by mixing it with sugar. The pale Italian Hybla
honey is lighter and is used in Neapolitan sweets and *pizza filiata,*
a coiled pastry filled with chopped nuts, candied fruits, spices,
and honey.

The famous honey cakes of the Levant, the Greek *baklava*
and the Turkish *kadaif* cannot be good unless rich pure honey is
included in the syrup. For years I've made Moroccan *tagines* with
fruit and honey in the sauce, never failing to be amazed how the

proper addition of freshly ground black pepper can balance the sweetness.

I have five Mediterranean honey dishes for you to make, each of them extraordinary, and, I think, unique. The first, the Provençal *poragneau coumtadino*, is my own adaptation of a most unusual dish served in Avignon at the famous Auberge de France. This restaurant is well known for its *charlotte aux noisettes et au miel de Provence*, and that same "honey of Provence" is part of the secret of the *poragneau*. But even if you make it with ordinary honey the result will be very good. Fillets of pork and lamb with slices of truffle between are bound together in caul fat and served in a sauce of wine, garlic, and honey. You only use a half tablespoon and as a result the dish is not sweet. But the honey is there, giving a subtle richness to the sauce.

Klandt bil Karmouss is a Moroccan pastry stuffed with chopped figs and dipped in honey. It's similar to the *shebbakia* described in my Moroccan cookbook, one of the many honey cakes eaten in North Africa to accompany the hot spicy soup used to break the Ramamdan fast. Here the honey is most apparent— the cake literally drips with it on the outside. I suggest you use Greek Mount Hymettus, which is easily obtainable and rather close to the country honeys of the Middle Atlas *souks*. This dish will produce marvelous little tea cakes which can be kept a long time if stored in a tin box.

Svingous me meli hymettus are puffed fried fritters saturated with honey syrup. You'll find similar confections in all mediterranean countries, but these Greek ones are especially good. I have cut down on the honey to suit American tastes, working for a sweet but not overly sweet honey-syrup blend.

Melipitta is a famous specialty of the island of Sifnos, known as the best island in the Cyclades for food. Honey and cheese is a great and classic combination, and here the Greek cheese is mezithra. A combination of cottage and cream cheeses gives a close approximation, and be sure to use a strong Greek honey such as Mount Hymettus.

Crème de miel, the honey cream of the French southwest is an unusual version of the more famous *crème caramel*. This is a good variation for those who like a lighter honey. It's served in a flat round dish but it can be made to fill six small individual ramekins. Serve it with a chilled Sauternes.

P O R A G N E U   C O U M T A D I N O

Pork and lamb scallops in white wine and honey sauce (France)

Ingredients

> 4 slices pork cut from the leg, ½ inch thick
> > and approximately 5 inches in diameter,
> > each weighing about 3½ ounces
> 4 slices lamb cut from the leg, ½ inch thick
> > and approximately 5 inches in diameter,
> > each weighing about 3½ ounces
> > Salt and freshly ground black pepper
> 12 thin slices black truffle
> 1 piece of caul fat (order from the pork butcher)
> > Flour
> 5 cloves garlic, peeled but left whole
> 1 tablespoon olive oil
> ¾ cup dry white wine
> ½ tablespoon honey, preferably imported from Provence

Equipment

> Cleaver or mallet · 14-inch skillet

Working time: 15 minutes

Cooking time: 30 minutes

Serves: 4

1. Place the pork and the lamb between sheets of wax paper and pound them with a mallet to make them thinner. Be sure to keep them of equal size.

2. Sprinkle the meat with salt and pepper. Place 3 slices of

truffle on each pork scallop and cover each with a lamb scallop. Wrap each in a piece of caul fat measuring approximately 9 inches by 9 inches.

3. Dust the prepared packages in flour. Gently sauté in olive oil with the garlic cloves 12 minutes on each side. Remove garlic cloves when golden brown and soft and crush them in a bowl; blend with the honey. Remove the meat packages and keep warm in the oven. Pour off the fat from the skillet. Add the wine to the skillet and cook over very high heat scraping up all the bits and pieces that cling to the pan. Reduce the wine by half. Stir in the garlic-honey mixture. Readjust the seasoning. Pour over the scallop packages and serve very hot.

KLANDT BIL KARMOUSS

Honey-dipped pastry stuffed with figs (Morocco)

Ingredients

¾ pound (36) dried figs, chopped
⅓ cup apricot preserves
½ cup chopped blanched almonds
    Ground cinnamon
½ pound phyllo leaves (14 sheets)
 8 tablespoons unsalted butter, melted and cooled
⅔ cup sugar
⅔ cup water
⅔ cup dark heavy honey
 3 tablespoons orange flower water (optional)
    Oil for frying (optional)

Equipment

Meat grinder · Mixing bowl · Damp towel ·
Baking sheet or deep-fat fryer · Heavy saucepan ·
Tongs and slotted spoons (optional)

Working time: 30 minutes

Baking time: 30 minutes
   or
Frying time: 20 minutes (approximately)

Makes: 28 pastries

1. Push the figs through a meat grinder with a little water. Combine the figs with the apricot preserves and the almonds. Add cinnamon to taste. Knead until well blended. Separate the mixture into 28 equal balls.

2. Unroll 1 sheet of phyllo, keeping the others under a damp towel. Brush the entire sheet sparingly with melted butter. Cut the sheet lengthwise into 2 equal parts, fold each in half, and place a portion of fig mixture at the bottom of each half. Fold the sides lengthwise over the filling. Fold the bottom over, and roll up like a rug. Fasten the last inch of pastry with a flour and water paste if necessary. Each stuffed pastry should measure 2 inches by 1¼ inches.

3. Preheat the oven to 350 degrees if you are going to bake the pastries.

4. To make the syrup: combine the sugar and the water in a heavy saucepan. Bring to a boil and cook 5 minutes at the simmer. Off heat stir in the honey, orange flower water, and a pinch of ground cinnamon. Return to the heat and keep on a low simmer.

5. Bake the *klandts* in the oven for 30 minutes or until puffed and golden on both sides or fry in not-too-hot oil until golden, turning once.

6. Transfer at once to the simmering honey syrup, allowing the hot syrup to penetrate the pastries for 2 to 3 minutes each. Remove to a flat dish to dry. Store when cool.

SVINGOUS ME MELI HYMETTUS

Puffed fritters with Mount Hymettus honey (Greece)

Ingredients

    1 cup water
    8 tablespoons unsalted butter
    1 tablespoon sugar
    Pinch of salt
    1 cup all-purpose flour, sifted
    1 teaspoon baking powder
    4 eggs

Honey syrup
    1 cup sugar
    ¾ cup water
    ½ cup Mount Hymettus honey
    2 tablespoons lemon juice
    Ground cinnamon

Equipment

Saucepans · Electric beater · Deep-fat fryer
or deep skillet · Slotted spoon · Fat thermometer

Working and cooking time: 40 minutes

Makes: 3 dozen

1. Combine water, butter, sugar, and salt in saucepan. Stir over medium heat until butter is melted and mixture boils. Remove from heat and immediately add the flour and the baking powder. Stir vigorously with a wooden spoon. Return pan to low heat, continue beating until a ball is formed in the middle of the pan and the sides are clean. This takes about 3 minutes. Cool slightly.

2. Using an electric beater beat in the eggs one by one, beating well. The batter should completely absorb one egg before the next is added. You will find that the third and fourth eggs will absorb very slowly. The batter is ready when it forms peaks upon raising the beater.

3. To make the syrup: combine sugar and water in a heavy saucepan. Bring to a boil and cook 5 minutes at the simmer. Off heat stir in the honey, lemon juice, and a pinch of ground cinnamon.

4. Heat the oil in the fryer to 350 degrees. Using 2 wet spoons, drop globs of batter into the hot fat, 4 to 5 at a time. Fry until golden, swollen to double in size, and crisp, turning them over once with a spoon. Drain on paper towels. Coat each hot fritter with tepid syrup. Serve hot or at room temperature with a sprinkling of ground cinnamon.

MELIPITTA

Honey cheese pie (Greece)

Ingredients

Pastry

1¾ cups all-purpose flour
2 tablespoons sugar
  Pinch of salt
6 ounces (12 tablespoons) unsalted butter
½ teaspoon grated lemon rind
¼ teaspoon ground cinnamon
1 egg, lightly beaten
2 tablespoons ice water (approximately)

Filling

10 ounces creamed cottage cheese
2 ounces cream cheese
¼ cup honey
⅓ cup sugar
  Ground cinnamon
3 large eggs, lightly beaten

Equipment

Mixing bowl   ·   10-inch tart mold   ·   Rolling pin

Working time: 20 minutes

Baking time: 35 to 40 minutes

Serves: 6

1. To make the pastry: mix the flour with the sugar and the salt. Rub in the butter. Mix egg, lemon rind, and ¼ teaspoon ground cinnamon. Stir into the flour. Quickly add enough ice water to form a ball of dough. Usually 2 to 3 tablespoons is enough. Work lightly until smooth, wrap in wax paper and chill 2 hours.

2. Preheat the oven to 350 degrees.

3. For the filling: combine the cheeses, honey, and sugar, mixing well until smooth. Gradually beat in the eggs then stir in 1 teaspoon ground cinnamon.

4. Roll out the pastry and line the tart mold. Trim and flute the edges. Transfer the honey-cheese mixture to the pastry shell and set in the oven to bake until golden brown and puffy. Sprinkle with a little ground cinnamon and serve when cool.

CREME DE MIEL

Honey cream (France)

Ingredients

> ½ cup sugar
> 2 teaspoons water
> 1⅓ cups sweet white wine
> ⅓ cup light honey
> Pinch of ground cinnamon
> 1 teaspoon grated lemon rind
> 2 egg yolks
> 4 whole eggs

Equipment

> Heavy skillet · Saucepan · 8-inch cake pan
> and a larger pan · Mixing bowl

Working time: 15 minutes

Cooking time: 45 to 50 minutes (approximately)

Serves: 6

1. Slowly heat the sugar and the water in a heavy skillet, stirring often, until the sugar has melted and turned into a caramel syrup. At once pour into a cake pan. Tilt so that the syrup covers the entire bottom of the pan. Cool.

2. Preheat the oven to 350 degrees.

3. Heat the wine and the honey in a saucepan, stirring until the honey dissolves. Stir in the cinnamon and lemon rind. Remove from the heat; allow to cool slightly.

4. In a mixing bowl beat the egg yolks and the whole eggs. Combine with the honey-wine mixture, beat until well blended, and pour into the caramel lined pan. Set the pan in a larger pan of hot water and bake about 45 minutes, or until set. Cool then refrigerate until ready to serve.

5. When ready to serve run a thin-bladed knife around the edges to loosen the sides. Invert onto a serving dish.

Lemons, Oranges, Figs, Dates, and Other Mediterranean Fruits

There's a mini-orchard in my garden in Tangier which I like to think of as a microcosm of the Mediterranean cornucopia of fruits. There are five old grape vines that grow along a stone wall, and then in clearings down a dozen grassy walks, quince trees, pears, apricots, sweet and bitter oranges, lemons, pomegranates, and figs. There's a pair of old grand-daddy palms that bear dates, but because of the climate the dates don't ripen. The same with the banana trees, though my mulberry tree explodes, and each fall I must ruthlessly cut it back. I've planted strawberries beside a field of day lilies, and I have an old tree that produces *nefle du Japon*. And the cactus along the bottom of the garden renders prickly pears, or "barbary figs" as we call them here.

There are many gardens in Tangier like mine—there's nothing exceptional about an orchard here. We don't have tangerines which amuses us, because that's what we call ourselves, and of course we don't have the fruit trees that need chill: apples, cherries, peaches, and plums. We don't have grapefruit, either, though they grow well further south. At the height of the winter harvest we can buy grapefruits and blood oranges for less than a dollar a case.

Fresh fruits, I think, make the best dessert to follow a Mediterranean meal. Like vegetables they appear in our markets only in their seasons—just as we're tiring of clementines the first strawberries come in. Wagon-loads of oranges flood our streets; great pyramids of lemons are erected beside market stalls. Mediterranean life is a festival of fresh fruit, and in the regions of the orchards it's impossible to starve.

We make sherbets of fruits and wonderful preserves, and we also cook with them. Not only desserts, but soups, fish, poultry, and stews. Moroccan shad stuffed with dates, Middle Eastern lamb and raisin pies, Greek *avgolemono* soup, French *épaule d'agneau à l'orange*, and sangría, the Spanish national drink—they are all based on fruit, as are hundreds of dishes more.

LEMONS

Lemons are a big crop in North Africa, Italy, and Spain. I'll never forget walking through the lemon groves that cover the slopes of Mt. Etna, and breathing in the tart fragrance of huge ripe lemons weighing down the boughs.

I think Mediterranean lemons are milder than California ones, and I've tried to compensate for this difference in my recipes. Also I haven't found the *cedrat* variety in America, though it is widely grown over here. It's shaped something like a quince and has a thick skin. The Greeks make preserves with it and in Corsica *cedrat* is the foundation of a liqueur called *cédratine*.

Lemons are used so widely that they are inevitably associated with Mediterranean cuisine. I've even seen their leaves put to use in Positano, where they're used to pack raisins in crates. Lemon juice is used in place of vinegar in dressings and sauces, and with oil as a Levantine sauce for fish. If your lemons don't seem particularly juicy let them sit in warm water for a while before squeezing them. You may get more out of them that way, but some lemons give very little no matter what you do. I have that problem just before Ramadan in Tangier—lemons are an indispensable ingredient in *harira* soup which North Africans use to break the fast, and someone always seems to corner the market on the juicy ones just before the holy month begins.

The Greeks use lemon slices as a bed for fish before putting them in the oven to bake. In Israel there's a liver ragout flavored with garlic and lemon, and in Italy lemon makes a famous veal scaloppine sauce. In Campania a little lemon peel is used in the meat ball mixture called *polpette*, and candied lemon peel is added to sweets and to sauces for game. In Tunisia bits of peel are often sprinkled over freshly grilled meat, and throughout North Africa preserved or pickled lemons are an important ingredient in *tagines*.

There are numerous lemon ices, lemon-flavored rice puddings, and lemon ice cream desserts, not to mention lemon-flavored preserves, *confits*, and candies. In the Balearic Islands they serve a lovely lemony dessert called *pastel de grachonera de Ibiza*, made of egg yolks, lemon, and milk, and thickened with *ensaimades*—a lard flavored spiral-shaped roll.

LIMOUN MARAKAD

Preserved lemons (Morocco)

Preserved lemons are an absolute necessity if you want to make North African food. They're used in salads, chicken and olive dishes, and many other things, including the recipe for *mohk* which follows. The famous sardines of Safi are often canned with a slice of preserved lemon on top, and in my opinion this makes them one of the best canned sardines in the world.

It's possible that a white lacy growth will appear in your pickling jar as the lemons spend 30 days on your shelf. Don't worry about it—simply discard it when you open the jar, and rinse the lemons before use.

Ingredients

    5–6 lemons, well scrubbed
    ¼ cup or more salt
        Freshly squeezed lemon juice, *not chemically produced*
           lemon juice

Equipment

    Sterilized pint-size Mason jar

Working time: 10 minutes

Ripening time: 30 days

    1. Quarter each lemon from the top to within ½ inch of the bottom, dust the pulp with salt, then reshape the lemon.
    2. Place 1 tablespoon salt in the jar. Pack in the lemons and push them down, adding salt between them. Press hard to make room for more lemons and to release as much of their juice as possible. The lemon juice must cover the lemons. If necessary add freshly squeezed lemon juice to fill to the top leaving some air space before sealing the jar.
    3. Allow to ripen in a warm place for 30 days. Turn the jar upside down each day to distribute the salt and the juice.
    4. Rinse each lemon, as needed, under running cold water.

Note: Preserved lemons keep up to one year if kept covered with plenty of lemon juice and salt.

MOHK

Brain salad (Morocco)

    Everyone likes this brain salad—even people who swear they can't eat brains. It's served cold as an hors d'oeuvre and also makes a delicious dip for Arab bread.

Ingredients

> 1 pound calf, lamb, or beef brains
> ¼ cup chopped parsley
> ¼ cup chopped fresh coriander
> ½ teaspoon ground cumin
> 1 teaspoon paprika
>   Pinch of cayenne
> 1 teaspoon finely chopped garlic
> ¼ cup olive or salad oil
> ⅓ cup fresh lemon juice
> 1 preserved lemon (see preceding recipe)
>   rinsed, pulped, and cubed
>   Salt

Equipment

Saucepan · 3-quart heavy enameled casserole with cover

Working time: 15 minutes

Cooking time: 1 hour

Serves: 4 to 6

1. Soak the brains for 30 minutes in lukewarm water, then remove the membranes and as much blood as possible. Simmer, partially covered, for 30 minutes with the herbs, spices, garlic, oil, and 1½ cups water.

2. In the casserole, off heat, using a wooden spoon, mash the brains into small pieces. Stir in the lemon juice. Cook at the simmer another 20 minutes, stirring often.

3. Add the preserved lemon and continue cooking 10 minutes, stirring often. Readjust the seasoning. Allow to cool completely before serving.

SOUPA AVGOLEMONO

Egg and lemon soup (Greece)

Avgolemono soup and the three recipes that follow all use the mixture of lemon juice and egg yolk that is so beloved by the Greeks. The mixture results in a tart creamy sauce that is rich but very hard to resist.

It's interesting that a similar liaison is used to bind sauces in Spain, but there vinegar replaces lemon juice. The Turks use egg-lemon sauce though not as much as the Greeks. Their name for it is *terbiye*.

Ingredients

1 quart rich chicken stock
¼ cup raw rice
2 eggs
¼ cup freshly squeezed lemon juice
Salt and freshly ground white pepper

Equipment

2-quart heavy saucepan · Medium-sized mixing bowl ·
Whisk

Working time: 5 minutes

Cooking time: 20 minutes

Serves: 4

1. Bring the chicken stock to the boil and add the rice. Partially cover the pan and allow to simmer 15 minutes.
2. Beat the eggs well in a small bowl until thickened then beat in the lemon juice. Gradually add 1 cup hot broth to the egg mixture, beating well after each addition. Slowly stir this mixture into the remaining soup and continue cooking, below the simmer,

beating constantly until the soup is smooth and thickened. If the soup is allowed to boil the eggs will curdle. Season the soup with salt and freshly ground white pepper. Remove from the heat and serve at once in hot soup bowls.

Note: The soup also can be chilled and served cold.

BRODETTO ALLA ROMANA

Poached lamb shoulder with egg and lemon soup (Italy)

Everyone knows about Greek *avgolemono*, but I was surprised to find something so similar in Rome. This combination of lamb and soup with a last minute whisking in of lemon juice and egg yolks is a specialty served on Easter.

I found another instance of the same thing in a hand-written recipe book belonging to a Piedmont family. The dish is for boiled tongue in a sauce based on capers, anchovies, parsley, and onion. The cooked tongue is reheated in the sauce, then removed and sliced, and just before serving egg yolks and lemon juice are beaten into the sauce to make it creamy and rich.

Ingredients

     2 pounds lamb shoulder in one piece, excess fat removed
     2 quarts hot degreased rich beef stock
  6–8 egg yolks
     3 tablespoons lemon juice
     3 tablespoons fresh marjoram leaves, or 1 tablespoon dried
   18 slices of Italian bread, toasted, buttered,
          and toasted under the broiler with a grated
          parmesan topping

Equipment

Large soup pot · Flameproof soup tureen

Working time: 25 minutes

Cooking time: 1½–2 hours

Serves: 6

 1. Place the lamb shoulder in the soup pot. Add the hot beef stock. Bring to the boil and cook at the simmer, partially covered, 1½ hours. Skim off any scum that rises to the surface.
 2. Remove the meat when well done. Cut into serving pieces. Keep moist with a few tablespoons stock. Meanwhile put the egg yolks and lemon juice in the soup tureen, whisking to combine. Slowly stir in 1 cup stock to raise the temperature of the egg yolks, then slowly pour in the remaining stock, whisking constantly. Set over low heat and cook, stirring, until thickened. Do not allow the mixture to come to the boil. Stir in the marjoram, correct the seasoning, and serve hot. Serve the lamb and the soup at the same time. Pass the toasted cheese bread slices.

DOLMADAKIA ME AVGOLEMONO
Stuffed grape leaves with lemon and egg sauce (Greece)

Ingredients

  1 cup finely chopped onions
  ¾ pound ground lamb
 1½ tablespoons oil
  ½ teaspoon salt
  2 pinches freshly ground black pepper
  ½ cup raw rice
  ½ teaspoon dried mint leaves,
    crumbled to a powder between fingertips
  ½ tablespoon finely chopped parsley
  1 8-ounce jar grape vine leaves in brine
  1 cup rich beef stock, or more
  1 tablespoon butter
  2 egg yolks
  2 tablespoons lemon juice

Equipment

    Large skillet · 3-quart heavy saucepan ·
    A plate with a weight to fit in the saucepan ·
    Small mixing bowl · Whisk

Working time: 45 minutes

Cooking time: 1 hour

Serves: 6

1. Stir-cook the onions and the lamb in oil in the skillet for 5 minutes. Sprinkle with salt and pepper then stir in the rice. Cook, stirring, for 5 minutes over gentle heat. Add ½ cup water and continue cooking until the water is completely absorbed by the rice. Add the herbs and toss gently to mix well. Set aside to cool.

2. Rinse the grape leaves under cold running water, carefully separating each leaf. Place the leaves shiny side down, a few at a time, on a flat work surface. Fill each in the following manner: put 1 heaping tablespoon filling on each grape leaf near the base. Starting at the base, fold bottom of leaf over filling. Fold sides over filling to center. Roll tightly toward tip of the leaf.

3. In a heavy 3-quart saucepan arrange rolls in layers, scattering a few torn grape leaves between each layer. When all the rolls are in the saucepan add enough beef stock to cover them. Weight them down using a heavy plate, just large enough to fit inside, on top of the rolls. Bring to the boil, cover saucepan, and cook over very low heat for 1 hour. Add additional stock if needed.

4. Whisk the egg yolks until thickened. Beat in the lemon juice then ½ cup of the hot cooking juices. Transfer the stuffed grape leaves to a warm serving dish and spoon over the sauce. Serve at once.

This recipe is from *International Home Dining*, edited by the author and published by CBS.

ARNAKI AVGOLEMONO

Fricassee of lamb with egg and lemon sauce (Greece)

Ingredients

2 pounds lamb shoulder, cut into 1½-inch chunks
2 medium onions, thinly sliced
¼ pound unsalted butter
2 tablespoons finely chopped parsley
½ teaspoon grated lemon rind
1 cup rich chicken stock
  Salt and freshly ground black pepper
8 small artichokes
2 tablespoons vinegar
3 egg yolks
¼ cup fresh lemon juice

Equipment

4-quart heavy casserole · Small mixing bowl · Whisk
  · Enameled sauté pan · Enameled saucepan

Working time: 20 minutes

Cooking time: 1 hour 50 minutes

Serves: 4

1. Remove and discard the excess fat from the lamb. In a heavy casserole brown the lamb and onions in 4 tablespoons butter. Add parsley and grated lemon rind to the casserole and cook, stirring, for 1 minute. Pour in the chicken stock and season with salt and pepper. Bring to a boil, reduce the heat, cover, and simmer 1½ hours or until the meat is tender.
2. Meanwhile prepare the artichokes by removing the outside leaves and trimming the bases. Halve each one and remove the hairy choke. Place in acidulated water (water with 2 table-

spoons of vinegar added) to keep from blackening while trimming the rest. Add enough water to cover the artichokes. Cook at the simmer for about 20 minutes or until just tender in an enameled saucepan. Drain and pat dry then sauté the artichokes in the remaining 4 tablespoons butter. Add to the casserole 10 minutes before serving.

3. In a small mixing bowl beat 3 egg yolks until slightly thickened. Beat in the lemon juice then ½ cup of the simmering meat juices by tablespoonsful. Pour this mixture over the meat and artichokes, lower the heat, gently shake the casserole, and continue cooking until the sauce thickens. Readjust the seasoning if necessary. Remove from the heat and serve at once.

KUZU ŞİŞ KEBAB

Skewered lamb (Turkey)

All through the Middle East cooks use lemon juice to tenderize chicken and meat. My own feeling is that even if you use good tender American lamb, your shish kebab will not be right unless it's marinated first.

Lemon juice marinades are popular in other parts of the Mediterranean, too. In Sète in France fresh raw anchovies and sardines are "cooked" in lemon juice as in the South American dish seviche. In Cephalonia, in Greece, rabbit, hare, and veal are all marinated overnight in a quart of lemon juice. Then they're dried, browned, and braised in a red wine, garlic, and oil sauce.

Ingredients

3 pounds boned leg of lamb, cut into 1-inch cubes
¼ cup virgin olive oil
⅓ cup freshly squeezed lemon juice
2 teaspoons salt
1 teaspoon freshly ground black pepper
1 teaspoon dried thyme
1 onion, quartered
2 green peppers, seeded and deribbed
2 small tomatoes, quartered

Equipment

> Porcelain or glass mixing bowl   ·   Skewers   ·
> Outdoor barbecue (optional)

Working time: 15 minutes

Broiling time: 10 minutes

Serves: 6 to 8

1. Place the lamb in the mixing bowl. Combine olive oil, lemon juice, salt, pepper, and herb and pour over the lamb. Separate the onion quarters into leaves and cut the green peppers into 1-inch squares. Add to the meat and toss to coat all the ingredients evenly. Cover and let marinate for several hours.

2. String the meat, onions, peppers, and quartered tomatoes alternately on the skewers. Grill over high heat basting with the marinade until done to your liking. In the Middle East lamb is served rather well done.

KOUSTILYAT MICHWI
Grilled lamb chops (Tunisia)

Ingredients

> 8 rib lamb chops, each about 1½ inches thick
> Salt and freshly ground black pepper
> 3–4 tablespoons olive oil
> 2 teaspoons finely chopped lemon peel
> ½ cup finely chopped onion
> 2 tablespoons chopped parsley
> 2–3 tablespoons freshly squeezed lemon juice

Equipment

> Outdoor barbecue or broiler

Working time: 5 minutes

Grilling time: 8 to 10 minutes

Serves: 4

1. Heat charcoal in an outdoor grill or heat up the broiler.
2. Trim the lamb chops to remove excess fat. Sprinkle with salt and pepper and brush with oil. Arrange chops over the coals on an oiled rack. After 4 minutes turn. Avoid overcooking the meat. Arrange the chops on a large serving dish. Scatter chopped lemon peel, onion, and parsley over them and sprinkle with lemon juice. Serve at once.

SCALOPPINE AL LIMONE

Veal scallops with lemon sauce (Italy)

Ingredients

1 pound veal scallops (8–12 thin slices of veal cut from
 the leg, each about 4 by 4 inches, pounded as thin
 as possible with the side of a cleaver
 between sheets of wax paper)
 Salt and freshly ground black pepper
 Flour
6 tablespoons unsalted butter
2 tablespoons oil
3 tablespoons lemon juice
1 tablespoon finely chopped parsley
 Lemon slices

Equipment

Large skillet

Working and cooking time: 10 to 15 minutes

Serves: 4

1. Dredge the scallops in seasoned flour.
2. Heat half the butter and 2 tablespoons oil in the skillet and in it cook the scallops quickly on both sides. Transfer to a heated serving dish. Discard the fat from the skillet. Stir the lemon juice into the remaining pan juices and scrape up all the bits and pieces that stick to the bottom of the skillet. Off heat beat in the remaining butter then pour the pan juices over the meat. Season. Decorate the dish with thin lemon slices and pinches of chopped parsley. Serve at once.

PERDICES ESCABECHADAS

Marinated partridges in piquant jelly (Spain)

Ingredients

  2 1-pound partridges, ready to cook
      Salt and freshly ground black pepper
  ¼ cup olive oil
  3 whole cloves garlic, peeled
  ⅓ cup wine vinegar
  2 cups dry white wine
  10 whole black peppercorns
  2–3 sprigs parsley
  2 bay leaves
  1 sprig thyme
      Pinch of sharp paprika
  6 thin slices of lemon
  4 thin slices of orange

Decoration
  8 very thin slices of orange

Equipment

  5-quart enameled or stainless steel casserole
  or a flameproof earthenware casserole with a tight-fitting lid

Working time: 10 minutes

Cooking time: 1 hour

Serves: 4

1. The day before you plan to serve, split the partridges in half, rinse, and wipe dry with a cloth. Rub all over with salt and freshly ground black pepper. In the casserole lightly brown the partridges in heated oil on both sides. Add the garlic cloves and gently fry for 1 minute without browning. Combine vinegar, wine, spices, herbs, lemon and orange slices and pour over the birds. Bring to a boil, reduce the heat to the simmer, closely cover the casserole, and cook for 45 minutes or until the partridges are tender.

2. Let the partridges cool in the liquid then refrigerate until ready to serve. Remove cooked orange and lemon slices and replace with fresh thin slices of orange.

BARBOUNIA LADOLEMONO

Red mullets with lemon oil dressing (Greece)

This is a superb way to serve broiled small fish. It's popular in Greece, Turkey, and throughout the Middle East. In some countries the fish are wrapped in leaves before broiling. The Palestinians and Lebanese use grape leaves, and sometimes Swiss chard.

Ingredients

> 2 1½-pound fish suitable for charcoal broiling such as
> red mullets, small bass, mackerel, porgies, or bluefish,
> split and cleaned, boned or left whole
> Salt and freshly ground black pepper
> ⅓ cup olive oil
> 3 tablespoons freshly squeezed lemon juice
> 2 good pinches of dried oregano, finely crumbled
> between fingertips just before using

Equipment

Outdoor barbecue or roasting pan for indoor broiling
Small bowl

Working time: 5 minutes

Broiling time: 10 minutes (approximately)

Serves: 4

1. Heat charcoal in an outdoor barbecue or heat up the broiler.
2. Sprinkle the fish inside and out with salt and freshly ground black pepper then rub all over with a little olive oil.
3. Combine remaining oil, lemon juice, and oregano in a small bowl. Place the fish on an oiled grid over hot coals. Brush with the prepared oil dressing and let cook, without turning, about 5 minutes. Turn and baste the fish.
4. Turn the fish onto a serving dish, pour over the remaining oil dressing, and serve at once.

ARROZ DOCE

Lemon and rice pudding (Portugal)

Ingredients

   ¾ cup medium-grain rice
   5 cups milk
 1½ tablespoons grated lemon peel
   3 tablespoons butter
   3 egg yolks
  ½ cup sugar
   3 tablespoons lemon juice
  ¼ teaspoon ground cinnamon

Equipment

Colander or large sieve   ·   Large heavy saucepan
Beating bowl and whisk   ·   1½-quart serving dish

Working time: 10 minutes

Cooking time: 1½ hours

Serves: 6 to 8

1. Bring 3 cups water to the boil and gradually add the rice. Cook, stirring, 2 minutes then remove from heat and drain the rice in a colander or sieve.

2. Combine 2½ cups milk, the lemon rind, and butter in a heavy saucepan. Bring to the boil and add the rice, stirring. Cook over very low heat, stirring frequently. After 30 minutes or when the rice absorbs all the milk, stir in the remaining milk and continue cooking until the rice is soft and the mixture looks like a thick creamy sauce.

3. Beat the egg yolks with the sugar until light and lemon colored. Add the lemon juice. Fold the egg mixture into the rice and set over low heat, stirring constantly for 4 or 5 minutes. Spoon the rice into a serving dish, allow to cool. Dust with ground cinnamon.

ORANGES

There were always bitter orange trees in Morocco, and the Moors brought them to Europe, but it took the Portuguese to import the sweet oranges they found in India and China.

Bitter oranges, or *bigarades*, or Seville oranges as we call them, are the basis for the best orange marmelade. You can find them in the middle of winter in Puerto Rican and Hispanic markets. The original duck *a l'orange* was first made with them in southern Spain where chocolate was also an ingredient. The dish spread to Languedoc where it was refined and the chocolate omitted, but bitter oranges remained the foundation of the sauce.

Finally when the *bigarade* was not available the good cooks of Paris changed the recipe and used vinegar to make sweet oranges tart.

Elizabeth David counsels that one of the best ways to use bitter oranges is in a tomato sauce as they do in southwestern France. A thick garlic-flavored tomato sauce is made, and then a handful of peeled *bigarade* pulp is added and cooked down. The sauce is used with broiled chicken or eggs.

Peel of *bigarade* is absolutely *de rigueur* in Provençal daubes, and in Perpignan they make *perdreaux à la Catalane*— partridge in orange and wine sauce.

In Spain pollock is served with an orange sauce, and in Murcia they bake hake with slices of orange and cinnamon.

In Turkey there is a salad of orange slices, black olives, and tiny sweet onions served in a dressing of lemon juice and olive oil. The Turks call it "The Emir's pearls" because of the colors of the dish.

Orange juice is used to flavor cookies, cakes, glazed fruits, berries, and soufflés. In Provence, Lebanon, and North Africa orange petals are distilled to make orange flower water used to flavor all sorts of sweets, as well as Moroccan salads and *tagines*.

In Tunisia they have a unique way of making *sole meunière*. Because wine can't be used in cooking on account of Koranic law, they use the juice of Seville oranges to glaze the pan drippings for the sauce.

CALDILLO DE PERRO

"Dog soup" with bitter oranges (Spain)

Alan Davidson describes this dish in his book *Mediterranean Seafood*, but he neglected to explain why it's called "dog soup." I'm rather curious about it, because it's an excellent dish, and certainly not "fit for a dog." But then I'm reminded of a famous restaurant in Taiwan on Formosa which is called, literally, "A Dog Wouldn't Eat Here!"

This dish is a specialty of Cadiz, which strictly speaking is not a Mediterranean town since it's on the Atlantic coast just outside the Straits of Gibraltar.

Ingredients

> 3 very fresh small whitings, head and tail intact, cut into 2½-inch-thick slices
> Sea salt
> 3 tablespoons olive oil
> 2–3 cloves garlic, peeled
> ½ cup chopped onion
> 3½ cups boiling water
> ¾ cup juice of bitter oranges
> ¼ cup cubed stale bread

Equipment

An earthenware, enameled, or stainless steel saucepan

Working time: 10 minutes

Cooking time: 25 to 30 minutes

Serves: 4

1. Salt the fish and let stand for 1 hour.
2. In a saucepan heat the oil and in it quickly brown the garlic cloves; discard them. In the same oil cook the onions without browning. Pour over boiling water and cook, covered, until the onion is soft. Bring the liquid to a rolling boil and add the fish, piece by piece, without losing the boil. Cook over high heat 15 to 20 minutes.
3. Just before serving stir in the orange juice. Serve with the bread cubes.

VIN D'ORANGE DE COLETTE

Orange flavored wine (France)

This recipe, adapted from Bifrous' *200 Recettes Secretes de la Cuisine Française*, was devised by the French writer Colette who also happened to be a very good cook.

Ingredients

    2 pounds oranges, quartered
    1 bottle dry white wine, preferably from Burgundy
    1 cup sugar
  2–3 tablespoons good cognac or *eau de vie*

Equipment

    1 large glass, porcelain, or earthenware jug
    or pitcher with a tight-fitting cover · Cloth strainer
    or cone filter paper · Enameled saucepan

Working and cooking time: 20 minutes

TO BE PREPARED 2 WEEKS BEFORE SERVING

1. Pack orange quarters into a jug or pitcher. Pour in the wine, cover, and set in a shady cool place for 1 week.
2. Strain into a saucepan, add the sugar then stir-cook over low heat until the sugar is completely dissolved. Cool. Stir in the cognac. Pour into a clean wine bottle, recork and let stand 1 week. Chill well before serving.

OAF TAPUZIM

Chicken with oranges (Israel)

Ingredients

> 1 3-pound chicken, quartered
> 4 teaspoons sharp mustard
>   Salt and freshly ground black pepper
> 2 tablespoons margarine
> ½ onion, finely chopped
> 1 cup orange juice
> ¼ cup brown sugar

Equipment

> A shallow baking pan, glass, porcelain, or stainless steel ·
> Saucepan

Working time: 10 minutes

Roasting time: 40 minutes

Serves: 4

1. Preheat the oven to 375 degrees.
2. Smear the chicken quarters with mustard and sprinkle with salt and pepper. Place the quarters skin side down in one layer in the baking pan. Add margarine, onion, and orange juice. Set in the oven to roast, basting often with the pan juices, for 20 minutes.
3. Turn the chicken quarters over, skin side up, add the sugar and continue roasting and basting until the chicken is tender and golden brown. Pour the pan juices into the saucepan. By way of boiling reduce to a thick sauce, stirring. Spoon part of the sauce over the chicken. Serve hot and pass the remaining sauce in a sauceboat.

ÉPAULE D'AGNEAU À L'ORANGE
Lamb stew with oranges (France)

This dish is from the southeast of France. The bouquet garni includes a dried orange peel which is typical of the region. To properly dry orange peel, peel off the zest of the orange and leave to dry three days in an airy place.

Ingredients

½ cup (about 4 ounces) lean salt pork, blanched, refreshed, drained, and cut into large dice
2 tablespoons olive oil
2 small onions, quartered
2 carrots, cut into 1-inch pieces
2 pounds lean shoulder of lamb, cut into 1½-inch chunks
Flour
1 cup dry white wine
1 cup beef stock or water
Bouquet garni: 1 bay leaf, a few parsley sprigs, thyme leaves, a few celery leaves, and a 2-by-1-inch piece of dried orange peel tied together with thread
1 tablespoon finely chopped garlic
2 teaspoons sugar
2–3 tablespoons freshly squeezed juice of a bitter orange or substitute orange juice mixed with 1 tablespoon lemon juice (see note)
8 peeled orange sections, preferably from bitter oranges
Cayenne (optional)
Chopped parsley

Equipment

Deep heavy skillet or small casserole with tight-fitting cover · 2 small enameled saucepans · Strainer with wooden pestle · Skimmer or slotted spoon · 3-quart saucepan with cover

Working time: 30 minutes

Cooking time: 2 to 2½ hours

Serves: 4

1. In a deep heavy skillet or casserole lightly brown the salt pork in olive oil. Add the onions and carrots, and cook, stirring, until golden brown and soft, about 15 minutes. Set aside the salt pork and vegetables.

2. Brown the meat in the same skillet on all sides. Sprinkle with flour and allow to brown nicely, turning the pieces of meat often. Add the wine, bring to the boil, stirring. Reduce the heat, add the beef stock, bouquet garni, and garlic. Return the vegetables and the salt pork to the skillet. Season the cooking liquid with salt and pepper. Cover tightly and cook over low heat at the simmer 1 hour.

3. After the first hour's cooking, lightly caramelize the sugar in a small saucepan. Stir in the orange juice and ¼ of the cooking liquid, mixing well. Add to the skillet and continue cooking, covered, an additional 45 minutes, or until the lamb is tender.

4. Transfer the lamb to a side dish, cover and keep warm. Strain the cooking liquid into a saucepan pressing down with a pestle on the vegetables to extract all their juices. Bring to the boil, reduce the heat, and simmer 15 minutes. Skim off all the fat that rises to the surface of the sauce. Correct the seasoning. Add the meat to the sauce. Add cayenne if desired. Simmer a few minutes to blend flavors. Add the peeled orange sections and allow to heat through. Serve hot dusted with freshly chopped parsley. Serve with rice pilaf.

Note: Bitter oranges are available in early February in Hispanic and specialty markets.

LOMO DE CERDO AL ESTILO DE IBIZA

Roast pork with oranges (Spain)

Ingredients

    4 pounds pork loin
    1 cup freshly squeezed orange juice
    Salt
    3 tablespoons sugar
    1 onion, quartered
    1 bay leaf, crumbled
    1 teaspoon chopped garlic
    ¼ teaspoon dried thyme
    2 oranges, thinly sliced
    2 apples, cored and thinly sliced
    2 tablespoons butter

Equipment

Deep stoneware, glass, enameled, or stainless steel bowl   ·
Shallow roasting pan   ·   Skillet

Working time: 10 minutes

Roasting time: 2½ hours

Serves: 8

    1. The day before you plan to serve, place the pork loin in a bowl. Combine the orange juice, ½ teaspoon salt, 2 tablespoons sugar, onion, and bay leaf. Pour over the meat, cover, and refrigerate for at least 12 hours, turning the meat once or twice,
    2. Preheat the oven to 450 degrees.
    3. Lift, drain, and wipe dry the meat, reserving the marinade. Rub the meat with a mixture of salt, garlic, and thyme. Place the roast fat side up in the roasting pan and set in oven.

Turn the oven heat down to 350 after 20 minutes. Baste often with the fat in the pan. After the first hour drain the fat from the pan. Add the marinade, strained, and continue basting the meat every 10 minutes.

4. Just before the end of the roasting time sauté the orange and the apple slices in butter in a small skillet. Sprinkle with the remaining tablespoon sugar and cook until nicely glazed.

5. When the meat is cooked remove and keep warm. Carefully skim off any fat from the pan. Boil down the remaining pan juices. Correct the seasoning with salt and pepper.

6. Place the meat, sliced, on a heated serving dish with alternating slices of orange and apple down each side. Pour the pan juices over the meat and serve at once.

GRANITA D'ARANCIA

Orange ice (Italy)

Like all Italian ices this *granita* should not be a frozen block, but light and mushy like snow.

Pureed strawberries and grapefruit juice plus a teaspoon of vanilla can be substituted for the orange and lemon juice. If you can get hold of some blood oranges the *granita* will be exquisitely beautiful and delicious.

Ingredients

> 2¾ cups sugar
> 2 cups water
> 1 quart orange juice, strained (use blood oranges
>   if available)
> ½ cup lemon juice, strained
> ½ tablespoon grated orange rind

Equipment

> 2-quart saucepan · Large mixing bowl · Electric beater
> · 6-cup ice cream mold

Working time: 10 minutes

Cooking time: 5 minutes

Makes: 6 cups

TO BE PREPARED 1 DAY IN ADVANCE

    1. Combine sugar and water in a saucepan and cook, stirring over medium heat, until the sugar is dissolved. Boil the syrup for 5 minutes. Pour into the mixing bowl and allow to cool.

    2. Stir the orange juice, lemon juice, and grated rind into the sugar syrup. Set in the freezer compartment until the mixture is mushy but set around the edges of the bowl. Use an electric beater and beat until smooth. Return to the freezer for 4 to 5 hours. Beat again, pour into mold, and freeze it until almost firm. If desired serve with whipped cream.

DIPLES

Deep-fried orange crullers (Greece)

Ingredients

    2½ cups all-purpose flour
    ½ teaspoon double-acting baking powder
    ⅛ teaspoon salt
    2 whole eggs
    1 egg yolk
    ½ teaspoon grated orange rind
    3 tablespoons orange juice
    3 tablespoons peanut oil
      Oil for deep frying
    1 cup liquid honey
  ¾–1 cup finely chopped walnuts
      Ground cinnamon

Equipment

Sifter · Large mixing bowl · Rolling pin ·
Fat thermometer (optional) · Deep skillet ·
Tongs or slotted spoon · Cake rack set over a wide pan
· Small saucepan

Working and cooking time: 1½ hours

Makes: 6 dozen crullers (approximately)

1. Sift the flour with the baking powder and the salt into a large mixing bowl. Lightly beat the eggs with the grated orange rind and orange juice. Press a deep hollow in the middle of the flour with your fist and pour in the egg mixture. Using your hands, gradually incorporate the flour into the center then gather the dough into a ball. Turn out onto a floured surface and vigorously knead the dough until very smooth and elastic, gradually working in the peanut oil by tablespoons. Put aside to rest for at least 1 hour in a cool place covered with a damp kitchen towel.

2. Divide the dough into 4 parts. Roll one part of dough out on a floured surface until paper thin. Cut into strips 6 inches long and about 1 inch wide. Loop them like bows or tie them into loose knots. Repeat with the remaining portions of dough.

3. Heat the oil to a depth of 1½ inches in a deep skillet. Fry 4 or 5 at a time until golden brown on both sides. This takes about 1 minute. With tongs or a slotted spoon, set the *diples* on cake racks to drain.

4. Heat the honey and dilute with ⅓ cup water. Dribble over the slightly cooled *diples* then sprinkle at once with the chopped walnuts and dust with ground cinnamon.

FIGS

In the Casbah of Tangier there's an old fig tree in the courtyard of a house that was once the home of Samuel Pepys. It's now owned by an elderly British gentleman who is accosted every summer by the women of his neighborhood just as the figs on his tree become ripe. They want the fruit because they think it will increase their fertility. The Englishman graciously complies.

Whether or not figs of old fig trees can perform miracles in marital beds, they are unquestionably a wondrous fruit. They're grown all over the Mediterranean region and used in a great variety of ways.

Italian kadota figs are pale green, the calmyrna of Smyrna are yellow and large, French bellons are purple with red pulp, and the figs of Marseilles—yellow-white with white pulp—are simply too good to be true.

In ancient Greece fig leaves were wrapped about fish before they were baked. Later many Mediterranean countries used them to wrap small birds.

The Phoenicians, it is said, first brought figs to France. Now the French use them with duck, the same way they use peaches, and make a medicinal drink of dried figs called *figuette*.

In Sardinia figs are stuffed into large woodcocks or partridges along with fresh white cheese and chopped mushrooms. Then the birds are wrapped in pork fat and fig leaves and baked over myrtle and juniper sticks. The dish is served with a puree of chestnuts, and is alleged by those who have tasted it to be divine.

The Italians, too, are great connoisseurs of figs. In Sicily there are a great number of fig desserts: fig ice cream, *buccelato* pastry stuffed with figs, and *cucidati* fig cookies. In Calabria *crocette* figs are half roasted, then stuffed with fennel seeds and almonds, and then roasted again. *Pestringolo* is the name of an Italian fig cake, and in Apulia there is a specialty called *fichi ripieni* in which large moist figs are stuffed with almond slivers, chopped walnuts, and candied fruits, baked, weighted, then sprinkled with liqueur and confectioners' sugar mixed with cinnamon.

In Yugoslavia there's a fig roll made with dried figs and yellow raisins soaked in rum. The fruits are chopped, then mixed with chopped almonds, walnuts, hazelnuts, and candied fruits— the whole mass is rolled into a sausage shape, powdered with cinnamon and sugar and left for a day to dry, after which it is cut into slices and served.

In southern Italy there's a confection of large dried figs each stuffed with a toasted almond and a small amount of diced candied orange peel. The figs are baked, then rolled in melted chocolate, and served when they are cool. In Portugal it's not uncommon to be served figs with an after dinner glass of port. Ground almonds and grated chocolate are blended and stuffed into the fruit, which are then baked and allowed to cool.

The Italians love to serve prosciutto rolled about halves of peeled ripe figs as an elegant and chic antipasto. In Malta fresh green figs are halved, peeled, sprinkled with sugar and liqueur, baked until they've caramelized, and then served cold with thick fresh cream.

The Syrians are famous for their fig jam, and through all the Middle East, too, there's a presentation of lamb stuffed with raisins, dates, and figs.

FRITTURA DI FICHI RUSPOLI

Hot fried figs (Italy)

Ingredients

    8 fresh firm black figs, peeled
    ½ cup dark rum
    ⅓ cup all-purpose flour
    ½ cup water
      Vegetable oil, lard, or olive oil

Equipment

    2 shallow bowls · Skillet · Slotted spoon

Working time: 5 minutes

Soaking time: 1 hour

Frying time: 3 minutes

Serves: 4

1. Soak the figs in rum for 1 hour, turning them often.

2. In a shallow bowl slowly stir the flour into the water. Beat until smooth and creamy. Heat enough oil or lard to the depth of ½ inch in the skillet. Dip the figs into the prepared batter then into the hot fat. Fry until golden brown on both sides. Serve very hot.

SAUTÉ D'AGNEAU AUX FIGUES FOURRÉES

Sautéed lamb with stuffed figs (France)

Ingredients

1½ pounds lamb shoulder, cut into 1½-inch chunks
    Salt and freshly ground black pepper
3 tablespoons oil
1 clove garlic, unpeeled
2 dozen dried figs, large and supple, each stuffed with
    1 shelled walnut
¼ cup lemon juice

Equipment

Large skillet with lid

Working time: 10 minutes

Cooking time: 1½ hours (approximately)

Serves: 4

Season the lamb with salt and pepper. Heat the oil and in it gently sauté the pieces of lamb until nicely browned on all sides. Add ½ cup water, the garlic clove, the stuffed figs, and ½ the lemon juice. Cook, covered, at the simmer until the lamb is very tender. Readjust the seasoning and stir in more lemon juice to taste. Serve very hot.

TEEN MAKOOD

Fig jam (Syria)

Ingredients

1½ pounds dried figs, washed
1¼ cups sugar
    Juice of ½ lemon
½ teaspoon ground aniseed
 1 cup mixed chopped nuts: walnuts, blanched almonds,
        and pine nuts

Equipment

Scissors · 4-quart enameled or stainless steel heavy
saucepan · 2 clean jars with tight-fitting lids

Working time: 5 minutes

Cooking time: 1 hour (approximately)

1. Cover the figs with cold water and let soak overnight. Drain but reserve the water. Cut the figs into small pieces with a pair of scissors.

2. Boil the soaking water, sugar, and lemon juice together 5 minutes. Add the figs, lower the heat, and cook at the simmer for about 1 hour, stirring often. When thick and jamlike add the aniseed and chopped nuts. Simmer gently 3 to 4 minutes then remove from the heat. Allow to cool. Pack into jars up to the top, cover tightly, and store in a cool place.

DATES

Dates, strictly speaking, are not a Mediterranean fruit. They're grown in the desert, where they're the dominant food. But the desert of North Africa is very near its coast, and dates have become so important to North African cuisine that it's really impossible to leave them out.

Algerian dates are absolutely the best I've ever had. On a long trip through the Algerian Sahara I literally lived on dates for two weeks. I bought kilos of the best I could find in the oasis of Bou-Saada, the half moist ones called *deglet nour*, and never tired of their sweet nutty smokey flavor.

The Moroccans make a date and orange salad that is a good accompaniment to a spicy *tagine*. They use dates to stuff fish, and often put them into couscous too.

The Tunisians have three types of stuffed dates called *tmar mikchi*. The dates are stuffed with apricot jam, or walnuts, or lightly toasted pine nuts and pistachios then dipped in syrup.

In Algeria there is a cookie called *makroud etmar*. A semolina-based pastry, it is filled with chopped dates flavored with orange flower water, cloves, cinnamon, and honey and fried in hot oil. Another Algerian date sweet is made with toasted semolina flour mixed with crushed dates, then blended with butter and oil. The mass is patted into a cake pan then cut into small pieces for serving.

For the two recipes that follow you can use California dates, which can really be very good. But I urge you to splurge on some good *biskra* or *bou-saada* Algerian dates next time you want to eat them plain. I think it will be a revelation.

TAGINE BI TEMAR

Date tagine *(Morocco)*

Ingredients

          2 tablespoons butter or oil
       2½ pounds lamb shoulder, trimmed of excess fat
               and cut into 1½-inch chunks
             Salt
        ¼ teaspoon turmeric
        ¼ teaspoon ground ginger
        ½ teaspoon ground black pepper
        ¼ teaspoon finely chopped garlic

   ¾ cup finely chopped onion
   6 sprigs fresh coriander
     Cayenne
¾–1 cup pitted dates
   ¼ teaspoon ground cinnamon

Equipment

   Large heavy casserole with cover · Round shallow
   ovenproof serving dish

Working time: 15 minutes

Cooking time: 2 hours

Serves: 4

   1. Melt the butter in the casserole and in it lightly brown the
meat on all sides. Add salt, spices, and garlic. Toss with the meat
and cook over low heat 5 to 10 minutes. Add the onion, coriander
sprigs, and 2 cups water. Bring to the boil, and simmer, covered,
1½ hours (adding more water if necessary), or until the meat is
very tender.
   2. Preheat the oven to highest setting.
   3. Spread the meat in one layer in the ovenproof serving
dish. Place the dates in between the meat. Remove the coriander
sprigs from the cooking liquid. Correct the seasoning adding
cayenne to taste. The sauce must be spicy. Pour the sauce over
the meat and sprinkle with ground cinnamon. Set on the highest
shelf of the oven and bake, uncovered, until the dates become
crusty—about 15 minutes. Serve hot.

SALATA LETCHINE

Date and orange salad (Morocco)

Ingredients

     1 head romaine lettuce
     3 navel or temple oranges
     2 tablespoons lemon juice
     2 tablespoons sugar
        Pinch of salt
        Ground cinnamon
     2 tablespoons orange juice
     1 tablespoon orange flower water
     ¾ cup chopped dates
     ¼ cup chopped blanched toasted almonds

Equipment

Mixing bowl · Salad bowl

Working time: 15 minutes

Serves: 4 to 6

1. Wash the lettuce after discarding the coarse outer leaves. Separate the tender leaves one by one. Drain, pat dry, shred, and place in a salad bowl. Keep chilled.

2. Pare the oranges and separate into sections. Mix the lemon juice, sugar, salt, ½ teaspoon cinnamon, orange juice, and orange flower water in a small mixing bowl.

3. Just before serving, pour most of the dressing over the lettuce and toss. Arrange the orange sections overlapping around the edges. Top with the dates and the almonds. Dribble over the remaining dressing and dust with a little cinnamon. Serve at once.

PEACHES

MARMELADE DE PÊCHES

Peach jam (France)

This recipe, from Elizabeth David's *French Provincial Cooking*, is wonderful, and my absolutely favorite preserve. This is not an adaptation. I give her recipe exactly as she wrote it herself.

When I do it I use 15 pounds of peaches which is just right for my 5½-quart preserving pan.

"Immerse the fruit in boiling water for a minute and then gently skin them. Extract the stones by pressing firmly with your finger on the stalk end. Cut the peaches in halves. Weigh them. For each pound measure ¾ pound of preserving or loaf sugar [granulated sugar] and ⅛ pint [5 tablespoons] of water. Put sugar and water into a preserving pan and bring to the boil. Put in the peaches, and when the sugar has once more come to the boil turn the flame low, and leave them very gently cooking, only just moving, for ¼ hour. Remove from the fire and leave until the next day, when the jam is to be boiled as before, very gently, for ½ hour. If the syrup sets when poured on a plate, the jam is cooked. If it is still too thin, remove the fruit, pack it carefully in jars, and continue cooking the syrup until it does set. Skim it when cool, pour it over the fruit, to fill the jars; tie down when cold. A dozen average size peaches will make sufficient preserve to fill two 1-pound jars.

"This method makes a rather extravagant but very delicious preserve. Unfortunately it tends to form a skin of mold within a very short time, but this does not affect the rest of the jam, some of which I have kept for well over a year, even in a damp house."

VIN DE PÊCHES

White wine flavored with peaches (France)

I once read a recipe in a cookbook for peach wine that called for 120 peach leaves. Thinking that most people probably don't have a peach tree, but nevertheless deserved to drink peach wine, I devised this recipe which requires no peach leaves, and only four good fresh Georgia peaches.

I suppose the converse of peach-flavored wine is wine-flavored peach. It's very Mediterranean to dip a piece of fresh peach into a little wine left in the glass.

Ingredients

> 4 yellow peaches, peeled
> 3 cups good dry white wine
> 2 cinnamon sticks
> 2 cloves
> ½ cup sugar
> ½ cup *eau de vie*, brandy, or vodka

Equipment

> 1-quart jar with cover · Filter paper or muslin bag
> or clean fine-mesh strainer · 2-quart enameled saucepan
> · Clean 1-quart bottle with an air-tight stopper

Working time: 10 minutes

Macerating time: 4 days

1. Drop the peaches one by one in boiling water for a few seconds; remove the peel and put them into a clean jar. Cover with all the wine. Add the spices, cover the jar, and set in a dark cool place to macerate for 4 days.

2. Strain the wine into the enameled saucepan. Add the sugar. Stir over low heat until the sugar is dissolved. Cool. Stir in the *eau de vie*. Bottle and plug tightly. Store in a dark cool place. Chill before serving. The peaches can be stewed for compote.

PESCHE RIPIENE
Stuffed peaches (Italy)

This recipe calls for yellow peaches, which appear in the market later than the white ones. If they're not ripe when you buy them you can ripen them at home by storing them wrapped in plastic in a dark place.

To facilitate peeling, lower peaches into boiling water for an instant. If the peaches are really ripe you may be able to peel them simply by rubbing them with the side of a knife.

Ingredients

> 8 firm ripe yellow peaches, peeled, halved, and stoned
> ½ cup shelled walnuts
> 6 macaroons or 6 whole *amaretti di Saronno*
> ¼ cup heavy cream
> 1 egg yolk
> 2 tablespoons cognac
> 1 tablespoon sugar

Equipment

> 12-inch baking dish, buttered · Electric blender ·
> Mixing bowl

Working time: 10 minutes

Baking time: 20 minutes

Serves: 8

1. Deepen the hollow in each peach half. Place the peaches hollow side up in the prepared baking dish.
2. Preheat the oven to 350 degrees.
3. In an electric blender grind the walnuts and the macaroons until crumbly. Combine with cream, egg yolk, cognac, and

sugar. Stuff each hollow with some of the filling. Any excess can be placed between the peach halves. Set in the oven to bake for 20 minutes. Serve warm.

SANGRÍA

Wine punch (Spain)

Ingredients

- 1 bottle (about 3¾ cups) red wine
- 1 cup fresh orange juice
- 1 cup fresh grapefruit juice
- ¼ cup sugar
- 2 cups mixed sliced fresh fruit: peaches, apples, melon, strawberries, and oranges
- 1 quart soda water
    Ice cubes (optional)

Equipment

Juice squeezer · Large jug or pitcher

Working time: 10 minutes

Serves: 10 to 12

Put wine, fruit juices, sugar, and mixed fruit in a large jug or pitcher. Stir until well combined. Chill 2 hours. Dilute with soda water just before serving. Serve over ice if desired.

GRAPES

There are vineyards in every country bordering the Mediterranean, producing vast quantities of grapes for the innumerable wines that are so necessary to Mediterranean life. From late August to October beautiful grapes flood the markets, to be eaten raw, used in cooking, for pressing to make wines, or for making an unfermented grape drink called must.

In France they call it *mout de raisin*; in Turkey *şira*. To make it, wash, stem, crush, and sieve ripe white grapes. Allow the juice to stand 24 hours in a glass jug in a cool place, then siphon off the clear juice from the sediment, sieve it through several layers of cheesecloth, and drink before it ferments.

On the Ionian Islands of Greece must is mixed with boiling cream of wheat, cinnamon, and fresh green grapes to make a custard called *mustalevria*. It's then decorated with nuts and sesame seeds, and either eaten fresh or put up in jars.

PICCIONI CON L'UVA

Squab with green grapes (Italy)

In southern France and Italy there are many recipes for pigeons and other small birds prepared with fresh green grapes. The addition here of navel oranges makes this *piccioni con l'uva* special.

Ingredients

> 4 squab, each weighing about 1 pound plus their livers
> Salt and freshly ground black pepper
> 2 tablespoons oil
> 3 tablespoons unsalted butter
> ½ medium onion, chopped
> 1 cup dry white wine
> ½ cup chicken stock
> 2 navel oranges
> A large bunch of Muscat grapes, peeled and pipped

Equipment

Heavy 5-quart enameled casserole

Working time: 10 minutes

Cooking time: 45 minutes

Serves: 4

1. Halve the squab then sprinkle with salt and pepper. Heat the oil and butter in the casserole and when hot lightly brown the squab on both sides. Add the onion and cook 5 minutes, over medium heat. Add ½ cup wine. Raise the heat, cook uncovered, until the wine reduces to a glaze. Continue cooking until the skin sides of the squab begin to crisp. Add the remaining wine and again reduce the wine to a glaze. Add the chicken stock and the livers. Cover the casserole, lower the heat, and cook for 30 minutes, or until the squab are tender.

2. Meanwhile peel and section the oranges. Remove the squab and keep warm. Skim off all the fat from the cooking liquid and discard. Add the orange sections and the grapes to the casserole and allow to heat through. Readjust the seasoning. Spoon some of the hot sauce over the squab and serve at once. Pass the remaining sauce in a sauceboat.

GRANITA D'UVA NERA ALLA SIMONETTA

Simonetta's black grape ice (Italy)

This is a recipe refined by my friend Simonetta Ponzone, who worked out the addition of ruby port wine by sniffing every bottle in her immense cabinet of liqueurs after tasting a black grape puree and deciding it needed "a little something."

Ingredients

> 1 pound black grapes
> 1 cup sugar
> ½ cup water
>   Juice of 2 lemons
> ¼ cup ruby port wine
>   Small bowl of whipped cream

Equipment

> Electric blender · Sieve · Small saucepan ·
> Mixing bowl · Whisk · Electric beater ·
> 6-cup ice cream mold

Working time: 10 minutes

Cooking time: 5 minutes

Serves: 6

1. The day before you plan to serve, puree the grapes in the blender and push through a sieve to remove skins and pips.

2. Combine sugar and water in a saucepan and cook, stirring over medium heat, until the sugar is dissolved. Boil the syrup 5 minutes. Pour into the mixing bowl and allow to cool; then stir in the grape puree and the juice of 2 lemons. Whisk until well blended. Pour into the mold and set in the freezer compartment until the mixture is mushy but set around the rim of the mold. Use an electric beater and beat until smooth. Return to the freezer and freeze overnight.

3. Remove from the freezer, beat again, add the port wine, and refreeze until firm. Turn out onto a serving dish and serve with whipped cream.

RAISINS

Raisins are used in Moroccan couscous, and all through Greece and the Middle East in vegetable stuffings, pilafs, and stuffed chickens, kids, and lamb. In Corsica eels are cooked with raisins, and in the Tunisian town of Sfax raisins, onions, and *ras el hanout* (a spice mixture of black pepper, roses, long pepper, cinnamon, and cloves) are made into a sauce for salted fish. There is also an interesting Roman dish called *coda all vaccinara*—oxtail stewed with tomatoes, herbs, raisins, pine nuts, and grated cheese.

CANETON À LA LANGUEDOCIENNE
Duckling with raisins (France)

This dish is normally made with raisins, but when green grapes are in season the Languedociennes use them instead.

Ingredients

    1 4½-pound duckling, ready to cook, with neck and giblets
        Salt and freshly ground black pepper
   ½ cup chopped carrots
   ½ cup chopped onion
    1 celery rib, chopped
    2 thick slices bacon, diced
    1 bay leaf
    1 sprig thyme
 2–3 sprigs parsley
   ¼ pound yellow raisins, soaked in water or cognac 30 minutes
    1 tablespoon sugar
   ½ cup dry white wine
    1 cup rich chicken stock
    1 lemon

Equipment

Kitchen string · Roasting pan with rack ·
Small heavy saucepan · Strainer

Working time: 20 minutes

Roasting time: 1½ hours

Serves: 4

1. Preheat the oven to 350 degrees.

2. Prick the duckling all over with the tines of a fork, rub the skin with salt and pepper, and truss the bird. Spread the neck, giblets, vegetables, bacon, and herbs in the roasting pan. Place the duckling on top and roast in the oven for 1½ hours or until tender, turning the duck at 20-minute intervals, basting with the pan juices.

3. In the heavy saucepan cook the sugar with the raisins over low heat, stirring constantly, until golden brown. Set aside.

4. Remove the duck, cover, and keep warm. Pour off all the fat and set the pan over high heat. Pour in the wine and reduce, scraping up all the bits clinging to the pan. Add the stock, bring to the boil, and simmer a few minutes to allow the sauce to reduce slightly. Strain the sauce pressing down hard on giblets, bacon, and vegetables to extract all their juices. Add the strained sauce to the raisins and reheat, stirring, to blend flavors. Add lemon juice to taste and readjust the seasoning.

5. Carve the duck, arrange on a heated serving dish. Spoon over the raisin sauce and serve at once.

PETITS PÂTES DE BÉZIERS

Little sweet lamb pastries from Béziers (France)

These little hot meat pies made of leftover lamb, brown sugar, and raisins mixed with meat fat baked inside a pastry shell are a favorite midday snack in Béziers. In the town of Pézenas, they are made the same way, with a little lemon rind added to the mixture.

Ingredients

> 2 cups all-purpose flour, sifted
> 1 teaspoon salt
> ¼ cup lard, chilled and cut into bits
> 3 tablespoons butter, chilled and cut into bits
> ⅓ cup ice water
> 2 cups ground cooked lamb
> ¼ cup finely chopped hard fat such as kidney fat, fat back, or lard
> 1 tablespoon brown sugar
> ¼ cup yellow raisins, soaked in brandy or rum
> Salt and freshly ground black pepper
> 1 egg yolk beaten with 1 teaspoon water

Equipment

Mixing bowl · Rolling pin · 1 8-cup muffin tin, well greased with lard · 2-inch cookie cutter

Working time: 30 minutes

Baking time: 30 minutes

Serves: 8

1. Mix the flour with the salt, rub in the lard and the butter. Mix in enough ice water to form a ball of dough. Quickly wrap in wax paper. Chill 1 hour.

2. Preheat the oven to 425 degrees.

3. Mix the ground lamb with the fat, sugar, raisins, brandy or rum, and salt and pepper to taste until well combined. Separate the mixture into 8 equal parts.

4. Roll out half the dough to ⅛ inch thickness. Use a cookie cutter to make 8 circles. Fit each circle into a muffin cup. Fill the pastry cases with the lamb mixture. Roll out remaining dough and cut into 8 circles. Moisten the pastry edges with cold water and cover each with a circle of dough. Crimp together to seal securely. Brush with beaten egg yolk. Bake on the lower middle shelf of the oven for 30 minutes. Serve hot.

QUINCE

KYTHONI GLYKO

Quince preserves (Greece)

Quince jelly is rather common in America, but quince preserves are rare. If you can get hold of fresh quince in autumn (not an easy task in many parts of the States) you might want to use this Greek method for making quince preserves, popular throughout the Levant.

Ingredients

    4½ pounds quince
     5 cups sugar
     2 sticks cinnamon
     3 whole cloves
       Juice of 1 lemon

Equipment

Electric grater (optional but time saving) · Cheesecloth
bag · Kitchen cloth or wax paper · Vegetable peeler
· Large heavy enameled or stainless steel saucepan ·
3 1-pint sterilized Mason jars

Working time: 30 to 50 minutes

Cooking time: 1¼ hours

Makes: 6 cups

1. Peel and halve the quince; remove the core, keep the
seeds to wrap in cheesecloth with the spices. Using an electric
grater, grate the quince. If you do not have an electric grater
count 20 minutes more for doing the job by hand.
2. Dissolve the sugar with 4 cups water over medium heat,
stirring. Add the quince, spices, seed bag, lemon juice. Bring to
the boil, reduce the heat, and cook at the simmer for about 1
hour, stirring often. When the quince has turned a lovely pink
color and the syrup tests firm—that is, when a drop of syrup
keeps its shape when dropped onto a dish—remove from the heat.
Lift out and discard the spice bag. Loosely cover the pan with the
cloth and allow to cool. Pour into clean jars up to the top, seal,
and store in a cool place.

MELON

MELON CON ANÍS DEL MONO
Melon with anisette (Spain)

Anís del mono, literally "the monkey's anise," is the name of a
famous Catalan anisette.

Ingredients

    2 ripe cantaloupe
    ½ tablespoon anisette
    1½ tablespoons confectioners' sugar
    3 tablespoons water

Equipment

    Melon-ball scoop · Glass serving dish

Working time: 10 minutes

Serves: 4

Halve the melon and remove the seeds. Scoop out the melon flesh in balls and place in a glass serving dish. Combine anisette, sugar, and water and pour over the melon balls. Allow to stand in a cool place about 1 hour before serving.

CHERRIES

SLATKO

Cherry jam (Yugoslavia)

Slatko can be made with almost any fruit, but this one, with sweet cherries, and one with Dalmatian *marascas* or with sour cherries are the most popular. (*Marascas* are the base of the famous maraschino cherry liqueur.)

Slatko is a big thing in Yugoslavia and Greece. No matter where you go, sooner or later your host will bring out Turkish coffee, and a tray with a bowl of *slatko* (in Greece *glyko*), a small plate, a glass of water, and a spoon. You help yourself to a spoonful of jam from the jam bowl, return the spoon to the plate, drink a little water to clear your mouth, and then you drink the coffee.

Slatko is very good with toast and butter too.

Ingredients

> 2 pounds dark sweet cherries
> 1½ pounds sugar
> Juice of ½ lemon

Equipment

> Cherry stoner · Cheesecloth bag · Preserving kettle
> or heavy large casserole · 2 12-ounce sterilized Mason jars

Working time: 30 minutes

Cooking time: 10 minutes

Makes: 1½ quarts

1. Wash and stone the cherries keeping them as whole as possible. Collect all the cherry juice as you work. Reserve a handful of stones and tie up in a cheesecloth bag.

2. Place stoned cherries, cherry juice, and the cheesecloth bag in the preserving kettle. Cook at the simmer 2 to 3 minutes. Add the sugar and cook, stirring, until it dissolves. Bring to the boil and cook, stirring often, at the boil until the syrup thickens. Stir in the lemon juice. Continue boiling about 5 minutes or until the syrup sets. Remove the cheesecloth bag and discard. Pour hot into 2 hot sterilized jars and seal when cool.

Suppliers and Sources for Ingredients and Materials

An asterisk (*) signifies mail orders will be filled.

EAST COAST

Connecticut

*Dimyans Market, 116 Elm Street, Danbury 06810
  Turkish, Greek, and Arab specialities.

Maine

*Model Food Importers, 115 Middle Street, Portland 04111

Massachusetts

*Cardullo's Gourmet Shop, 6 Brattle Street, Cambridge 02138
  Imported cheeses, honeys, phyllo leaves, and olive oils.

Martiginetti, 84 Salem Street, Boston 02113
  Italian specialties.

Syrian Grocery Import Co., 270 Shawmut Avenue, Boston 02116

Euphrates, 726 Harrison Avenue, Boston 02118

Demoulas Supermarkets: Lowell, Methuen, Lawrence, Haverhill

New Hampshire
Joseph Brothers Market, 196 Lake Avenue, Manchester 03103

New Jersey
Michael Nafash & Sons, 2717 Bergenline Avenue, Union City 07087
    Middle Eastern specialties.

New York
*H. Roth & Sons, 1577 First Avenue, New York 10022
    Almonds, mortar and pestles, olives, spices, phyllo pastry
    leaves, semolina flour, couscous, honey, dried beans, cooking
    implements, tahini, grape leaves, bulghur, olive oils, and im-
    ported rice.
*Casa Moneo, 210 West 14th Street, New York 10011
    Spanish specialties: olive oil, *chorizo* sausages, *turron*, im-
    ported rice, *paellera*, and bean pots.
*Bloomingdale's Delicacies Shop, Lexington Avenue at 59th
    Street, New York 10022
    Imported cheeses, honeys, couscous, black and white truffles,
    imported wine vinegars, and olive oils.
*Sahadi Importing Company, Inc., 187 Atlantic Avenue, Brooklyn
    11201
    Olives, spices, sumac, couscous, grape leaves, orange blossom
    water, rose water, and other Arab and Middle Eastern spe-
    cialties.
Trinacria Importing Company, 415 Third Avenue, New York
    10016
    Phyllo pastry leaves, olives, spices, halvah, and fresh green
    coriander.
The Athens Food Market, 542 Ninth Avenue, New York 10036
    Greek olives, phyllo pastry leaves, honey, Greek cheeses, and
    tarama.

*Karnig Tashijian Middle East and Oriental Foods, 380 Third Avenue, New York 10016
  Ful medames in tins, phyllo pastry leaves, sumac, grape leaves, and other Turkish and Middle Eastern specialties.

*Maryland Market, 412 Amsterdam Avenue, New York 10024
  Partridges, squab, pigeons, quail, and game.

*The Bremen House, 218 East 86th Street, New York 10028
  Goose fat in tins.

*Manganaro Foods, 488 Ninth Avenue, New York 10018
  Italian specialties: pasta, cheeses, sausages, prosciutto, dried beans, white truffles, imported Arborio rice, *pancetta, amaretti di Saronno,* and olives.

*The Bridge Company, 212 East 52nd Street, New York 10022
  Pots, earthernware dishes, and many cooking implements.

Pennsylvania

*Savarese, 2011 Pennsylvania Avenue, Pittsburgh 15222

Stamoolis Brothers, Grocers, 2020 Pennsylvania Avenue, Pittsburgh 15222

*European Grocery Store, 520 Court Place, Pittsburgh 15219

*Lucio Mancuso & Sons, 1902 East Passyunk Avenue, Philadelphia 19148

Rhode Island

*Near East Market, 602 Reservoir Avenue, Cranston 02910

Vermont

*Izzo Market, 77 Pearl Street, Burlington 05401
  Italian specialties.

MIDWEST

Illinois

Czimer Foods Co., 953 West 63rd Street, Chicago
  Game birds.

D'Andrea & Son Italian Foods, 5825 Roosevelt, Cicero 60650

Columbus Food Market, 5534 West Harrison Street, Chicago 60644
  Middle Eastern specialties.

Gekas Brothers, 4655 North Lincoln Avenue, Chicago 60625

The Schiller and Asmus Company, 1525 Merchandise Mart, Chicago
  Cooking implements.

Indiana
*Guy Montani Fine Foods, 12 West 27th Street, Indianapolis 46208

Iowa
Swiss Coloney, Lindale Plaza, Cedar Rapids 52402

Fancy Food Shop, Younker Bros., Seventh and Walnut, Des Moines 50309

Michigan
*Lombardi Food Company, 1466 E. Vernor, Detroit 48214

Delmar & Co., 501-11 Monroe Avenue, Detroit 48226

Acropolis Market, 8441 Joy Road, Detroit 48204

Stemma Confectionery, 514 Monroe Avenue, Detroit 48226

Continental Gourmet Shop, 210 South Woodward Avenue, Birmingham 48011

Missouri
*Italio American Importing Company, 512 Franklin Avenue, St. Louis 63101

Volpi Italian Foods Inc., 6256 Daggett Avenue, St. Louis 63110

Demmas Shish Kebab, 5806 Hampton Avenue, St. Louis 63109

Heidi's Around the World Food Shop, 1149 South Brentwood Boulevard, St. Louis 63117

Nebraska

A. Marino, 1716 S. 13th Street, Omaha 68108

Leon's Food Mart, Winthrop Road, Lincoln 68502

Ohio

*Athens Pastries Import, 2545 Lorain Avenue, Cleveland 44113

Ellis Bakery, 577 Grant Street, Akron 44115

*Bruno Foods, 4970 Glenway Avenue, Cincinnati 45238

Spanish and American Food Market, 7001 Wade Park Avenue, Cleveland 44103

SOUTH

Florida

*Baratta Italian Grocers, 2503 Southwest Eighth Street, Miami 38103

*Gus Panos' Grocery, 515 N. Main Street, Miami 32202

Arabic Grocery and Bakery, 1615 Southwest Eighth Street, Miami 33135

Greek American Grocery Store, 2961 Coral Way, Miami 33134

Grecian Mart, 3244 South Dixie Highway, US 1, West Palm Beach 33405

Georgia

George's Delicatessan, 1041 North Highland Avenue N.E., Atlanta 30309

Barrett & Leach, 3771 Roswell Road, Atlanta 30305

Davison's Gourmet Shop, 180 Peach Tree Street, N.W., Atlanta 30303

*Pine Hills Herb Farm, P.O. Box 307, Roswell 30075

Kentucky

Strohm Market, 921 Barrett Avenue, Louisville 40205

Arimes Market, 216 Walton Avenue, Lexington 40502

Louisiana
*Progress Grocery, 915 Decatur, New Orleans 70116
   Greek, Turkish, Italian, and Spanish specialties.

Maryland
*Sorrento Grocery, 7212 Harford Road, Baltimore 21214

Mario's Italian Specialities, 5050 River Road, Bethesda 20016

North Carolina
James Heonis Company, 218 South Blount Street, Raleigh 27601

East Trade Grocery, 402 East Trade Street, Charlotte 28202

Tennessee
*Barzizza Brothers, 351 South Front Street, Memphis 38103

Morris Zager, 230 Fourth Avenue, Nashville 37207

J. Goldsmith & Sons, 123 South Main Street, Memphis 38103

The Cheese Market, 503A Clinch Avenue, S.W., Knoxville 37902

Virginia
Galanides Inc., 902 Cooke Avenue, Norfolk 23504

Nick's Produce and Importing Co., 504 East Marshall Street, Rich-
   mond 23219

The New Yorker Delicatessen, 2602 Williamson Road, N.W., Ro-
   anoke 24012

Washington, D.C.
*Acropolis Food Market, 1206 Underwood Street, N.W. 20012

*Wine & Cheese Shop, 1413 Wisconsin Avenue, N.W. 20007

*Skenderis Greek Imports, 1612 Twentieth Street, N.W. 20009

Pena's Spanish Store, 1636 17th Street, N.W. 20009

Safeway International, 1110 F Street, N.W. 20004

West Virginia
Haddy's Food Market, 1503 Washington Street, Charleston 25312

R. A. Medovic, 2201 Market Street, Wheeling 26003

WEST

California

*Mediterranean & Middle East Import Company, 223 Valencia Street, San Francisco 94103

*Bezjian's Grocery, Inc., 4725 Santa Monica Boulevard, Los Angeles 90029

*Greek Importing Company, 2801 West Pico Boulevard, Los Angeles 90006

Manley Produce, 1101 Grant Avenue, San Francisco 94133

Istanbul, 247 Third Street, San Francisco 94103
　　Oriental pastries.

Tony's Market, 2190 Union Street, San Francisco 94123

Sunnyland Bulghur Company, 1435 Gearhart Street, Fresno 93707

Colorado

*P. C. Mancinelli, 3300 Osage Street, Denver 80211

*Pinelli & Sons, 1409 15th Street, Denver 80202

Economy Grocery, 1864 Curtis Street, Denver 80202

Oregon

Maletis Bros., 100 Northwest Third Avenue, Portland 97209

Texas

* Simon David, 7117 Inwood Road, Dallas 75209
　　Italian and French specialties.

Jamails, 3114 Kirby Drive, Houston 77006

Washington

*Angelo Merlina & Sons, 816 Sixth Avenue So., Seattle 98134

De Laurenti & Co., Stall 5, lower floor, Pike Place Market, Seattle 98101

Nick Carras, 422 North 48 Street, Seattle 98103

Weights and Measures

1 teaspoon	⅓ tablespoon
3 teaspoons	1 tablespoon
4 tablespoons	¼ cup
5⅓ teaspoons	⅓ cup
8 tablespoons	½ cup
12 tablespoons	¾ cup
16 tablespoons	1 cup
2 cups	1 pint
4 cups	2 pints

Bibliography

Arab Information Office. *A collection of Arab recipes.* Washington, D.C.: 1972.

Boni, Ada. *Italian Regional Cooking.* New York: E. P. Dutton, 1969.

Courtine, Robert J. *La vrai cuisine française.* Paris: 1953.

David, Elizabeth. *A Book of Mediterranean Food.* Baltimore: Penguin Books, 1966.

———. *Italian Food.* Baltimore: Penguin Books, 1969.

———. *French Country Cooking.* Baltimore: Penguin Books, 1944.

———. *French Provincial Cooking.* Baltimore: Penguin Books, 1969.

Davidson, Alan. *Mediterranean Seafood.* Baltimore: Penguin Books, 1972.

Dumay, Raymond. *Guide du gastronome en Espagne.* Paris: 1970.

Eren, Neset. *The Art of Turkish Cooking.* Garden City: Doubleday, 1969.

Escudier, Jean-Noël and Peta Fuller. *The Wonderful Food of Provence.* Boston: Houghton Mifflin, 1968.

Ferhi, Youcef. *Grandes recettes de la cuisine algerienne.* Paris: 1957.

Francesconi, Jeanne Carola. *La cucina napoletana.* Naples: 1965.

Giobbi, Edward. *Italian Family Cooking.* New York: Random House, 1971.

Gosetti della Salda, Anna. *Le ricette regionali Italiane.* Milan: 1967.

Herrera, Ana Maria. *Manual de cocina.* Madrid: 1960.

Karsenty, Irene and Lucienne. *Le livre de la cuisine pied noir.* Paris: 1969.

Khawam, Rene R. *La cuisine Arabe.* Paris: 1970.

Kouki, Mohammed. *Poissons Mediterranées.* Tunis: no date.

———. *La cuisine Tunisienne.* Tunis: no date.

Landry, Robert. *Les soleils de la cuisine.* Paris: 1967.

Montagné, Prosper. *Larousse Gastronomique.* Translated by Nina Freud, et al. New York: Crown, 1961.

Markovic, Spasenija-Pata. *Yugoslav Cookbook.* Belgrade: 1966.

Perl, Lila. *Rice, Spice and Bitter Oranges.* New York: World Publishing, 1967.

Pomiane, Edouard de. *Cooking with Pomiane.* Translated by P. Benton. London: 1962.

Rayess, George. *The Art of Lebanese Cooking.* Beirut: Librairie du Liban, 1966.

Roden, Claudia. *A Book of Middle Eastern Food.* New York: Alfred A. Knopf, 1974.

Root, Waverly. *The Food of Italy.* New York: Atheneum, 1971.

———. *The Food of France.* New York: Alfred A. Knopf, 1958.

Ruspoli, Mario. *Petit Bréviaire de la Cuisine.* Paris: 1975.

Tarhan Bookstore. *Turkish Delights.* Ankara: 1958.

The Women of St. Paul's Greek Orthodox Church. *The Art of Greek Cooking.* Garden City: Doubleday, 1961.

Wolfert, Paula. *Couscous and Other Good Food from Morocco.* New York: Harper & Row, 1973.

———, ed. *International Home Dining.* New York: CBS, 1971.

Index to Recipes by Course and Country

FRANCE

HORS D'OEUVRE

Anchoïade Corse (Corsican anchovy oil canapés)   7
Pissaladière (Onion, anchovy, and olive tart—Provence)   50
Salade de fenouil et noix (Walnut and fennel salad—
    Languedoc)   252
Tapenade (Provençal olive paste)   52

SOUPS

Crème à l'ail (Garlic soup from Southwestern France)   10
Pistou marseillaise (Vegetable soup with basil)   173

FISH

Brandade de morue en croustade (Salt cod mousse in puff
    pastry shells with poached eggs—Provence)   25
Filets de sole à la façon Provençale (Poached fish with
    herbal oil—Provence)   185

FISH SOUPS, STEWS, AND CHOWDERS

"*L'aïgo-sau*" (Simple Provençal fish soup) 18
Bourride des pêcheurs (Provençal fishermen's soup) 13
Soupe de poissons (Kathy Jelen's fish soup) 19

POULTRY

Caneton à la languedocienne (Duckling with raisins) 326
Poulet à la camarguaise (Chicken prepared in a style of the
  Camargue) 62
Poulet au fromage (Chicken with cheese and tarragon) 236
Poulet aux 40 gousses d'ail (Chicken with 40 cloves of garlic) 27
Tourte Tante Vivienne (Chicken and sausage pie from
  Languedoc) 166

MEAT

Poragneu Coumtadino (Individual pork and lamb scallops
  in white wine and honey sauce—Provence) 277
Cassoulet toulousaine (White beans with pork, pork sausages,
  and lamb in the style of Toulouse) 132
La daube de bœuf Provençale (Provençal beef, wine, mush-
  rooms, and olive stew) 70
Épaule d'agneau aux figues fourrées (Sautéed lamb with
  stuffed figs—Provence) 314
Épaule d'agneau à l'orange (Shoulder of lamb stew with
  oranges—Provence) 306
Gasconnade (Leg of lamb with garlic sauce—Languedoc) 33
Gigot d'agneau, sauce aux olives (Roast leg of lamb with
  black olive sauce in the style of Provence) 69
Gigot d'agneau farci (Stuffed boned leg of lamb—
  Languedoc) 31
Petits pâtés de Béziers (Little sweet lamb pastries from
  Béziers) 328

VEGETABLES AND SAUCES

Artichauts aux anchois (Artichokes with anchovies) 109
Aubergines à la toulousaine (Stuffed eggplants in the style
  of Toulouse) 87

Ratatouille (Provençal vegetable stew) 85
Tourte Corse (Corsican herb and cheese pie) 246
Beurre Montpellier (Green butter of Languedoc) 184
Coulis de tomates à la Provençale (Fresh tomato sauce in the style of Provence) 93
Mayonnaise 41
Sauce Rouille (Hot red pepper and garlic sauce for Provençal fish soups) 15

DESSERTS

Crème de miel (Honey cream—Languedoc) 282
Croquets de Languedoc (Hazelnuts crisps) 271
Figues fraîches au fromage (Figs and cream cheese) 250
Pouding au nougat (Nougat pudding with chocolate sauce) 268

PRESERVES

Marmelade de pêches (Peach jam—Provence) 319

BEVERAGES

Vin de pêches (White wine flavored with peaches) 319
Vin d'orange de Colette (Orange-flavored wine) 304

ITALY

HORS D'OEUVRE

Fagioli con tonno (White beans with tuna—Tuscany) 121
Fagioli con caviale (White beans with caviar—Rome) 122
Mozzarella in carrozza (Italian cheese sandwiches—Rome) 231
Insalata Caprese (Italian tomato, mozzarella and basil salad) 94

SOUPS

Acqua cotta di maremma ("Cooked water" Tuscan vegetable soup with olive oil and sage) 11
Brodetto alla romana (Poached lamb shoulder with egg and lemon soup) 291

FISH

Pesca (spada) a ghiotta alla messinese (Swordfish pie in the style of Messina—Sicily 56

Sarde a beccaficu (Sardines stuffed with nuts and raisins—Sicily) 254

Cacciucco de polpi (Fricassee of squid, cuttlefish, or octopus in the style of the region of Populonium) 22

POULTRY

La gallina del ghiottoni ("Box" chicken or chicken with cheese sauce—Piemonte) 235

Pollo alla cacciatora con peperoni (Sicilian style chicken *cacciatora* with sweet peppers) 106

Pollo tonnato (Poached chicken with tuna fish sauce) 30

Anitra con olive (Genovese duck with green olives) 65

Anitra con lenticchie (Braised duck with lentils) 131

Palombacci alla perugina (Wood pigeons or squabs with polenta as prepared in Perugia) 67

Piccioni con l'uva (Pigeons with green grapes) 323

MEAT

Fritto misto alla marchigiana (Mixed fry as prepared in the Marches) 63

Scaloppine al limone (Veal scallops with lemon sauce) 297

Fegato di vitello con foglie di lauro (Calf's liver with laurel leaves) 176

Costata di manzo alla romana (Rib steaks in the style of Rome) 195

RICE, VEGETABLES, AND COLD SAUCES

Risotto con tartufi bianchi (Risotto with white truffles) 206

Gnocchi di spinachi al gorgonzola (Spinach and cheese dumplings with gorgonzola sauce) 242

Torta di cavolo (Italian cabbage, cheese, and pork pie) 243

Tortino Ripieno di scarole e olive (Neapolitan "cake" stuffed with escarole and black olives) 48

Caponatina (Seafood and vegetable medley in the style of Syracuse)   89

Spinaci aglio olio (Spinach with garlic and oil)   37

Spinaci con parmigiana (Spinach with parmesan cheese)   110

Frittata di fiori di zucca (Omelet with stuffed zucchini blossoms)   112

Pomodori ripieni alla Calabrese (Hot stuffed tomatoes in the style of Calabria)   95

Salsa Vende (Green sauce)   40

PASTA

Pasta   141

Spaghetti alla puttanesca (Spaghetti with olive sauce and 2 variations)   53

Spaghetti con le melanzane (Spaghetti with tomato and eggplant sauce)   84

Pasta e ceci (Pasta and chick peas)   126

Panzarotti (Fried stuffed ravioli with tomato and cheese sauce)   145

Agnolotti da vigilia (Stuffed pasta with spinach and cheese for Fridays)   144

Agnolotti toscani (Stuffed pasta with meat)   143

Pasta con mollica di pane (pasta with breadcrumbs)   147

Pasticcio di maccheroni alla piemontese (Macaroni pie with chicken livers, sweetbreads, quenelles, truffles, and mushrooms)   148

Aia (Ligurian walnut sauce for green pasta or *agnolotti di magro*)   263

Salsa di noci (Walnut sauce)   264

Pesto (Ligurian basil sauce from Nervi)   172

Olio verde (Genoese herbal oil for spaghetti)   38

Burro rosso (Red butter sauce)   142

DESSERTS

Frittura di ricotta Pasqualina (Ricotta cheese fritters)   248

Granita d'uva nera alla Simonetta (Simonetta's black grape ice)   324

Pesche Ripiene (Stuffed peaches)   321

Frittura di fichi Ruspoli (Hot fried figs)   313
Granita d'Arancia (Orange ice)   309
Soufflé dolce di amaretti (Almond macaroon soufflé)   269

LEBANON, EGYPT, SYRIA, AND ISRAEL

HORS D'OEUVRE

Salatit Michoteta (Egyptian cheese salad)   233
Mahammara Labni (Lebanese *labni* with dill and pimiento)   212
Tamiya (Egyptian bean patties)   123
Hummus bi taheeni (Pureed chick peas with sesame seed
    paste)   124
Lahm bi ajim (Lebanese meat pies)   162
Tabbouleh (Lebanese cracked wheat salad)   164
Baba Ghanoush (Eggplant cream with *Tahini*; Syrian ver-
    sion with yogurt)   82

SOUP

Looz shorba (Almond soup)   253

POULTRY

Farareej Mashwi (Broiled chicken with oil, lemon, and garlic
    sauce—Egypt)   29
Oaf Tapuzim (Chicken with oranges—Israel)   305
Oaf Sum Sum (Fried chicken with sesame seeds—Israel)   200

MEAT

Kafta Snobar (Lamb patties with pine nuts—Lebanon)   261
Laban Ŏummo (Lamb cooked in its mother's milk)   222
Shish barak bi laban (Lebanese meat dumplings and kibbee
    in yogurt sauce)   217

RICE AND VEGETABLES

Roz snobar (Syrian rice pilaf with pine nuts)   265
Fistuquia (Green beans with yogurt and taklia)   215

CHEESE

Labni (Lebanese fresh white cheese made from yogurt)   212

PRESERVES

Teen makood (Syrian fig jam)   315

NORTH AFRICA

HORS D'OEUVRE

Batenjal m'charmel (Algerian eggplant salad)   83
Limoun marakad (Preserved lemons)   287
Mohk (Moroccan brain salad)   288
Salata letchine (Moroccan orange and date salad)   318

BRIKS

Briks bil mohk (Brain and egg turnovers—Tunisia)   160
Briks bil sthun (Anchovy and egg turnovers)   161
Briks bil djej (Chicken and egg turnovers)   162
Sweba (Ground meat and egg turnovers)   161

FISH

Hancha bil salsa ou zeetoon (Eel with tomatoes and olives—
   Tunisia)   58
Hout Makli (Fried fish with zucchini and tomato sauce—
   Tunisia)   114
Scabetch (Pickled fried fish—Algeria)   23

POULTRY

Djej bil zeetoon meslalla (Chicken smothered in green
   olives—Morocco)   61
Djej bil zeetoon (Chicken with olives, Tangier style—
   Morocco)   59
Djej matisha mesla (Moroccan chicken *tagine* with sweet
   tomato jam)   100

Djej bil hamus (Moroccan chicken *tagine* with chick peas)   129
Djej bil looz (Moroccan chicken *tagine* with almonds)   258
H'mam M'Douzane (Squab with coriander and spices—Algeria)   179
Sfirya (Algerian chicken *tagine* with potato–cheese croquettes)   238

MEAT

Tagine Sebnakh (Lamb and spinach *tagine*—Tunisia)   203
Aijja (Brains and eggs in tomato sauce—Tunisia)   204
Koustilyat michwi (Tunisian grilled lamb chops)   296
Tagine bi temar (Moroccan date *tagine*)   316
Tagine nana (Lamb and *tagine*—Tunisia)   188
Tagine bi gouta (Tunisian lamb and cheese *tagine*)   240

COUSCOUS

Seksu Tanjaoui (Lamb and vegetable couscous in the style of Tangier)   154
Kouski bil hout (Tunisian fish couscous with fish, quince and raisins)   156

VEGETABLES AND SAUCES

Marka Ommalah (Tunisian pickled vegetables with spiced ground beef)   115
Bisbas michchi (Tunisian stuffed fennel bulbs)   111
Slata Toonsia (Mixed salad—Tunisia)   189
Slata kera (Zucchini salad—Tunisia)   178
Harissa (Hot pepper sauce—Tunisia)   182
Smen (Herb flavored butter—Morocco)   201

DESSERT

Klandt bil Karmouss (Moroccan pastry stuffed with figs and dipped in honey)   278

SPAIN AND PORTUGAL

HORS D'OEUVRE

Gambas al ajillo (Shrimp in garlic sauce) 5

SOUPS

Caldillo de perro ("Dog" soup with bitter oranges) 302
Gazpacho (Spanish cold vegetable soup) 97
Gazpacho ajo blanco (Gazpacho with garlic, almonds, and
 green grapes from Malaga) 9

FISH

Calamares en su tinta # 1 (Squid in its own ink with garlic
 and almonds) 21
Calamares en su tinta # 2 (Squid in its own ink with tomato
 sauce) 98
Gambas a la menorquina (Shrimps in tomato sauce with almonds and pine nuts) 255
Mero a la chiclanera (Fried halibut or pollock with parsley
 sauce) 192

POULTRY

Perdices escabechadas (Marinated partridges in piquant
 jelly) 298
Pavo relleño a la menorquina (Stuffed roast turkey with pine
 nuts and raisins) 259

MEAT

Chuleta de cordero a la brasa con ali oli (Lamb chops with
 oil, garlic, and egg sauce) 35
Lomo de cerdo al estilo de Ibiza (Roast pork with oranges) 308
Carne fiambre (Stuffed beef roll—Spain) 72
Cocido con judias blancas (Lamb and pork with white
 beans) 128
Cocido a la Andaluza (Boiled meat and vegetables with
 pumpkin and *pimentón* sauce) 193

RICE, VEGETABLES AND SAUCES

Paella (Paella) 197
Arroz en caldero (Rice with green or red peppers in the style of Murcia) 108
Acelgas con piñones (Swiss chard with pine nuts) 266
Garbanzos a la Catalana (Chick-peas with tomatoes, sausage, and peppers) 136
Salsa Romesco (Almond and hot pepper sauce from Catalonia) 262

DESSERTS AND BEVERAGES

Polvorones (Spanish almond cookies) 272
Arroz doce (Portuguese lemon and rice pudding) 300
Melon con anís del mono (Melon with anisette) 330
Sangria (Sangria) 322
Horchata (Earth almond drink) 274

TURKEY, GREECE, AND YUGOSLAVIA

HORS D'OEUVRE

Tiropitakia (Greek cheese triangles with dill or fresh marjoram) 230
Peynirli kabak (Zucchini stuffed with cheese—Turkey) 249
Dolmadakia me avgolemono (Greek stuffed grape leaves with lemon and egg sauce) 292
Elyes (Marinated olives—Greece) 47
Ajvar (Eggplant and green pepper relish—Yugoslavia) 78
Taramasalata (Carp roe dip—Greece) 6
Çerkez Tavuğu (Circassian chicken) 256

SOUPS

Yogurt Çorbasi (Turkish yogurt soup) 213
Tarator (Yugoslav yogurt and cucumber soup) 214
Soupa avgolemono (Greek egg and lemon soup) 290

FISH

Garidhes à la turkolimano (Shrimps in tomato sauce with feta cheese in the style of Turkolimano) 234
Barbounia ladolemono (Red mullets with lemon oil dressing—Greece) 299
Psari plaki (Baked fish with tomatoes and onions—Greece) 99

POULTRY

Ortikia skara (Grilled quails—Greece) 36

MEAT

Ćevapčići (Yugoslav skewered ground beef) 80
Bosanske ćufte (Bosnian meatballs with yogurt—Yugoslavia) 219
Stifado (Greek beef stew with onions and cheese) 239
Arnaki avgolemono (Fricassee of lamb with egg and lemon sauce—Greece) 294
Kuzu şiş kebab (Turkish shish kebab) 295
Moussaka (Baked meat and eggplant casserole with yogurt sauce) 221
Keftaidakia me saltsa (Small meatballs in tomato sauce—Greece) 102
Sarma (Yugoslav way of stuffing cabbage) 116

EGGS, CHEESE, AND YOGURT

Çilbir (Poached eggs with yogurt—Turkish) 216
Yogurt (Homemade yogurt) 211
Gibanica (Yugoslavian cheese pie) 228

VEGETABLES AND SAUCES

Hunkar begendi (Sultans Delight—Turkish eggplant cream) 80
Hunkar begendi (Greek eggplant cream with oil) 80
Zeytinyagli Domates Dolmasi (Cold stuffed tomatoes—Turkish) 96
Punjene paprike (Hot stuffed peppers—Yugoslavia) 105

Biber dolmasi (Cold stuffed green peppers—Turkish)   104
Skordalia (Garlic sauce—Greece)   39

DESSERTS

Diples (Greek deep fried orange crullers)   310
Svingous me meli Hymettus (Puffed fritters with mount hymettus honey—Greece)   280
Istarske fritule (Istrian hazelnut fritters—Yugoslavia)   267
Karidopitta (Greek honey walnut cake)   273
Melipitta (Greek honey cheese pie)   281

PRESERVES

Slatko (Yugoslav cherry jam)   331
Kythoni glyko (Greek quince preserves)   329

Index

Acelgas con piñones, 266
Acqua cotta di maremma, 11
Adas be sabanigh, 127
Agnolotti
    toscani, 143
    da vigilia, 144
Aia, 263
Aijja, 204
Ajvar, 78
Almond(s)
    chicken with, 258
        Circassian, 256
    cookies, 272
    drink, earth, 274
    gazpacho with garlic, green grapes, and, 9
    and hot pepper sauce, 262
    macaroon soufflé, 269
    and pine nuts, shrimp in tomato sauce with, 255
    soup, 253
Anchoïade corse, 7
Anchovy(ies)
    artichokes with, 109

and egg turnovers, 161
oil canapés, 7
onion, and olive tart, 50
spaghetti with olive sauce, 53
    variation #1, 54; #2, 55
Aniseed, general data on, 170–171
Anisette, melon with, 330
Anitra
    con lenticchie, 131
    con olive, 65
Appetizers
    anchoïade corse, 7
    anchovy oil canapés, 7
    cheese
        with dill and pimento, 212
        sandwiches, 231
        triangles with dill or marjoram, 230
    chicken
        Circassian, 256
        poached, with tuna fish sauce, 30
    coccarda, 94
    eggplant and green pepper relish, 78

355

Appetizers (*cont'd*)
  fagioli
    con caviale, 122
    con tonno, 121
  grape leaves, stuffed, with lemon
      and egg sauce, 292
  lemons, preserved, 287
  meat pies, 162
  mozzarella in carrozza, 231
  olives, marinated, 47
  onion, anchovy, and olive tart, 50
  pissaladière, 50
  salade de fenouil et noix, 252
  shrimp in garlic sauce, 5
  squid in its own ink, with garlic
      and almonds, 21
  swordfish pie, 56
  tapenade, 52
  white beans
    with caviar, 122
    with tuna, 121
  zucchini stuffed with cheese, 249
  See also Dips, Salads, Soups
Arnaki avgolemono, 294
Aromatics, general data on, 169–170
Arroz
  en caldero, 108
  doce, 300
Artichauts aux anchois, 109
Artichoke(s)
  with anchovies, 109
  hearts, seafood and vegetable
      medley, 89
Aubergines à la toulousaine, 87

Baba ghanoush, 82
Barbounia ladolemono, 299
Basil
  general data on, 171–172
  sauce for pasta, 172
  tomato, and mozzarella salad, 94
  vegetable soup with, 173
Batenjal m'charmel, 83
Bay leaves
  general data on, 175
  calf's liver with, 176
Beans, dried
  general data on, 119–121

fava, patties, 123
white
  with caviar, 122
  lamb, pork, and stew, 128
  with pork, sausage, and lamb,
      132
  with tuna, 121
  See also Green beans
Beef
  boiled meat and vegetables with
      pumpkin and pimentón sauce,
      193
  daube Provençale, 70
  ground
    baked meat and eggplant cas-
        serole with yogurt sauce, 221
    and egg turnovers, 161
    finely, skewered, 80
    macaroni pie, 148
    meat pies, 162
    meatballs, Bosnian, with yogurt,
        219
    meatballs in tomato sauce, 102
    moussaka, 221
    spiced, pickled vegetables with,
        115
    stuffed cabbage, 116
    stuffed fennel bulbs, 111
    stuffed green peppers, 105
  mixed fry, 63
  rib steaks with rosemary, 195
  roll, stuffed, 72
  stew
    with onions and cheese, 239
    wine, mushroom, and olive, 70
Beurre Montpellier, 184
Beverages
  earth almond drink, 274
  sangria, 322
  wine
    orange-flavored, 304
    punch, 322
    white, flavored with peaches,
        319
Biber dolmasi, 104
Bisbas michchi, 111
Bosanske cufte, 219
Bouillabaisse, general data on, 17
Bourride des pêcheurs, 13
Brodetto alla romana, 291

Brain(s)
  and eggs
    in tomato sauce, 204
    turnovers, 160
  salad, 289
Brandade de morue en croustade, 25
Breadcrumbs, pasta with, 147
Briks
  general data on, 159
  bil djej, 162
  bil mohk, 160
  bil sthum, 161
  sweba, 161
Burghul, cracked wheat salad, 164
Burro rosso, 142
Butter
  green, 184
  herb-flavored, 201
  sauce, red, 142

Cabbage
  cheese, and sausage pie, 243
  stuffed, 116
Cacciucco de polpi, 22
Cake
  honey walnut, 273
  stuffed with escarole and black
    olives, 48
Calamares en su tinta: #1, 21; #2,
  98
Caldillo de perro, 302
Calf's liver with laurel leaves, 176
Canapés
  anchovy oil, 7
  See also Appetizers
Caneton à la languedocienne, 326
Capers, general data on, 177
Caponatina, 89
Caraway seeds
  general data on, 177
  zucchini salad, 178
Carne fiambre, 72
Carp roe dip, 6
Cassoulet toulousain, 132
Caviar, white beans with, 122
Çerkez tavuğu, 256
Ćevapčići, 80
Cheese
  general data on, 225–228

appetizers
  with dill and pimento, 212
  sandwiches, 231
  triangles with dill, 230
beef stew with onions and, 239
cream, see Cream cheese
creamed, figs and, 250
feta, shrimp in tomato sauce with,
  234
fresh
  with dill and pimento, 212
  from yogurt, 212
fritters, Easter ricotta, 248
labni, 212
mozzarella, tomato, and basil
  salad, 94
parmesan, spinach with, 110
pie, 228
  cabbage and sausage, 243
  herb and, 246
  honey, 281
-potato croquettes, chicken tagine
  with, 238
salad, 233
sandwiches, 231
sauce, chicken with, 235
and spinach dumplings, with gorgonzola sauce, 242
tagine, lamb and, 240
triangles with dill or marjoram,
  230
zucchini stuffed with, 249
Cherry jam, 331
Chicken
  with almonds, 258
  appetizers
    Circassian, 256
    poached, with tuna fish sauce,
      30
  cacciatora, 106
  with cheese sauce, 235
  with chick-peas, 129
  Circassian, 256
  with cream cheese and tarragon,
    236
  and egg turnovers, 162
  with 40 cloves of garlic, 27
  hunter's, with sweet peppers, 106
  livers, macaroni pie, 148
  mixed fry, 63

Chicken (cont'd)
  with oil, lemon, and garlic sauce,
    broiled, 29
  with olives
    Camargue style, 62
    Tangier style, 59
  with oranges, 305
  paella, 197
  and sausage pie, 166
  with sesame seeds, fried, 200
  smothered in green olives, 61
  tagine
    with potato-cheese croquettes,
      238
    with sweet tomato jam, 100
  with tuna fish sauce, poached, 30
Chick-peas
  general data on, 119–121
  chicken with, 129
  couscous
    fish, 156
    lamb, 154
  pasta and, 126
  with sesame seed paste, 124
  with tomatoes, sausage, and pep-
    pers, 136
Chocolate sauce, for nougat pudding,
  268
Chuletas de cordero a la brasa con
  ali-oli, 35
Çilbir, 216
Cocida
  a la andaluza, 193
  con judías blancas, 128
Cookies
  almond, 272
  hazelnut crisps, 271
Coriander
  general data on, 178–179
  seeds, ground, for paste for Moroc-
    can roasted lamb, 180
  and spices, squab with, 179
Costata di manzo alla romana, 195
Coulis de tomate à la provençale,
  93
Couscous
  general data on, 151–154
  fish, 156
  lamb, 154
Cracked wheat salad, 164

Cream cheese
  pastry, for meat pie, 164
  and tarragon, chicken with, 236
Crème
  à l'ail, 10
  de miel, 282
Croquets de Languedoc, 271
Croquettes, potato-cheese, chicken
    tagine with, 238
Crullers, deep-fried orange, 310
Cucumber soup, yogurt and, 214
Cumin, general data on, 180–181
Cuttlefish, fricassee of, 22

Date(s)
  general data on, 315–316
  and orange salad, 318
  tagine, 316
Daube de boeuf provençale, 70
Desserts
  almond
    cookies, 272
    macaroon soufflé, 269
  cookies, almond, 272
  crullers, deep-fried orange, 310
  figs
    and creamed cheese, 250
    hot fried, 313
  fritters, 280
  hazelnut
    crisps, 271
    fritters, 267
  honey
    cheese pie, 281
    cream, 282
    -dipped pastry stuffed with figs,
      278
    walnut cake, 273
  ices
    orange, 309
    Simonetta's black grape, 324
  melon with anisette, 330
  peaches, stuffed, 321
  puffed fritters with honey, 280
  pudding
    lemon and rice, 300
    nougat, with chocolate sauce,
      268

Dill, cheese triangles with marjoram
    or, 230
Dips
    baba ghanoush, 82
    brain salad, 288
    carp roe, 6
    chick-peas with sesame seed paste,
        124
    eggplant cream, 80
        Greek variation, 82
        Lebanese variation, 82
        Syrian variation, 82
    hummus bi taheeni, 124
    olive paste, 52
    taramasalata, 6
Diples, 310
Djej (Chicken)
    bil hamus, 129
    bil looz (tarfaya), 258
    bil zeetoon, 59
        meslalla, 61
    matisha mesla, 100
"Dog soup" with bitter oranges, 302
Dolmadakia me avgolemono, 292
Duck(ling)
    braised, with lentils, 131
    with green olives, 65
    with raisins, 326
Dumplings
    lamb, and kibbe in yogurt sauce,
        217
    spinach and cheese, with gorgon-
        zola sauce, 242

Earth almond drink, 274
Easter ricotta cheese fritters, 248
Eel with tomatoes and olives, 58
Egg(s)
    and lemon sauce
        lamb fricassee with, 294
        stuffed grape leaves with, 292
    and lemon soup, 290
        poached lamb shoulder with,
            291
    omelet with stuffed zucchini blos-
        soms, 112
    poached, with yogurt, 216
    in tomato sauce, brains and, 204
    turnovers

anchovy and, 161
brain and, 160
chicken and, 162
ground meat and, 161
Eggplant
    general data on, 77–78
    casserole with yogurt sauce, baked
        meat and, 221
    cream, 80
        Greek variation, 82
        Lebanese variation, 82
        Syrian variation, 82
    and green pepper relish, 78
    moussaka, 221
    salad, 83
    sauce, spaghetti with tomato and,
        84
    seafood and vegetable medley, 89
    stuffed, 87
    vegetable stew, 85
Elyes, 47
Épaule d'agneau à l'orange, 306
Escarole and black olives, "cake"
    stuffed with, 48

Fagioli
    con caviale, 122
    con tonno, 121
Farareej mashwi, 29
Fegato di vitello con foglie di lauro,
    176
Fennel
    general data on, 181
    bulbs, stuffed, 111
    salad, walnut and, 252
Fenugreek, general data on, 181–182
Feta cheese, shrimp in tomato sauce
    with, 234
Fig(s)
    general data on, 311–313
    and creamed cheese, 250
    honey-dipped pastry stuffed with,
        278
    hot fried, 313
    jam, 315
    stuffed, sautéed lamb with, 314
Figues fraîches au fromage, 250
Filets de sole à la façon provençale,
    185

Fish
  baked, with tomatoes and onions, 99
  couscous with quince and raisins, 156
  "dog soup" with bitter oranges, 302
  fillets with herbal oil, poached, 185
  fricassee of squid, cuttlefish, or octopus, 22
  fried
    pickled, 23
    with zucchini and tomato sauce, 114
  scabetch, 23
  soup
    Kathy Jelen's, 19
    Provençal, 13, 18
  See also Seafood, *and names of fish and shellfish*
Fishermen's soup, 13
Fistuquia, 215
Frittata di fiori di zucca, 112
Fritters
  Easter ricotta cheese, 248
  hazelnut, 267
  puffed, with honey, 280
Frittura
  di fichi ruspoli, 313
  de ricotta pasqualina, 248
Fruit
  general data on, 285–286
  wine punch, 322
  See also names of fruit

Gallina del ghiottoni, 235
Gambas
  al ajillo, 5
  a la menorquina, 255
Garbanzos a la catalana, 136
Garidhes a la turkolimano, 234
Garlic
  general data on, 3–5
  chicken with 40 cloves of, 27
  and oil, spinach with, 37
  sauce, 39
    hot pepper and, 15
    lamb with, 33
    shrimp in, 5

soup, 10
Gasconnade, 33
Gazpacho, 97
  ajo blanco, 9
Gibanica, 228
Gigot d'agneau
  farci, 31
  sauce aux olives, 69
Gnocchi de spinaci al gorgonzola, 242
Gorgonzola sauce, spinach, and cheese dumplings with, 242
Grains, general data on, 139–141
Granita
  d'arancia, 309
  d'uva nera alla Simonetta, 324
Grape(s)
  general data on, 322–323
  black, ice, Simonetta's, 324
  green
    gazpacho with garlic, almonds, and, 9
    squab with, 323
  leaves, stuffed, with lemon and egg sauce, 292
Green beans with yogurt and taklia, 215
Green pepper(s)
  relish, eggplant and, 78
  stuffed, 105
    cold, 104
  vegetable stew, 85
Green sauce, 40

Halibut, fried, with parsley sauce, 192
Hancho bil salsa ou zeetoon, 58
Harissa, 182
Hazelnut
  crisps, 271
  fritters, 267
Herb(s)
  general data on, 169–70
  -flavored butter, 201
  mixtures, 183
  oil for spaghetti, 38
  pie, cheese and, 246
Hmam m'douzane, 179

Honey
   general data on, 275–277
   cheese pie, 281
   cream, 282
   -dipped pastry stuffed with figs, 278
   puffed fritters with, 280
   walnut cake, 273
   and white wine sauce, pork and lamb in, 277
Horchata, 274
Hors d'oeuvre, *see* Appetizers
Hout makli, 114
Hummus bi taheeni, 124
Hunkar begendi, 80
   Greek variation, 82
   Lebanese variation, 82
   Syrian variation, 82

Ices
   orange, 309
   Simonetta's black grape, 324
Insalata Caprese, 94
Istarske fritule, 267

Jam
   cherry, 331
   fig, 315
   peach, 319
Juniper berries, general data on, 186

Kafta snobar, 261
Karidopitta, 273
Kathy Jelen's fish soup, 19
Kaftaidakia me saltsa, 102
Kibbe, lamb dumplings and, in yogurt sauce, 217
Klandt bil karmouss, 278
Kouski bil hout, 156
Koustilyat michwi, 296
Kuzu şiş kebab, 295
Kythoni glyko, 329

La kama, 202
Laban oummo, 222
Labni, 212

Lahm bi ajim, 162
Lamb
   chops
      grilled, 296
      with oil, garlic, and egg sauce, 35
   cooked in its mother's milk, 222
   couscous, 154
   dumplings and kibbe in yogurt sauce, 217
   fricassee with egg and lemon sauce, 294
   gasconnade, 33
   ground
      meat pies, 162
      stuffed fennel bulbs, 111
   leg of
      with garlic sauce, 33
      with olive sauce, 69
      stuffed boned, 31
   pastries, 328
   patties with pine nuts, 261
   and pork
      and sausage, white beans with, 132
      and white bean stew, 128
      in white wine and honey sauce, 277
   sautéed, with stuffed figs, 314
   shoulder, poached, with egg and lemon soup, 291
   skewered, 295
   stew with oranges, 306
   tagine
      cheese and, 240
      mint and, 188
      spinach and, 203
Lemon(s)
   general data on, 286–287
   and egg sauce
      for lamb fricassee, 294
      for stuffed grape leaves, 292
   and egg soup, 290
      poached lamb shoulder with, 291
   lentils with spinach and, 127
   oil dressing, for red mullets, 299
   preserved, 287
   and rice pudding, 300
   sauce, for veal scallops, 297

Lentils
  general data on, 119–121
  braised duck with, 131
  with spinach and lemon, 127
Limoun marakad, 287
Liver, calf's, *see* Calf's liver
Lobsters, seafood and vegetable
    medley, 89
Lomo de cerdo al estilo de Ibiza, 308
Looz shorba, 253

Macaroni
  pasta and chick-peas, 126
  pie, 148
Macaroon soufflé, almond, 269
Mahammara labni, 212
Marjoram
  general data on, 186–187
  cheese triangles with dill or, 230
Marka ommalah, 115
Marmelade de pêches, 319
Mayonnaise
  general data on, 41–42
  homemade, 43
Meat
  boiled, and vegetables, with
      pumpkin and pimentón sauce,
      193
  Bosnian meatballs with yogurt,
      219
  cassoulet toulousain, 132
  and eggplant casserole with yo-
      gurt sauce, baked, 221
  ground
      and egg turnovers, 161
      stuffed cabbage, 116
      stuffed fennel bulbs, 111
      stuffed green peppers, 105
  macaroni pie, 148
  moussaka, 221
  pies, 162
  stuffed pasta with, 143
  See also Beef, Brains, Calf's liver,
      Lamb, Pork, Sausage, Steak,
      and Veal
Melipitta, 281
Melon
  con anís del mono, 330
  with anisette, 330

Mero a la chiclanera, 192
Miloukia, general data on, 187
Mint
  general data on, 187–188
  mixed salad, 189
  tagine, lamb and, 188
Mohk, 288
Moussaka, 221
Mousse, salt cod, in puff pastry
    shells, 25
Mozzarella
  in carrozza, 231
  tomato, and basil salad, 94
Myrtle, general data on, 190

Noodle dough, homemade, 141
Nougat pudding with chocolate
    sauce, 268
Nuts
  general data on, 251–252
  Circassian chicken, 256
  fig jam, 315
  and raisins, sardines stuffed with,
      254
  See also Almond(s), Hazelnut(s),
      Nougat, Pine nuts, Walnut(s)

Oaf
  sum sum, 200
  tapuzim, 305
Octopus, fricassee of, 22
Oil, olive
  general data on, 4–5
  green sauce, 40
  herbal, for spaghetti, 38
  mayonnaise, 43
  vegetable soup with sage and, 11
Olio verde, 38
Olive(s)
  general data on, 45–47
  black, "cake" stuffed with escarole
      and, 48
  chicken with,
      Camargue style, 62
      Tangier style, 59
  eel with tomatoes and, 58
  green
      chicken smothered in, 61

duck with, 65
marinated, 47
oil, *see* Oil, olive
onion, and anchovy tart, 50
paste, 52
sauce
    leg of lamb with, 69
    spaghetti with, 53–55
Omelet with stuffed zucchini blossoms, 112
Onion(s)
    anchovy, and olive tart, 50
    baked fish with tomatoes and, 99
    and cheese, beef stew with, 239
Orange(s)
    general data on, 301–302
    bitter, "dog soup" with, 302
    chicken with, 304
    crullers, deep-fried, 310
    and date salad, 318
    -flavored wine, 304
    flower water, general data on, 190–191
    ice, 309
    lamb stew with, 306
    roast pork with, 308
Oregano, general data on, 186–187
Ortikia skara, 36

Paella, 197
Palombacci alla perugina, 67
Panzarotti, 145
Paprika
    general data on, 191
    boiled meat and vegetables with pumpkin and pimentón sauce, 193
    stuffed green peppers, 105
    See also Pimentón
Parmesan cheese, spinach with, 110
Parsley
    general data on, 191
    sauce, fried halibut or pollock with, 192
Partridges, marinated, in piquant jelly, 298
Pasta
    general data on, 140–141

agnolotti, 143, 144
basil sauce for, 172
with breadcrumbs, 147
and chick-peas, 126
e ceci, 126
gnocchi, 242
green, walnut sauce for, 263
homemade noodle dough, 141
macaroni pie, 148
con mollica di pane, 147
ravioli, fried stuffed, with tomato-cheese sauce, 145
red butter sauce for, 142
con salsa di noci, 264
spaghetti
    herbal oil for, 38
    with olive sauce, 53–55
    with tomato and eggplant sauce, 84
stuffed
    with meat, 143
    without meat, 144
with walnut sauce, 264
Pasticcio di maccheroni alla piemontese, 148
Pastry(ies)
    lamb, 328
    stuffed with figs, honey-dipped, 278
Pavo relleño a la menorquina, 259
Peach(es)
    jam, 319
    stuffed, 321
    white wine flavored with, 319
Pepper(s)
    general data on, 103–104
    chick-peas with tomatoes, sausage, and, 136
    and garlic sauce, hot, 15
    green, *see* Green peppers
    rice with, 108
    sauce, hot, 182
        almond and, 262
    seafood and vegetable medley, 89
    sweet, hunter's chicken with, 106
Perdices escabechadas, 298
Pesca (spada) a ghiotta alla messinese, 56
Pesche ripiene, 321
Pesto, 172

Petits pâtes de Béziers, 328
Peynirli kabak, 249
Piccioni con l'uva, 323
Pickled
  fried fish, 23
  vegetables with spiced ground beef, 115
Pie
  cheese, 228
    cabbage, and sausage, 243
    and herb, 246
    honey, 281
  macaroni, 148
  swordfish, 56
Pigeons, wood, with polenta, 67
Pimentón
  general data on, 193
  sauce, boiled meat and vegetables with pumpkin and, 193
Pine nuts
  and almonds, shrimp in tomato sauce with, 255
  lamb patties with, 261
  and raisins, stuffed roast turkey with, 259
  rice pilaf with, 265
  Swiss chard with, 266
Pissaladière, 50
Pistou marseillaise, 173
Polenta, wood pigeons or squab with, 67
Pollo
  alla cacciatora con peperoni, 106
  tonnato, 30
Pollock, fried, with parsley sauce, 192
Polvorones, 272
Pomodori ripieni alla calabrese, 95
Poragneu coumtadino, 277
Pork
  ground
    stuffed cabbage, 116
    stuffed green peppers, 105
  and lamb
    and sausage, white beans with, 132
    and white bean stew, 128
    in white wine and honey sauce, 277

paella, 197
  roast, with oranges, 308
  See also Sausage
Potato-cheese croquettes, chicken tagine with, 238
Pouding au nougat, 268
Poulet
  à la camarguaise, 62
  au fromage, 236
  aux 40 gousses d'ail, 27
Poultry, see Chicken, Duck, Partridges, Pigeons, Quail, Squab, Turkey
Preserve(s)
  cherry jam, 331
  fig jam, 315
  lemons, 287
  peach jam, 319
  quince, 329
Psari plaki, 99
Pudding
  lemon and rice, 300
  nougat, with chocolate sauce, 268
Pumpkin and pimentón sauce, boiled meat and vegetables with, 193
Punch, wine, 322
Punjene paprike, 105

Quail, grilled, 36
Quince
  preserves, 329
  and raisins, fish couscous with, 156

Raisins
  general data on, 325
  duckling with, 326
  fish couscous with quince and, 156
  and pine nuts, stuffed roast turkey with, 259
  sardines stuffed with nuts and, 254
Ratatouille, 85
Ravioli with tomato-cheese sauce, fried stuffed, 145

Red mullets with lemon oil dressing, 299
Relish, eggplant and green pepper, 78
Rice
  with green or red peppers, 108
  and lemon pudding, 300
  pilaf with pine nuts, 265
  risotto with white truffles, 206
Ricotta cheese fritters, Easter, 248
Risotto con tartufi bianchi, 206
Roses, general data on, 196
Rosemary
  general data on, 195
  rib steaks with, 195
Rouille sauce, 15
Roz snobar, 265

Saffron
  general data on, 196–197
  paella, 197
Sage
  general data on, 199
  vegetable soup with olive oil and, 11
Salad
  brain, 288
  cheese, 233
  cracked wheat, 164
  date and orange, 318
  eggplant, 83
  mixed, 189
  tabbouleh, 164
  tomato, mozzarella, and basil, 94
  walnut and fennel, 252
  zucchini, 178
Salade de fenouil aux nois, 252
Salata letchine, 318
Salatit michoteta, 233
Salsa
  romesco, 262
  verde, 40
Salt cod mousse in puff pastry shells, 25
Sangría, 322
Sandwiches, cheese, 231
Sarde a beccaficu, 254
Sardines stuffed with nuts and raisins, 254

Sarma, 116
Sauce
  chocolate, for nougat pudding, 268
  egg and lemon
    for lamb fricassee, 294
    for stuffed grape leaves, 292
  garlic, 39
  gorgonzola, for spinach and cheese dumplings, 242
  green, 40
  hot pepper, 82
    almond and, 262
    garlic and, 15
  lemon, for veal scallops, 297
  pimentón, for boiled meat and vegetables, 193
  red butter, 142
  rouille, 15
  tahini cream, 199
  tomato, 93
  walnut
    for green pasta, 263
    pasta with, 264
Sausage
  chick-peas with tomatoes, peppers, and, 136
  pie
    cheese, cabbage, and, 243
    chicken and, 166
  pork, and lamb, white beans with, 132
Sauté d'agneau aux figues fourées, 314
Scabetch, 23
Scaloppine al limone, 297
Seafood
  paella, 198
  and vegetable medley, 89
  See also Fish and names of fish and shellfish
Seksu tanjaoui, 154
Sesame seeds
  general data on, 199–200
  fried chicken with, 200
  tahini sauce, 199
Sfirya, 238
Shellfish, see Lobsters, Seafood, Shrimp
Shish barak bi laban, 217

Shrimp
  in garlic sauce, 5
  seafood and vegetable medley, 89
  in tomato sauce
    with almonds and pine nuts,
      255
    with feta cheese, 234
Simonetta's black grape ice, 324
Skordalia, 39
Slata
  kera, 178
  toonsia, 189
Slatko, 331
Smen
  general data on, 201
  recipe for, 201
Soufflé
  almond macaroon, 269
  dolci di amaretti, 269
Soup
  almond, 253
  avgolemono, 290
  "dog soup" with bitter oranges,
    302
  egg and lemon, 290
    poached lamb shoulder with,
      291
  fish, 13
    Kathy Jelen's, 19
    simple Provençal, 18
  garlic, 10
  gazpacho, 9, 97
  pistou marseillaise, 173
  tarator, 214
  vegetable
    with basil, 173
    cold, 97
    with garlic, almonds, and green
      grapes, 9
    with olive oil and sage, 11
  yogurt, 213
    and cucumber, 214
Soupa avgolemono, 290
Soupe de poissons
  "l'aïgo-sau," 18
  "Kathy Jelen," 19
Spaghetti
  with breadcrumbs, 147
  herbal oil for, 38
  con le melanzane, 84

alla puttanesca, 53–55
  with tomato and eggplant sauce,
    84
Spice(s)
  general data on, 169–170
  See also names of spices
Spice mixtures
  general data on, 202
  la kama, 202
  tabil, 202
Spinach
  and cheese
    dumplings with gorgonzola
      sauce, 242
    and herb pie, 246
  with garlic and oil, 37
  and lemon, lentils with, 127
  with parmesan cheese, 110
  tagine, lamb and, 203
Spinaci
  aglio olio, 37
  con parmigiana, 110
Squab
  with coriander and spices, 179
  with green grapes, 323
  with polenta, 67
Squid
  fricassee of, 22
  in its own ink
    with garlic and almonds, 21
    with tomato sauce, 98
Steaks, rib, with rosemary, 195
Stifado, 239
"Sultan's delight," 80
Sumac, general data on, 205
Svingous me meli Hymettus, 280
Sweba, 161
Swiss chard with pine nuts, 266
Swordfish pie, 56

Tabbouleh, 164
Tabil, 202
Tagine
  bi temar, 316
  bil gouta, 240
  nana, 188
  sebnakh, 203
Tahini cream sauce, 199

Taklia, green grapes with yogurt and, 215
Tamiya, 123
Tapas, *see* Hors d'oeuvre
Tapenade, 52
Taramasalata, 6
Tarator, 214
Tart, onion, anchovy, and olive, 50
Teen makood, 315
Thyme, general data on, 205
Tiropitakia, 230
Tomato(es)
    general data on, 92
    -cheese sauce, fried stuffed ravioli with, 145
    chick-peas with sausage, peppers, and, 136
    and eggplant sauce, spaghetti with, 84
    jam, sweet, chicken tagine with, 100
    mozzarella, and basil salad, 94
    and onions, baked fish with, 99
    sauce, 93
        brains and eggs in, 204
        fried fish with zucchini and, 114
        shrimp in, 234, 255
        small meatballs in, 102
        squid in its own ink with, 98
    stuffed
        cold, 96
        hot, 95
    vegetable stew, 85
Torta di cavolo, 243
Tortino ripieno di scarole e olive, 48
Tourte
    corse, 246
    tante Vivienne, 166
Truffles, white Italian
    general data on, 206
    risotto with, 206
Tuna
    fish sauce, poached chicken with, 30
    white beans with, 121
Turkey, stuffed roast, with pine nuts and raisins, 259
Turnovers, egg
    anchovy and, 161
    brain and, 160

    chicken and, 162
    ground meat and, 161

Veal
    macaroni pie, 148
    scaloppine with lemon sauce, 297
Vegetable(s)
    boiled meat and, with pumpkin and pimentón sauce, 193
    dried, general data on, 119–121
    Mediterranean, general data on, 75–77
    mixed fry, 63
    pickled, with spiced ground beef, 115
    ratatouille, 85
    and seafood medley, 89
    stew, 85
    soup
        with basil, 173
        cold, 97
        with olive oil and sage, 11
    See also names of vegetables
Vin
    d'orange de Colette, 304
    de pêches, 319

Walnut(s)
    cake, honey, 273
    Circassian chicken, 256
    and fennel salad, 252
    sauce
        for green pasta, 263
        pasta with, 264
Wine
    orange-flavored, 304
    punch, 322
    white, flavored with peaches, 319

Yogurt
    general data on, 209–210
    Bosnian meatballs with, 219
    çorbasi, 213
    homemade, 211
    lamb cooked in its mother's milk, 222

Yogurt (*cont'd*)
   poached eggs with, 216
   sauce
      baked meat and eggplant cas-
         serole with, 221
      lamb dumplings and kibbe in,
         217
   soup, 213
      and cucumber, 214
   and taklia, green beans with, 215

Za'atar, general data on, 186–187
Zeytinyagli domates dolmasi, 96
Zucchini
   blossoms, stuffed, omelet with,
      112
   salad, 178
   stuffed with cheese, 249
   and tomato sauce, fried fish with,
      114
   vegetable stew, 85